NATURE KNOWS NO COLOR-LINE

Nature Knows no Color-Line

RESEARCH INTO THE NEGRO ANCESTRY
IN THE WHITE RACE

by

J. A. ROGERS

Beauty, thou wild fantastic ape
Who dost in every country change thy shape
Here black, here brown, here tawny and there white.
Abraham Cowley (1618-1677)

"Thou are white and I am black but day must join
with night to bring forth the dawn and the twilight
which are more beautiful than they."
Victor Hugo.

Wesleyan University Press
Middletown, Connecticut

Wesleyan University Press
Middletown CT 06459
www.wesleyan.edu/wespress

First Wesleyan University Press edition 2014
ISBN 978-0-8195-7510-4

Manufactured in the United States of America
5 4

CONTENTS

FOREWORD 1

I. WHERE DID THE COLOR PROBLEM ORIGINATE?
    AND WHY 6

II. COLOR PREJUDICE AMONG WHITES
    THEMSELVES 17

III. NEGROES IN ANCIENT EUROPE—GREECE 27

IV. WHITES AND BLACKS IN ANCIENT ROME 43

V. RACIAL INTERMIXTURE IN SPAIN AND
    PORTUGAL 55

VI. THE NEGRO AS "MOOR." ARISTOCRATIC
    EUROPEAN FAMILIES 69

VII. WHITES AND BLACKS IN GREECE, TURKEY,
    ITALY, GERMANY 111

VIII. NEGRO ANCESTRY IN THE FRENCH 143

IX. NEGRO ANCESTRY IN THE ANGLO-SAXONS 156

X. NEGRO ANCESTRY IN WHITE AMERICA 189

XI. RECENT MIXED MARRIAGES 208

    APPENDIX—MISCELLANY ON RACE MIXTURE 214

    APPENDIX—GENERAL MISCELLANY 218

    INDEX 235

NATURE KNOWS NO COLOR-LINE

"In the historical amplitude of life on earth races have been in a state of flux. Authorities on prehistoric races point to this as a fact and even the brief span of historic record affords instances as illustrations of how races have fallen. It does not need the prophetic eye then to see that races will continue to change. In consequence race as something permanent becomes an artificial notion, a myth. What we call races are merely temporary eddies in the history of human kind." T. R. Garth. (1)

"Everyone alive is, I am convinced, of mixed ancestry but some of us are more white, some of us more Negro, some of us more Chinese." H. G. Wells. (2)

What was the first man like and of what "race"? Was he Caucasian or Negro, black or white? Or are both the evolution of some other type? The ancient Greeks believed that black man was white man darkened by the sun. Their mythology says that Phaeton, son of Helios, the Sun-God, induced his father to let him drive the chariot of the sun one day and in his lack of skill drove it too near certain lands and burnt black with intense heat the peoples there. Their poet, Theodectes, attributed the "sooty" skin and "curled" hair of the Ethiopians to this mishap, and Caedman, Anglo-Saxon poet of about 670 A.D., called the Ethiopians "a race burned brown by the heat of the sun."

This belief held until the discovery of the New World in the fifteenth century when it gradually shifted to the theory that man originated in the tropics; that some peoples, either because they migrated into cold snowy lands, or because the climate changed to that, lost some of their color and their hair grew longer to protect the scalp. Among the earlier writers who were inclined to this theory were Pallas, Lacepede, Hunter, Dornik and Link. Later ones were Prichard, Schopenhauer, Chambers, and Darwin. Chambers whose "Vestiges of the Natural History of the Creation," was to have immense influence on Darwin, said that, man begining as a Negro, passed through Malay, Indian and Mongolian and finally reached Caucasian. "The leading character, in short." he said, "of the various races of mankind are simply representations of particular stages of development of the highest. or Caucasian type." (3)

Among recent ones who thought that white man evolved from a much darker type are Von Luschan, Finot, Verneau, Griffith Taylor W. K. Gregory and Binet-Sangle. Sergi thought Europeans

1. Race Psychology, p. 220, 1931.
2. World of William Clissold, Vol. 2, p. 431.
3. pp. 226-7. 1844. Prichard said, "The primitive stock of men were probably Negroes and I know of no argument to be set on the other side." Physical History of man, p. 289. 1913. See also: Binet-Sangle, Les Ancetres de l'Homme, pp. 86, 103. 1931.

were originally Africans. (4) This is certain: Abundant evidences that African Negroids once inhabited Europe as far north as Russia have been found and are to be seen in the museums of Europe and the United States.

Still stronger proof is that the oldest human skulls found are Negroid (prognathous) not Caucasian (orthognathous). Life Magazine in an article "Up From The Ape," on the finding of skulls in South Africa by Professors Broom and Dart and especially of one found on an island in Lake Victoria by Dr. L. S. Leakey, shows "Modern Man" (white) as descended from Boskop Man, a Bushman with pepper-corn hair, of about 20,000 years ago.

Whatever be the point of view regarding which came first, black or white, both religion and science agree on a common human origin, which origin anatomy and the X-Ray confirm. The points of unlikeness between so-called races are as nothing compared with those in which they are alike.

Unlikeness is most observed in the faces of human varieties. But even here fundamental alikeness remains. Nose, eyes, mouth, ears, hair, are located in the same places in the head and function alike. Furthermore, one is likely to find some point of facial resemblance in individuals of widely different so-called races. Studying faces has been a life-long habit with me. Now and then I see Chinese, Japanese, Indians, Caucasians, Negroes as well as Frenchmen, Spaniards, Germans, Italians. Americans, Englishmen, and Jews, with a nose here or a mouth there, or a facial expression which reminds me of those I have seen in the above-mentioned peoples no matter how far apart they were thought to be racially. The same is true when I study sculpture, paintings and photographs. Whether they be reconstructions of prehistoric man, or from ancient Egypt, Greece, Rome, India, pre-Columbian America, the Renaissance, or in a museum of modern art, I am always seeing resemblances not only among them but among living persons, including acquaintances. (5)

4. Sergi says, "The primitive populations of Europe after Homo Neanderthalensis originated in Africa, these constituted the entire population of Neolithic times." He calls the European, Eur-African. The Mediterranean Race, p.v. 1901.

5. See, for instance Beethoven's nose, as it appears on his life-mask (reproduced, Sex and Race, Vol. 3, p. 308) and the nose of the Olmec Negro god of pre-Columbian America in this book. Both are very much alike. One sees, too noted white Americans in whom the Negro strain is evident—a fact which candid pictures of them, (of which I have a collection), show up more clearly. Of one of America's most distinguished white women of a family in which the Negro strain is evident, the Cincinnati Union said, "A colored woman of New York, wife of a prominent Cuban, has often been greatly annoyed by being mistaken for her." In fact, certain of her friends sometimes call her by that lady's name.

Exterior differences as color, hair, facial form are adaptations to climate, which, in turn, is determined by the amount of sunlight. We are, as one astronomer said, blossoms of the sun. And as blossoms owe their color to sunlight so do human beings.

To understand the force of this start in Norway and travel south. Humanity which is generally blond there gets perceptibly darker the further one goes until when southern Europe is reached brunettes are common and blonds are rare. Go on to the equator where the sun is hottest and most constant and the natives are jet-black. (6)

That it was degree of sunlight over thousands of years which produced the "original" so-called five races of the anthropologists of the last century is inescapable. Some give food as the cause but are not kinds of foods also determined by degree of sunlight? Racial intermixture. in turn, from these "five" produced thousands of other varieties, which by still more intermixture produced such an infinity of others until of the two and a half billion souls on the earth no two are alike. "Nature," says Inman, "is always attempting to breed new races and varieties and appears to abominate sameness. This being so there is a strong resistance to breed back to the same ancestral form." The evident truth is that each human being is a "race," a variety in himself — a variety through which runs fundamental unity.

However, there have ever been those who have never been able to realize this essential oneness. Even so great a thinker as Voltaire could not.

Certain anthropologists (some of them of our times) (7) could not either. Dominated by the slave-holding interests, or other exploitation, they dubbed mixed-bloods "mongrels" and preached "race purity." But we know now that the nearly "pure" peoples as the Pigmies of the Congo, the Andaman Islanders and the Ainos are the farthest down and that the "impure" — the so-called mongrels are not only more advanced but are among those highest up.

As regards mixture of so-called Negro and Caucasian we have heard much of the white strain in the black man and almost nothing of the black strain in the white man. But intermixture of

6. On a recent visit to Denmark I was struck with the difference in the complexion of the Danes and the English. Brunets were very rare among the Danes. Of scores of school children I saw only one whose hair was a trifle darkish; the rest were almost cottony white. In London and to the south, on the other hand, the people were considerably darker. Among American whites the difference to the Scandinavians is still more noticeable.

7. This, for example from W. D. Boyce, writing in 1925. He presents a chimpanzee and a Negro together and says, "Here is evidence for the evolutionist. Which is more intelligent, the African native or the African chimpanzee? Those who know them best say that given equal opportunities the chimpanzee will make faster progress." Illustrated Africa, p. 472. 1925.

the two has not been a one-way street. Hence the sub-title of this book, "Negro Ancestry In The White Race.

I have chosen this with the full consciousness that it will offend very many. But I know, too that in man's march towards emancipation from falsehood and fear the sacred cows of today have ever become the incredible stupidities of tomorrow.

I know also that many white Americans, like most Europeans, will not be offended but will rather welcome the truth. Their number will increase with the years.

Let me add, too, that this work is intended not only to show intermixture but to give some idea of the Negro's contribution, biologically and culturally in Europe, itself. In my "World's Great Men of Color" I have given what certain Negroes as Dumas, Pushkin, St. George, Coleridge-Taylor and others, have acomplished there. In Volume One of Sex and Race I have given more. It is to be hoped that some day added information will be collected and presented in a single volume. Negro contribution inside Europe is very much more than is generally believed.

As I said, probably many will be offended by this book and there are those who will not. All human beings, through the ages may be roughly divided into egotists and altruists. The egotists, feeling insufficient in themselves, need someone to be better than — a sort of dope as it were to provide courage to carry on. On the other hand the altruists, with their inner strength giving them a sense of mental well-being, endeavor to see the good, rather than the evil, in others and how that good might be increased. The altruists, in short, see in other human beings but another version of themselves, have always recognized the fundamental oneness of humanity.

Socrates of the fifth century B.C., said, "I am not a Greek or an Athenian but a citizen of the whole world." "I am a man," said Terence of Rome, "and nothing human is alien to me."

"There is neither Greek nor Jew, circumcision nor uncircumcision, Barbarian, Scythian, bond nor free, but Christ is all in all," said St. Paul. "In the variety of your languages and your complexions," said Mohamet, "verily therein are signs unto men of understanding." Shakespeare, whose all-embracing mind saw the whole earth as a unit, whose every atom was related to every other, said, "One touch of nature makes the whole world kin." And he was specific as regards "race." Of white and Negro he said in Troilus and Cressida, "I care not an she were a blackamoor;! 'tis all one to me." (Act 1, Sc. 1).

And so on down the ages. "The world is my country," said Thomas Paine, "and to do good is my religion." Buffon (1707-1788) French anthropologist, wrote, "There are in nature only individuals. Races, orders, classes, exist only in imagination."

Darwin showed the growth of every living thing from a common organism. Nietzsche said, "Have no intercourse with people who partake of this hypocritical race humbug."

Walt Whitman in his magnificent "Salut au Monde" wrote: "You daughter or son of England
You of the mighty Slavic tribes and empires! You Russ in Russia!
You dim-descended black, divine-souled African, large, fine-headed, noble formed, superbly destined on equal terms with me.
You Norwegian! Swede! Icelander! You Prussian!
You Spaniard of Spain. You Portuguese. You Frenchwoman and and Frenchman of France.
Each of us inevitable.
Each of us limitless — each of us with his or her rights upon the earth
Each of us allowed the eternal purports of the earth
Each of us as divinely as any is here."

And Abdul Baha, greatest modern advocate of the brotherhood of man, said, "The earth is but one country and mankind its citizens."

However, I shall not rely on humanitarian or religious sentiment nor on deductions from pre-history or anthropology for support of my thesis. To show Negro ancestry in the white "race" I go to direct historical evidence from early writers and sculptors— Egyptians, Greeks, Romans down through the centuries to those of our times. This is only a minor part of what could be given. Moreover in the three volumes of Sex and Race will be found much additional. I have drawn here from that work only what was essential to round out my point.

Before giving these facts I however, shall discuss how and why color prejudice began.

CHAPTER ONE

WHERE DID THE COLOR PROBLEM ORIGINATE? AND WHY

The two varieties of humanity which have intermixed the most and longest are so-called Negro and Caucasian. There is some evidence that they mated in prehistoric times; that a Negro, or Negroid, people inhabited Europe when it was joined to Africa and was still tropical. As for the historic period, or about eight thousand years there is abundant evidence they did, especially in the Americas since Columbus.

In so-called racial intermixture there are usually two forces: exogamy or out-breeding and endogamy, or inbreeding. In colonial lands, the first is called miscegenation; the second, race purity. However, in those lands as in all lands where one's partner in marriage is not selected by his parents, like and dislike generally determine one's choice of a mate. Which qualities attract or repel are quite beyond precise definition, so much depends upon the individual, regardless of race, caste or religion. As Shakespeare said:

Strange is it that our bloods
Of colour, weight and heat, poured all together
Would quite confound distinction, yet stand off
In differences so mighty.

Some of these "mighty" differences are not all physical. They are economic, social, educational and religious, also. Any of the latter can operate as strongly as the racial, which is supposed in colonial, or former colonial lands, to be the strongest of all objections. The peculiar thing about miscegenation is that some of its most vociferous objectors practise it.

In certain colonial and former colonial lands as in the United States, South Africa, and the West Indies, color of skin, (which is accepted as normal in Europe, where the population is white, or Central Africa where it is black) is a "mighty" difference, influencing not only mating but life in some of its most unexpected phases. For instance, the matter of the blonde and the brunette among white women. When one reads in American papers of a man having an affair with some gorgeous girl, she is always blonde. When blunettes are mentioned it is almost with some sort of apology. Is this depreciation of the white brunette an extension of the prejudice against the Negro's color? Whiteness of skin has become a symbol of purity, goodness, and fine Christian living. "Wash me and I shall be whiter than snow," runs the hymn. Thus the more bleached the skin, the more bleached the character —Negro albinos, not included, of course.

But whatever be the reason the blondes are raved over in America, and the brunettes aren't. However, in the Scandinavian lands, where as one visitor remarked, "Blondes are a dime a thousand," blonde skin and hair count for no more than does black among the blacks of Central Africa or yellow among the Chinese. Unmixed blacks in Scandinavia, I have noticed, attract attention and are usually welcome. They offer some variety to the color scheme, in certain villages in the West Indies where the people are dark I have noticed similar welcome given to a white visitor for the same reason.

Is color in sexual selection a factor only in colonial and former colonial lands? Evidently not. It probably goes back to the time when variety of skin coloring began to appear in the human race, or many hundreds of thousands of years ago. Since the first human beings were all of the same color it is clear that difference of color of skin is an important factor in human evolution. All human beings, except albinos, have some degree of color in their skins.

Another question. When and where was color first used as a social, economic and political factor? Many who have given thought to that say it started with the invasion of the dark men's lands — Asia, Africa, America — by the whites in the fifteenth century. Lord Cromer, distinguished statesman, thought however, that the question had never been competently examined. "I am not aware," he said, "that any competent scholar has ever examined into the question of the stage in history at which difference of color . . . acquired the importance it now possesses as a social and political factor." (1) I think he is right. If it has been done I have not seen it.

The first recorded instance of color prejudice I have been able to find is in India of some five thousand years ago when the Aryas, or Aryans, invaded the valley of the Indus and found there a black people — the Dasysus, or Dasyus. In any case we find very clear evidences of it in Aryan writings. In the Rig-Veda (Book IX, Hymn, 42: 1) Indra, their national god, is depicted as "Blowing away with supernatural might from earth and from the heavens the black skin which Indra hates." Hymn 42:1, tells of "Driving the black skin far away." The blacks were called "Anasahs" (noseless people). Book v. Hymn 29:10, tells how Indra "slew the flat-nosed barbarians."

1. Ancient and Modern Imperialism, p. 140. 1910.

India's caste system was based on color. (2) The word varna (caste) literally means "color." Arya varna (white skin); Krishna varna (black skin). (3)

"The Aryans of India," says the Encyclopedia of Religion and Ethics, "prided themselves on their fairer skins and more aquiline features and held in derision the black color and flatter physiognomies of the aborigines, regarded them much as conquering whites regarded blacks in Africa."

Thanks, however, to time and the Moslem invasion of the eleventh century color prejudice weakened. Aryan and Dasyu; and Negro and white Moslems from Africa and the Near East amalgamated into the present Indian population. Later, the incoming of the Europeans, did much to revive it.

The next evidence of it I have been able to find is in Ancient Egypt. Gerald Massey, perhaps the greatest of all authorities on ancient Egyptian lore, said, "On the monuments the dark people are commonly called 'the evil race of Kush' but when the Ethiopian

2. The aborigines were not the barbarians Aryan legends say they were. These blacks, now known as Dravidians, had a mighty civilization of their own. From them came the Buddhas. James Bird (Historical Researches on the Origin of the Buddhas, pp. 5, 8, 12. 1847) says, "Buddhas of a black complexion are common in the Fresco paintings of Ajunta and that of the Arishtanemi, or race of vishnu, who is the twenty-second Jain saint is described as of a black complexion on the authority of the Hemachandras vocabulary."

Of one black Buddha in the case of Aurangabad, he says, "Its features are large, its hair curly, its whole resemblance is so much allied to that of the African as to have given origin to the opinion of some that Buddhism had an extra Indian origin." In this cave there is also, he says the drawing of "an Abyssinian prince seated on a bed along with a fair woman to whom he appears to be married."

Godfrey Higgins says, "The religion of Buddha of India is well-known to have been very ancient. In the most ancient temples scattered throughout Asia where his worship is yet continued he is found as yet with the flat face, thick lips and curly hair of the Negro. Several statues of his may be met in the Museum of the East India Company . . . The religion of the Negro God is found in the ruins of his temples and other circumstances to have been spread over an immense extent of countries,even to the remotest parts of Britain and to have been professed by devotees, inconceivably numerous . . . That the Buddhists were Negroes the icons of their God clearly prove.' Anacalypsis, Vol. 1, pp. 52. 1866.

For additional facts on the Negro Buddhas together with pictures of them and the evolution of Christianity from the black Buddhas see Sex and Race, Vol. 1, pp. 265-8. 2nd ed. 1940.

3. Rabindranath Tagore, Indian poet and Nobel Prize winner, says of color prejudice, "Our own history began with it and though India desperately tried some kind of mechanical race adjustment she has failed in giving birth to a living political organism owing to this abnormal caste consciousness that obstructs the strain of human sympathy and spirit of mutual cooperation. This is the reason why, in spite of the fact that India

element dominates the dark people retort by calling the light complexions, the pale, degraded race of Arvad." (4) But this prejudice of fair for dark and the converse was, it is safe to say, never nearly as strong as in India. The whites did not come in any considerable number to Egypt until the Ptolemaic invasion of the third century B.C., by which time intermixture had already taken too firm a root for any appreciable degree of color prejudice, as I shall show later.

The third instance of color prejudice is to be found in the rabbinical writings. The early rabbis did very definitely and abundantly say that a black skin was the result of a "curse" on Ham by Noah. The signs of this "curse" said certain rabbis were "a black skin, misshapen lips, and twisted hair." The Bible says the "curse" was placed on Canaan, Ham's son, but some rabbis said it was placed directly on Ham. Rabbi Huja said that he came forth from the Ark "black-skinned." (5) This would mean that Ham who

had produced a series of great minds, she has not produced a great organic history; and it has yet to be seen if such history is in the making in which peoples of different colours can have a perfect bond of life from across the seas. "Spectator, May 9, 1931, p. 739.

Rice says, "In India, itself today a fair skin is considered desirable." Hindu Customs and Their Origins, p. 39. 1937.

The Spectator says, "To this day a high caste Hindu may speak disparagingly of a low caste man 'as a very black fellow' and may avoid pollution by his touch." May 28, 1931, p. 501.

P. L. Prattis says of his visit to India in 1949: "I talked with the editor of the Hindustani Times about matrimonial advertisements in which girls mention their fair and white complexions as desirable attributes in seeking a husband. It was my impression that this dispositon was a carryover from the long British occupation. The editor said this was not true, that it has long been the tradition of Indians to place a premium upon a fair skin that fairness has been a sort of ideal written into India's literature by the poets."

The Indian movies, said Prattis, had "a mik-white cast." How could Indians, I asked myself, make a picture with a cast so unrepresentative of Indians, themselves? All the members of the cast looked like Italians and Greeks. They were a white set . . . But India is just running over with brown, dark brown and black peoples. The yellows and the fair are a minority so small that you don't even meet them on the streets. Take any handful of Indians and they are dark . . . But you couldn't tell that from seeing one of their motion pictures . . ." Seventeen Days in Independent India. Pittsburg Courier. Aug. and Sept. 1949.

Moslem India—Pakistan—thanks to its faith, is less concerned about color than India. When Islam invaded India about the ninth century A. D., Negroes were in the Moslem armies and tdeir numbers increased as the conquest of the peninsula proceeded. Some Negroes rose to be sultans, two of the principal ones bbeing Malik Ambar (1548-1628) and Malik Andeel (1494). There were also great generals, admirals, prime ministers and builders. Many of these blacks, says C. Stewart, "who, if they had fallen into the hands of Europeans, would have been condemmed to service drudgery became the associates of princes and governors of provinces." (History

had gone into the Ark fair skinned had undergone this change of color in the only one hundred and ninety days that had been in the Ark. Ham it appears, had been guilty of some sexual infraction while in there from having intercourse with his wife to sodomy.

Topinard, French anthropologist, thinks, too, that the rabbis of the first century were the first to stress differences of race and color. Race, as we now use it, he says, was unknown in far antiquity, at least in the West. He correctly notes that Aristotle, Father of Natural History, and Hippocrates, Father of Medicine, do not mention "race" though both studied anatomy and the then known varieties of the human race. including the Negro.

The Greek had two distinct divisions of humanity — Greek and Barbarian, or citizen and alien. An Athenian who married an alien, regardless of color, was sold into slavery. It was for a long time the same in Rome. "Race" as based on color and physique is, in fact comparatively recent. The King James Bible of the seventeenth century does not mention it. Shakespeare used it only for family lineage or contests. So also do the first English dictionary by Nathaniel Bailey in 1736; and the second by Dr. Samuel Johnson in 1750.

To quote Topinard, "In the first century when Christianity was beginning to seat itself in Rome the doctrine of a separate creation for whites and blacks was defended by the Babylonian rabbis and later by Emperor Julian. In 415 A. D. when one council was debating whether the Ethiopians were descended from Adam and the theory they weren't was making progress, St. Augustine in his 'City of God' intervened and declared that no true Christian would doubt that all men, of no matter what form, color, or height were of the same protoplasmic origin." (6)

Emperor Julian, The Apostate (c. 331-363 A. D.) said on race, "For different natures must have existed in all those things that among the nations were to be differentiated. Thus, at any rate is seen, if one observes how very different in their bodies are the Germans and Scythians from the Libyans and Ethiopians." (7) The first were whites; the latter two, blacks.

of Bengal, pp. 100-08. 1813). For Malik Ambar, Andeel and names of other eminent Negroes of the Moslem past see Rogers, J. A. Sex and Race, Vol. 1, 96-99. 1946.

4. A book of the Beginnings, Vol. 1, p. 454. 1881.

5. Ginsberg L. Legends of the Jews. Consult the Index, Vol. 7 for HAM, HAMITE, ETHIOPIAN, EGYPTIAN, CAIN (1938). See also Sex and Race, vol. 3, pp. 316-17. Also Freeman and Simon's Midrash Rabba for Story of the Ethiopian maid who thought herself fairer than her white mistress (Song of Songs, p. 690) ; and the story of the Negro slave to whom his Jewish master left his entire wealth except one thing in order to trick him, in Rapoport S. Tales and Maxims from the Midrash, pp. 223-4, also p. 167. 1907.

Also in a letter to a priest he said that "facts bear witness that many men came into the world at once I shall maintain elsewhere, and precisely, but for the moment it will be enough to say this much that if we were descended from one man and one woman, it is not likely that our laws would show such divergence; nor in any case is it likely that the whole earth was filled with people by one man; nay, not even if the women used to bear many children at a time to their husbands like swine." (8)

St. Augustine replied that all human beings even "monsters" — so-called freaks of nature — were of "the stock of Adam's or Noah's sons" and that, "whosoever is anywhere born of a man, that is, of a rational mortal animal, no matter what unusual appearance he presents in colour, movement, sound, nor how peculiar he is in some power, part, or quality of his nature no Christian can doubt he springs from a single protoplast." He added, "All the varieties of mankind . . . unquestionably trace their pedigree to that one first father of all." (9)

As a result of this dispute, monogenism, or a single origin for the human race, became a fixed Christian doctrine; and, says Topinard, more than one doubter paid the supreme penalty for disbelief.

The fourth stage in the development of color prejudice seemed therefore to have occurred in Rome of the first century A. D. as a phase of the fight between Christianity and Paganism. Prior to that, however, Pagan masters held the belief that humanity regardless of color, were either Roman or Barbarian. Christianity, the new religion, decided that "of one blood" God made all the peoples of the earth and that all men were brothers in Christ. Moreover, the earliest Christians pictured the Virgin Mary and Christ as black, both being an evolution of the worship of Isis and Horus which was once common in Rome.

Before proceeding to the fifth stage in the growth of color prejudice let us endeavor to see why the rabbis made the "curse" on Ham a black skin. This is certain: Next to the Aryans the Jews were more color conscious than any of the ancients. Why? They had been slaves to the Egyptians and Ethiopians who are described in their legends as Negroes. Again, after they had established themselves in Palestine they were twice invaded by Egyptians and Ethiopians. Shishak, Ethiopian ruler of Egypt, ravaged the land, plundered Solomon's Temple, and took a great number of Jews slaves to Egypt. (II Chronicles, 12). Another Ethiopian King, Zerah, who came with "a host of a thousand thousand and three hundred chariots" was beaten off. (II Chronicles, 14).

6. De la notion de race en anthropologie. Revue d'Anthrop 2nd ser. Vol. 2, p. 589. Paris 1879.

It could be that the Jews before they left Egypt imbibed some of the color prejudice mentioned by Massey but it could not have been strong among them because they were dark, or even black. One rabbi does say they were black at that time, that the passage "black but comely" from the Songs of Solomon means. "I was black in Egypt but comely in Egypt." (10) There is no doubt that after four centuries in Egypt the Jews had mixed much with Egyptians and Ethiopians, whom their legends describe as "black" and wooly-haired." Thus the main difference between Hebrew and Egyptian was not racial but religious, the form which economic exploitation then took. Miriam's objection to the Ethiopian wife of Moses, Zipporah, was not on color but on religion and more likely on culture. Talk of Semitic and Hamitic as "race" is sheerest nonsense and is used only by "parrot" anthropologists.

Furthermore we have no proof that the original seventy Jews who went to Egypt were white. According to their legends they originated in Chaldea and there is considerable evidence the inhabitants of that region in earliest times were Negroid. In fact, some writers said the Jews were an African people. Strabo said many of his time believed they were.

How then was it possible for them to place a "curse" on a black skin? The answer is that centuries after they had left Egypt and being somewhat whitened by mixing with fairer skinned people to the north and with Europeans, they could now look back on the unchanged color of the Ethiopians and Egyptians in comparison with themselves; and their rabbis, that is their "scientists," endeavoring to explain how black people came about tacked on that bit of folk-lore of the "curse" on Ham. It is very important to remember here that the Masoretic text, regarded as the correct one of the ancient Hebrew writings, (called by Christians "The Old Testament"), says nothing whatever of Ham or Canaan's color. It merely says that a curse was placed on Canaan. So, too, does the Old Testament. (Genesis, 10:25). That the "black" skin was a later addition is indisputable.

Strongest reason of all is that the curse on a black skin could now be used as proof of retribution on the blacks for having enslaved them. "The Egyptians," said one rabbi, "were descended from Ham, who was pronounced to be a slave of slaves." Other rabbis say likewise.

7. Works of Emperor Julian, Vol. 3 (Against the Galileans) p. 357. 1903. Trans. by Wright.
8. Julian, Vol. 2 (Fragmentum Epistolae), p. 297.
9. Works of Aurelius Augustine. City of God. Vol. 2. Book 16 pp. 117-18. Edited by Marcus Dods. 1871.
10. Freedman and Simon. Midrash Rabba, Song of Songs p. 51. 1939. See also their Genesis, Vol. 2, p. 293.

Still clearer proof that this legend was used later as retribution is that the "curse" on Ham and "blessing" on Shem by Noah worked in reverse. The Hebrews, sons of Shem, were enslaved for centuries by the Egyptians, while there is no proof that Hebrews enslaved the Egyptians, whom they call the sons of Ham. Moreover, according to the Masoretic version, the curse is on Canaan. But the Canaanites lived in Palestine which is in Asia, not Africa. Being Asiatics and nearer to the whites of the north, they were doubtless lighter in color than the Egyptians. Why then the curse of blackness on the offspring of Canaan? Well, they owned the land of Canaan, which the Hebrews claimed Jehovah had given them. In olden times one way of inciting one group against another was to place a curse on it. The modern parallel is "excommunication."

The Arabs, who are ethnically related to the Jews and are largely Negroid, had their version of the Ham legend, which they applied to the blacks of the Sudan. Mohamet, they said, once stopped at a woman's house and asked her how many sons she had. She had three but fearing that Mohamet would take one to carry his baggage, she hid one and brought out two. The Prophet of God, knowing she had lied, placed a curse on the hidden son. While the other two would have fair-skinned offspring, who would be wealthy and be lords of the earth, that of the hidden one would be as black as "darkness," be sold like cattle, and be perpetual slaves to the offspring of his brothers." (11) Of course the Arabs also captured white Circasians in Asia and sold them like cattle but here again logic and facts give way to belief, inspired by gain, in this case, enslavement of the blacks.

And just here an observation as regards the lighter Negoid Arabs and what they said of the unmixed blacks since it will explain the case of the Negroid Jews towards the latter also. It is not necessary for a people to be unmixed white to have prejudice for a black sin. Sometimes those with only an eighth of white ancestry have this prejudice, too. I have known dark mulattoes, especialy in the West Indies, who were much more prejudiced than many European-born whites there. Lighter mulattoes in France had much more prejudice for African blacks than any white Frenchman.

Incidentally, the blacks had their theory of the origin of the whites, also. Thin lips, straight hair and a white skin, they said, originated from an albino ape, who was the ancestor of the whites. Christianized Negroes, dipping into the Bible, had their origin of

11. Speke. J. H. What led to the Discovery of the Blue Nile, p. 341. 1864. Sir Thomas Browne examined this belief about Ham nearly three centuries ago and showed its falsity (Works, Vol. 3, pp. 242-8. 1928).
12. Reade, W. Savage Africa, p. 24. 1864.

the whites, too. All men, they said were originally black but that when God shouted at Cain in the garden of Eden for having killed Abel, he turned white from fright. (12) The rabbis, on the other hand, said that Cain turned black as a curse. Xenophanes of 550 B. C. rightly observed that men made their gods in their own image and that the gods of the Ethiopians were black and flat-nosed like themselves. Marco Polo said that the "natives of Malabar make their devils white and their saints black" like themselves.

Mungo Park said that the Africans accounted for his white skin by saying that as a baby he had been continually dipped in milk. The prominence of his nose, they said, was due to its being pinched daily "until it acquired its present unnatural and unsightly shape." (13) Parkyn, a white traveller, said that Ethiopians said he had "cat's" eyes and "monkey hair" and that he had "lost his skin." (14)

Another belief was (and still is) that a white skin was the result of leprosy. Voltaire thought that African albinos were decended from "a race that had been whitened by leprosy." Many East Indians still believe that white people are the descendants of lepers. T. S. Ramanujam says, "An Indian villager after seeing an Englishman for the first time asked me whether the gentleman 'was tainted with leprosy.' " (15) Harold Cox tells of a high-caste Indian woman who on seeing white persons for the first time, said, "Why they have no skins."

Certain American Negroes also believe that a white skin was caused by leprosy. The ancestor of the whites, they say, was Gehazi, servant of Elisha, who was "cursed" with leprosy for having solicited money from Naaman (II Kings, 5:21).

Some Negro preachers and expounders of the Bible have even "proved" that white people will not go to heaven because Jesus placed a curse on their hair. As authority they quote the parable of the sheep and the goats (Matthew 25:32), where Christ said that when he comes again in all his glory he shall separate the sheep from the goats, place the sheep on his right hand and say to them, "Come ye blessed of my Father, inherit the kingdom prepared for you from the foundation of the world." Now there is this distinction: The goats have straight hair like the whites; the sheep, wool, like Negroes.

13. Park. Travels in the Interior of Africa, p. 56, 1799. Marco Polo, India, Vol. 2, p. 291. (Yale ed. 1871.) Fernandez reported the same of the Ethiopians. See Sex and Race, Vol. 3, p. 122. See also Spectator, May 28, 1931, p. 531. Other Indians have said the same.

14. Parkyn, M. Life in Abyssinia (Lond. Quar. Rev. Vol. 1. pp. 178-9; Vol. 3, 1854-55, p. 49).

15. Spectator, March 14, 1931, p. 402.

Of course, all these versions of the origin of color whether
originated by unlettered blacks or by learned theologians show
a common kinship. Theology, whether it be Jewish, Christian,
Buddhist, Moslem, Shinto, or just plain heathen, is largely an ex-
cursion of the folk-mind into the realm of the unsubstantiated, and
the incoherent. Ideas picked up here and there are patched up
into a system. The theologian of whatever faith is largely a
romancer. For him miracles do happen as in pagan myths and
in fairy-tales.

SOME SOURCES OF CONTACTS OF WHITE AND BLACKS IN PREHISTORY.

Marett, P. R. Race, Sex and Environment. 1936.

Delisle, F. Sur une crane Negroide trouve au Carrefour de Revelon,
pres d'Epehy (Somme pp. 13-18. Jan. 22, 1909.)

Verneau, R. La race de neaderthal et la race de Grimaldi: leur
role dans l' Humanite." Huxley Memorial Lecture for 1924. Royal
Anthrop Instit. of Gt. Britain, vol. 54, pp. 211-230. 1924. Bull. et
Mem. Soc. l'Anthrop. de Paris. Nov. 5, 1902, pp. 771-79; Feb. 18,
1904, pp. 119-121; Jan. 22, 1909, pp. 13-18, Dec. 6, 1894. Boule M.
Les Hommes Fossiles. 2nd ed. Paris 1923. pp. 245, 274-285, 470,
277, 278, 312, 318, 498, 403, p. 340. on race de Mugem.

L. Manouvrier, Sur L'Aspect Negroide de quelques cranes
prehistorique trouves en France. Bull. et. Mem. pp. 119-121. Feb. 18,
1904.

E. Piette. Gravure du Mas d'Azil et Statuettes de Menton tells
of five statuettes found in Southern France. He says (Bull. et Mem.
Soc. d'Anthrop. de Paris) "The most remarkable one is a head
in several fragments that I have picked up. It has a head-dress
similar to that of certain Pharaohs of the Louvre Museum and
appears to belong to the Neanderthaloid. The forehead is very
low and forms an angle slightly obtuse with the face; the eye-
brows are prominent, a little oblique, the nose flat like that of a
Negro, the mouth, large and fleshy; the chin, short, slightly protruding, the face therefore is indisputably Negroid.

Chasseloup Laubat. Art Rupestre Hoggar, pp. 21, 47. On
Negroes in pre-dynastic Egyptian civilization. "Here again one
is reminded of Egypt and the lengthened heads of the daughters
of Amenhopis IV but thinks also of the numerous ochre paintings of
South Africa the work of ancient Negroids, the Bushmen; the
coloring, movements and techniques are the same. (p. 21).

"We have now seen that the 'resemblance' between the
archaic arts of the Hoggar and those of pre-dynastic Upper Egypt,
explain each other by a tie direct from the same source and that

in all logic it is necessary rather to admit an influence of the former upon the latter, that is to say, a migration from west to east, which brings one to say that the ancestors of the Egyptians and their art, arose, like their race, from the meeting of the people of the South with those of the North, may be considered as being at the base of the grand Art Egyptian."

Negro skull from ancient Portugal (Mugem). Negro soldier from ancient Spain in Louvre with a white soldier beside him. Negro skull of about 1500 B. C. from Spain (Sex and Race, vol. 1, p. 160. 1941.)

Encyc. Francaise. Comparison of Grimaldis and Bushmen (VII, 52, 8 & 9. 1936.

Frobenius, Leo. Prehistoric Rock Pictures in Europe and Africa. Bull. Museum of Modern Art, N. Y. Figures on p. 26.

Illustrated London News, Apr. 6, 1929, pp. 568-70: Apr. 13, pp. 613-15 and Apr. 20, pp. 652-3, which says of African art, it "helps to make a perfect connection between European and prehistoric African cultures."

Prehistoric Negroid Type in valley of the Tagus. Revue Anthrop. Vol. 40. pp. 325-337. 1930. by G. Herve.

Fossil Man of Asselar. Arch. Institut de Paleontologie, Humaines. Memoires 9, 1932.

Bulleid A. & Gray, H. The Glastonbury Lake Village, Vol. 2, p. 405. 1917. Wilson, D. Archaeology of Scotland, p. 309, 1851.

Van Riet Lowe, C. South Africa in the Stone Age. Illus. London News p. 606. Apr. 29, 1933.

Higgins, G. Anacalypsis, Vol. 1, p. 50. 1927.

Massey, G. A Book of the Beginnings, vol. 1, pp. 18, 218. 1881.

CHAPTER TWO

COLOR PREJUDICE AMONG WHITES AND AMONG DARKER PEOPLES FOR THEIR OWN KIND

It is quite possible also that the color prejudice of white for black began in prejudice among the whites for shades of their own color. I refer to the so-called science of Physiognomy, which rates individuals as good or bad, desirable or undesirable, on their physical traits.

This pseudo-science probably originated in the East. A very ancient Indian work, Elem-I-Kaifa, (1) tells how to judge character by the eyes, height, hair, color, and so on. But the work to which it owes development and power in the West was Aristotle's Physiognomica of the fourth century B. C.

Soft, silky hair, said Aristotle, was a sign of cowardice. Coarse one meant courage provided it curled gently at the ends. If it curled too much, or was "wooly like that of the Ethiopians" then it signified the same as the soft, silky one.

A full voice, deep and round, indicated courage; a languid or high-pitched one, cowardice. Short arms showed addiction to gambling and dancing. A pale complexion, small eyes, and thick black hair on the body showed lasciviousness. Big feet meant strength of character, provided the toes did not curve at the ends in which case it indicated impudence. Bony buttocks showed strong character; fat ones, a weak mind. A large head was quickness; a small forehead, stupidity; grey eyes, cowardice.

As for the nose, its shape, size, width, had great effect on one's character.

Blondness so much valued in the United States was no more desirable to the Greeks than jet-black, according to Aristotle. He said, "Too black a hue marks the coward as witness Egyptians and Ethiopians; so also, does too white a complexion as you may

1. Anthrop. Soc'y. Jour. Bombay, Vol. 7, pp. 440-7 1901-07.

see from women. So the hue that makes for courage must be intermediate between these extremes. A tawny color indicates a bold spirit as in lions but too ruddy a hue makes a rogue." (2) That is, the Greeks seem to have thought that the most desirable color was a dark brunet, or mulatto one. By too white a color he undoubtedly meant the fair whites of the north. In his Politics he classed them as inferior.

The Greeks admired physical strength and muscles do show up better in a dark skin than a fair one. Julian Huxley, a great living scientist, says, "Why does a good physique look better when the skin over the muscles is black than when it is white?" (2a) And we say, today, not tall, blond and handsome, but tall, dark and handsome.

In Ancient India, also, at least among the Brahmins, a very fair skin and a very dark one were not considered desirable. Their love precepts as recorded in the Kama Sutra say that among women "not to enjoyed" are "the very white" and "the very black." (3) The early Arabs did not admire a blond skin either. They "drew the distinctions that we draw between blonds and brunettes but reversed the values," says Toynbee. (4) In no dark men's lands today is a blond skin admired over a brunette one. This is true, at least for males in certain white countries interested in athletics, as Germany.

In the earlier Islamic writings one finds now and then expressions of prejudice for a black skin. Mohamet found it necessary to caution against this. He said that all men, regardless of color,

2. Physiognomy. 812a. 15. (Trans. by Loveday and Forester). Politics VIII, 7. Red hair was a sign of evil. Typhon, monster of Greece and Rome, was said to have red hair; likewise Nebuchadnezzar and Judas Iscariot. Poyntz A. World of Wonders, p. 86, 1845. Hertz F. thinks the Greeks were dark-complexioned and despised blondness. Race and Civilization, p. 108. 1928. This pseudo-science is still used by some whites in judging other whites. Dr. John B. Watson said, "There is another group of fakers advertising also in our best magazines, who agree to pick your employees on the basis of hair, color, texture of the skin, and color of the skin. To dismiss such claims, I need only mention here the fact that in some of our larger experimental laboratories we have been trying for years to correlate general intelligence, special abilities an dthe like with the color of the individual's skin, the texture and color of hair and the like. All the findings show that there is not the slightest scientific evidence supporting any of these claims." The Ways of Behaviorism, pp. 130-31. 1928.

2a. Africa View, p. 38. 1931.

3. Vatsayana. Kama Sutra, p. 46. Paris.

4. Toynbee A. Study of History, vol. 1, p. 226. 1934. See also excerpt from Said of Andalusia quoted in this present book.

were one in God; that one whose hair was even like "dried grapes" should be respected if ever he came to authority. (5)

Even in Ethiopia where a white skin was never admired and is hardly so now, a very dark skin, especially when accompanied by pronounced Negro features are somewhat looked down on. (6) The more desirable color seems to be that of the northern Ethiopian as the Shoan. The complexion of the latter is usually that of a dark mulatto and is probably due to mixture with the Portuguese who occupied that region from 1490 to 1653. But at no time in the East from Alexander the Great to now has the prejudice of whites been as strong as that of mulattoes in the British West Indies for blacks.

Except for the wars between Aryans and Dasyus in India and occasional revolts in the Islamic empire (which were not due to color alone) it is safe to say that there has been no conflict in the East nearly as serious as that between blacks and mulattoes in Haiti as late as 1850 under Emperor Soulouque.

Belief in Physiognomy grew so strong among whites and was such a power in the hands of charlatans that Pope Paul IV in 1559 placed books on it on the Index (7) and in 1743 the British Parliament outlawed it. (8)

These laws lessened this pseudo-science in Europe. But it had been developing meanwhile in the American colonies where difference in skin-color was so much more marked. With no restraining hand there, Physiognomy mounted the throne. What the whites had been saying about one another's color and features they now applied with double force to the blacks.

This began the fifth and present stage of color prejudice. And since it was a time when it was considered most awful not to be a Christian and one went to the Bible as authority for most

5. Sources in Sex and Race, Vol. 3, p. 26.

6. Asfa Yilma in her book, Haile Selassie, p. 23. 1936, says "a third race whose hair is wooly and thick. There are no Negroes in Abyssinia except as slaves." The inference is that the only Negroes there are those with "wooly hair." Yet it is the rare Ethiopian from the Emperor and his family down, whose hair is not Negroid. In 1936, I went into a room where the daughters of upper-class Ethiopians were making Red Cross bandages and I was struck with the blackness (I mean real black) of skin of all of them and such wooly hair as one would never see among American Negroes. The exception in Ethiopia are some of the Somalis who have East Indian-like hair.

7. Thorndike L. Hist. of Magic and Experimental Science, Vol. 5, p. 147. 1941.

8. Encyl. Britannica. See PHYSIOGNOMY. "All persons pretending to have skill in physiognomy were deemed rogues and vagabonds and were liable to be publicly whipped. . . . "

everything, the colonists picked up the story of Ham, tacked on the obscure Jewish legends already mentioned and used them as God's own orders to enslave the blacks. The legend of the Gibeonites doomed by Joshua to be hewers of wood and drawers of water" (Joshua 9, 23) was also woven in. Differences of color, hair and features were pushed to extreme length as in Hinton Rowan Helper's Nojoque, published 1867, where even the color of buildings was adduced to prove the "inferiority" of the black skin. Of course, the motive was production of tobacco, cotton and sugar.

This doctrine of Negro inferiority was supported by several European thinkers, among them the great Voltaire. In reply to the belief held by some that the white man was descended from the black, he said that only a blind man was permitted to believe such nonsense. "The round eyes of the Negroes," he said, "their flat noses, thick lips, ears of different shape, the wool on their heads, the measure of their intelligence, place between them and the other species prodigious differences." (9)

The spirit prevailing then was best expressed by Montesquieu (1698 - 1775) jurist and philosopher, who said ironically, "Those creatures are all over black and with such a flat nose can scarcely be pitied.

"It is hardly to be believed that God, who is a wise Being, should place a soul, especially a good soul, in such a black, ugly body. It is so natural to look upon color as the criterion of human nature. . . ." (10)

The belief in the inherent inferiority of Negroes was strengthened by a revival in the doctrine of plural human origins, which had once been outlawed by the Church. But the amazing geographical discoveries by Columbus and others had revealed varieties of humanity, hitherto undreamed of. How otherwise explain, for instance, the American Indian living on an isolated continent?

In 1520, Paracelsus, a Swiss physician, boldly declared that such people could not have been descended from Adam. In 1591, Giordano Bruno declared that no intelligent person could believe that Negroes and Jews had a common origin. At that time, the Jews, descendants of Shem, were believed by some to be the foot down. Bruno was burnt alive for this and other heresies. ancestors of European whites. But once again the Church put its

One of the next to advance this doctrine was Lucilio Vanini, who said that "Ethiopians had apes for ancestors because they had the same color" (11) and that the first men walked all-fours like

9. Essai sur les Moeurs, Vol. 1, p. 7. 1829.
10. Spirit of Laws, Book XV, Chap. 5.

apes. He excluded the whites but was nevertheless burnt alive in 1619.

The next most important work on the theory of plural origins was "The Pre-Adamite" by Isaac de la Peyrere in 1655. Peyrere proved his from the Bible. Composing chapters one and two of Genesis, he showed very logically there were two creations of man. Chapter One records a man and woman who were given dominion over the earth and over every living thing. Chapter Two says "there was not a man to till the ground." So God made a man out of dust of the earth, and later gave him a woman as companion in the Garden of Eden. This man is mentioned as Adam and the woman, Eve. Peyrere says that the man and the woman in Chapter One were therefore pre-Adamites and that it was from that stock "Cain got his wife." The Bible clearly says that Cain was sent off to another country and how could he have got a wife there if there were then on earth only three persons — Adam, Eve and Cain?

Adam and Eve, said Le Peyrere, were consecrated exclusively by God to be ancestors of His chosen people, the Jews. This idea in naming the Jews as the object of a special creation was said to be so flattering to them that La Peyrere, who was a Protestant, was accused of wanting to be their leader.

Pope Alexander VIII thought this rank heresy and had him thrown into a dungeon at Versailles. However, thanks to the intervention of Prince de Conde, the book, not himself, was burnt. Prostrating himself before the Pope the following year, he abjured his doctrine.

It was otherwise in the colonies. Racial heresies took root freely and were even preached from Christian pulpits. In the Anglo-Saxon colonies the blacks were called pre-Adamites(that is offspring of Cain), and Ham. The Catholics still taught a common origin of all men but in time accepted the Ham legend and of Noah's curse on blacks.

Color prejudice was never so strong among Spaniards and Portuguese in the Americas as among the Anglo-Saxons. They had not only been living among black people from the earliest times (as will be seen later) but were considerably mixed with them. The Spaniards treated the dark-skinned Indians of the West Indies very cruelly but this was not so much white imperialism as it was Christian imperialism. The Indians were "ungodly heathen" and the Spaniards felt that God had delivered them into their hands, precisely as did the dark-skinned Jews when they entered Canaan, firmly believing that their Jehovah had

11. Oeuvres Philosophiques, p. 214. 1842. Revue Anthrop. Vol. 25, p. 21. 1915.

1. Neolithic youth. 2. Osiris. 3. General Uah-ah-Ra (Brit. Museum).
4. Akhenaton (Louvre).

delivered the Amalekites, Jebusites and other in their hands to be slaughtered.

For cruelty, based on color, the French in Haiti came first; the Dutch in Guiana, second; and the English in the West Indies, third. The last, greater sticklers for law and morality found greatest justification for their treatment of the blacks in the "curse" on Ham.

I have given something of the where and when of the birth and growth of color prejudice. As a preliminary to dealing directly with race mixture something now of the why.

I said that the faint beginnings of color prejudice existed in Egypt and quoted Massey to that effect, therefore my theory of its origin there is this: The first colonizers of Egypt were probably the "black, wooly-haired Ethiopians" — the "blackest of all peoples" as writers of the times, as Strabo, called them. Diodorus Siculus, first of the world historians, said the Ethiopians claimed they had colonized Egypt and archaeology seems to confirm them. In fact, the earliest known Egyptians, the Badarians, a neolithic people, were Negroid. (12)

To this black colony migrated fairer peoples from the north. There is at least one instance of these white savages landing there and being made prisoners immediately. In time a mulatto "race" arose. More whites came in until in time a struggle for power between lighter and darker Egyptian grew. This much is certain, however: At no time did color rivalry become strong enough to prevent native Egyptian blacks, or even Nubian blacks, from holding positions of high power. In fact, this would have been difficult to do since most of the military was black. Also in the eighth century B. C., the Ethiopians, or unmixed blacks not only dominated all Egypt but swept into Asia Minor. If certain of the earlier Pharaohs of native stock as Thotmes III, Seti the Great, Amenophis III, and Akhenaton were not unmixed black they were very near it. (13) Others as Ramases III were undoubtedly white. Egyptian pharaohs ranged in color from white to jet-black.

Another cause of color prejudice is sexual selection, which is always and everywhere at work. Even in white men's lands there is rivalry between blonde and brunette, dark and fair. This degree of color selection in Egypt, where climatic conditions call for darker complexions, was slight. Thus the fairer and the darker intermarried pretty freely. One such marriage in royal circles was that of a Negro princess of the Cheops family with a prince

12. "Negroid traits of the Badarians." Childe, V. G. The Most Ancient East, p. 61, also, pp. 52, 144. 1928.
13. See portraits of Egyptian rules in Sex and Race, Vol. 1 & 3.

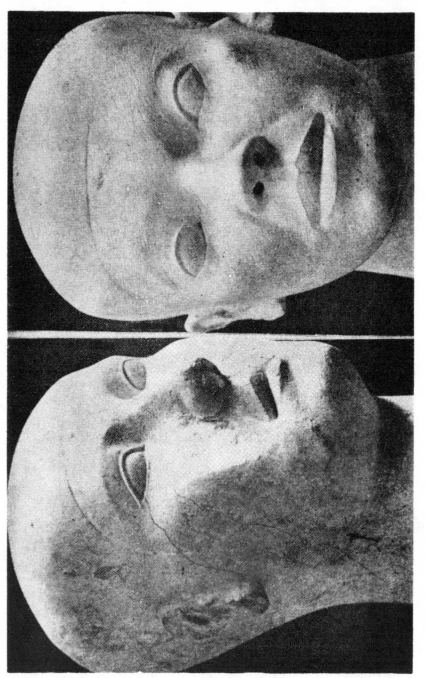

A "MIXED MARRIAGE OF 3700 B. C." Prince, evidently white, and Princess of the Cheops, famiy. Cheops was builder of the Great Pyramid (Courtesy Boston Museum of Fine Arts).

24

to all appearances European, at least in features. (14) Cheops was builder of the Great Pyramid.

But the greatest reason for color prejudice is avarice. I said that the Arabs, themselves, of Negro stock, used their version of the Ham story to exploit and enslave Central African blacks. The mulattoes of Haiti were also cruel exploiters of the blacks. One factor contributing greatly to the success of the exploiters of the blacks is the inferiority complex of large numbers of whites who compensate for the frustrations of life by looking down on Negroes. They need someone to be better than in order to feel really alive. This in time develops into hatred and mob violence.

Incidentally when whites look down on Negroes are they being so superior as they think? Well, black slaves who had been born in America used to look with contempt not only on the newly-arrived ones from Africa but on poverty-stricken whites for whom they coined the term, "poor white trash." (15) In the British West Indies are still mulattoes who look on blacks with as much contempt as certain American whites do on both.

After the blacks and mulattoes of Haiti and the Djukas, or Bush-Negroes of Dutch Guiana, had won their freedom, the United States led in cruelty to Negroes. Physiognomy blossomed into a science and actually dominated anthropology until the end of the first world war. Folk beliefs about Ham and the Gibeonites are still common in parts of the South, even as they are in the Dominion of South Africa and Kenya Colony.

The chief surviving dogma of the slave era on race is that regarding so-called intermarriage. Intermixture is "bad," especially that of the Negro and the white woman. Mating of white man and Negro woman is not so objectionable provided there is no marriage. Twenty-eight states still penalize mixed marriages. The economic motive here is clear. Slave masters were great promoters of miscegenation, especially after the abolition of the slave-trade in 1808 when they went in for slave-breeding on a large scale. White men, including students, were encouraged to cohabit with Negro women. Mulattoes meant more mammies.

14. Stevenson-Smith M. says, "The aquiline type of face so characteristic of some members o fthe family appear in the head of the prince." The wife of the prince, he says, "is of the Negroid type with thick lips wide nostrils and full cheeks." American Jour. of Archaeol. Vol. 45, Oct. Dec., p. 32. 1941.

15. Documentary Hist. of Amer. Indus. Soc'y, Vol. 2, p. 53. 1910, quotes Atlantic, Ga. Daily Intelligencer, Mar. 9, 1859, on how Negro slaves who had arrived earlier in America treated those who were then being smuggled in, with contempt. "Our common darkies treat them with sovereign contempt." Negroes continued to be smuggled in till 1861.

concubines, and butlers, who usually fetched a higher price than the unmixed Negro of the fields. Mating of Negroes and white women on the other hand helped to smash exploitation as based on color of skin.

In the chapters to follow I shall show that the issue of intermarriage belongs to the same class of rubbish as the "Physiognomy" of Aristotle and the Ham legends of the rabbis. Furthermore that if so-called instinctive repugnance to it is proof of its validity that certain mulattoes, a class that is looked down on by the whites, do also object to the marriage of unmixed blacks and white women because it threatens their position of "superiority." A writer on Haiti says that once when a black man arrived from America with a white wife the occasion called forth from the mulatto clerks remarks "very similar to those uttered on the occasion by the American shipmasters in the harbor." (16) Also upper-class mulattoes in the British West Indies do not relish the sight of black students who go to England and return with white wives. I have heard their pungent remarks on such unions. Finally, I shall show that Europe, original home of American and South African whites, had an abundance of intermarriage, or other racial admixture, from the days of Greece and Rome.

16. See Sex and Race, Vol. 2, p. 112.

CHAPTER THREE

NEGROES IN ANCIENT EUROPE — GREECE

A very singular fact about color prejudice. Where you would expect to find it most, it is least, namely in Europe, homeland of the whites. This is true of the most ancient times to the present. And contrary to popular belief, as I shall show, Negroes were, in certain areas, abundant. Moreover, whites especially of the upper classes, were fascinated by them. There was a great vogue — a fad for having them about long before the Christian era and down to the middle of the nineteenth century. Most royal and noble palaces from Sicily to Northern Russia had them. Tall, coal-black Negroes of magnificent physique were a feature of the palaces of the Czars as late as 1917. R. W. Wood (House and Garden, April 1933) tells of the great popularity of Negroes with the noble ladies of England, France, Venice and Spain.

Nowhere in earlier European literature have I been able to find any such sentimental appeal to "racial" kinship as exists in the United States and South Africa even when the Negroes came into Europe as conquerors. This appeal is a pure invention of the colonial whites to bind themselves together to further the exploitation of darker peoples.

Today, even in England, the European country where color prejudice is strongest, the black man who would be jim-crowed in the United States, refused service in Brazil, or dare not step on a sidewalk in South Africa, may enter the best hotel or restaurant and receive the finest courtesy. The average Englishman at home, has, in fact, much less prejudice towards unmixed blacks than some mulattoes in the West Indies and South America.

But this freedom from prejudice for a black skin in the earlier centuries in Europe was not due to any particular benevolence towards minorities and weaker groups. If it happened that a Negro, like a white, belonged to one of these groups, he, too, felt the iron heel, indiscriminately. Even those of his own color who were on top joined in the oppression.

Whites oppressed other whites in Europe as cruelly as they later treated Indians and Negroes in the New World. Nor was the absence of color prejudice in Europe due to the reason generally given: fewness of Negroes.

European animosities were chiefly those of sex, class, religion and nationality. Women were the first to be oppressed. They had, on the whole, no rights that a man was bound to respect. Herodotus tells how every virgin, regardless of rank, had

27

to give herself in the temple of Venus Mylitta to any man who wanted her. (1) This happened not only in Babylonia but in Cyprus and other parts of Europe. R. H. Bell rightly says that women were driven to the temple "to be ravished by the loitering horde of human boars and lascivious goats."

Everything, however, bad and shameful, that whites of the colonies said about Negroes can be equalled by what white men said about white women. Most of the earlier writers, Pagan and Christian, were contemptuous of them. An old Latin proverb ran, "Nux, asinus, muliere verbere opus habent" (A nut, a donkey and a woman need the whip). Eschylus, Greek dramatist, said, "O God, what a breed thou hast given us in womankind." Menander: "There is nothing worse in the world than a woman be she never so good." Simonides: "This is the greatest evil that Zeus has made." And Seneca, one of the most liberal of Roman writers said, "The leader of all wickedness is woman." (2)

The Jews, also, had contemptuous sayings about women, such as: "Small as an ant though your husband may be he nevertheless confers on you rank and dignity."

"Ten measures of idle talk were given the world — nine of these the women took."

"From a woman was the beginning of sin and because of her we all die." (3)

Throughout Christian Europe, generally, woman was considered an evil, an enemy of faith. A common saying was, "Woman is the gateway to hell." The Latin, femina (woman) was interpreted as "minus faith" (fe, faith; mina, minus).

In the matter of religious prejudice, Christians were thrown to the lions in Rome. When the Christians came to power they tortured not only non-Christians but other Christians. Henry VIII, head of the Protestant Church of England, sent over 70,000 Catholics and other Christians to the stake. His daughter, Bloody Mary, a Catholic, burnt or beheaded even more Protestants. The Jews in Europe were hounded, harassed, massacred. In Spain, a Jew who had carnal intercourse with a Christian woman, though she were a prostitute, was killed. (4) In Avignon, France, under the Popes, the penalty for same was the loss of a leg and a heavy fine for "each similar offense. (5) In eighth century Saxony one

1. Herodotus. Book I, chap. 199 (Rawlinson).
2. Stevenson B. Home Book of Proverbs. See WOMAN.
3. Zucrow, S. Women Slaves, and the Ignorant in Rabbinic Literature, pp. 43, 105, 120. 1932.
4. Benavides. Memorias de Fernando IV. Chap. II, 20. Cited by Lea, C. H. Spanish Inquisition, Vol. 1, p. 90. 1922.
5. Le Pileur. Prostitution du XIII a XVI siecle. Documents. Art XV, pp. 15-16. 1908.

who married a woman of a rank higher than his own was killed. (6) Under Edward III an Englishman who so "lowered" himself as to have intercourse with an Irishwoman was guilty of high treason the penalty for which was to be half-hanged, disembowelled, and quartered. English and Irish were then of the same faith — Catholic. (7)

On the other hand, persecution as based on the simple difference of color was extremely rare, even though in parts of Europe Negroes were proportionately as many as in any of the large Northern cities of the United States. Lisbon in the eighteenth century had a higher percentage of Negroes than New York.

Prejudice against Negroes and Negroids did not develop even though the latter came in at times as invaders. In spite of diligent research I have been able to find only one passage in which invading blacks are called "a cursed race," that is, in the Chanson of Roland, which will be mentioned later.

Negroes were first worshipped in Greece and Rome. White masses bowed down to black deities. The rites of Apollo were founded by Delphos and his Negro mother, Melainis; and the worship of black Isis and Horus was popular in Rome, and the Roman colonies as far north as Britain. When this latter evolved into the worship of the Black Madonna and Black Christ, Christian whites also bowed down to them. (8) In fact, one of these black

6. Ross, Class and Caste. Amer. Jour. of Social. Vol. 22, pp. 745-50. 1917. Gurowski A. Slavery in History, p. 186. 1860.

7. Kilkenny Statutes. Cited by Prendergast, J. P. in Chomwellian Invasion of Ireland, pp. 40, 143. 1868.

8. Sources cited in Sex and Race Vol. 1, p. 273-93, 239. 1940. 2nd ed. Auvergne, France, is noted for its Black Madonnas. Gostling, M. Auvergne and its people (pp. 269-70. 1911) says cf the Black Mother of Rocamadour, who is probably the ancient Negro goddess, Soulivia, "The Black Mother . . . signified to those pre-Christian worshippers at Rocamadour the highest ideal of which they were able to conceive and to her they sacrificed their best—and what can man do more?" Of another, the Black Madonna of the Vallee Tenebreuse, he says that St. Louis, King of France, his three brothers, and his queen, Blanche, came to her shrine with rich offerings. Also Henry II of England, Charles le Bel and Philippe de Valois and Louis XI. This Black Mother was called "La Reine de France" (Queen of France) p. 273. Other Virgins mentioned are that of Orcival, p. 12 ; of Marsat, p. 53 ; of Ferrand, p. 81 ; Mt. Dore, p. 83 ; Puy de Dome, perhaps most famous Black Virgin now, p. 170 ; Aurillac, 219 ; and Capelou.

Costello, L. S. Pilgrimage to Auvergne, pp. 64-73, mentions Notre Dame de Liesse, the black woman of the Crusades, Ismeria, who was later worshipped as a Madonna, and adds, "There is scarcely a celebrated Virgin throughout France who is not black." Louis XI Charles VII, Francis I, and Louis XIII, all thought there was a special virtue in the Black Virgins, he says.

For additional sources on the Black Madonna see: Durand-Lefebvre,

Madonnas was a Sudanese woman of the thirteenth century A. D. There were also Negro saints of the Catholic Church in Europe. (9)

After considerable research I have been able to find only three instances of laws aimed at Negroes in Europe. The first was in 1689 in France, when under the influence of white Haitian planters, marriage of whites and Negroes was forbidden; (10) the second, also in France, when Louis XV ordered the expulsion of Negroes from France because of the 1500 mulatto foundlings in Paris alone, (11) a decree which was not carried out. (The anti-marriage law was repealed during the Revolution). The third was in London in 1731, when the city council forbade the teaching of trades to Negroes. (12)

A seeming fourth was when the Moors of Granada were forbidden to bring in more blacks from Africa in 1560. (13) That reason, however, was religious, not racial, as the prohibition did not apply to Christians, regardless of color. This lack of color prejudice existed even though the Negroes had been engaging in warfare with whites on European soil perhaps even before Hannibal. In fact, there were even saying and proverbs in favor of black people. An old English saying was: "To see a black man the first thing on waking up in the morning is an omen of good luck."

M. Etude sur l'origine des Vierges noires. Paris 1937. He gives a list of the black Virgins, some 230 in France, and 36 elsewhere. pp. 11-39. Latin America also has some famous black Virgins, chiefly in Mexico and Costa Rica.

Pommerol, M. F. Cultes des vierges noires. Soc. D'Anthrop. de Paris. Bull. Jan. 17, 1901.

Jones, T. W. S. The Queen of Heaven (Mamma Schiavona, or the Black Mother) 1898.

L. Bertrand says of the Virgin of Font-Romeu, Catalonia. "She has the figure of a peasant woman with a great flattish nose . . . . The Child Jesus looks like a little wooly-haired African with low forehead and large ears," p. 42 1931. See also the extensive documentation I have given on the Black Madonna in the appendix of Sex and Race, Vol. 1.

9. Baring-Gould. S. Lives of the Saints (Moyses the Ethiopian) Vol. 9. pp. 348-50; Vol. 12 Pt. 2, pp. 659-668 (St. Elesbaan). For St. Maurice of Aganaum see Rogers, J. A. World's Great Men of Color, Vol. 1, pp. 290-95. 1947.

10. Lespinasse, B. Histoire des Affranchis de St. Domingue, Vol. 1, p. 38. 1882.

11. See sources in Sex and Race, Vol. 1, p. 223. 1940 (2nd ed.)

12. Notes and Queries, Vol. 161, p. 272.

13. Marmol Carvajal. Rebelion y Castigos de Moriscos, Vol. 1, p. 161.

(14) Shakespeare speaks of the "sweet colour" of the "Ethiopes," and in Sonnet 130 rapturously of a black skin and wiry hair. Negroes became the favorites of royalty as far north as Russia. Adopted by royalty they were given royal surnames, married persons of rank; and in some cases became virtual rulers and ancestors of European royalty. (15) Byron satirized this custom in Don Juan: ". . . blacks and such like things that gain their bread as favorites and ministers."

Negroes, as was said, were deified in early Greece. They appear as gods in Greek mythology. The chief title of Zeus, greatest of the Greek gods, was "Ethiops," that is, "Black." (16) And from the descriptions of Ethiopians in early Greek writings there can be no doubt of their identity with living Negroes. Xenophanes of about 550 B. C. spoke of their black skin and flat noses; and Herodotus (450 B. C.) not only does the same but adds that the Egyptians were like them. (17) Again, Strabo, (first century B. C. geographer), wrote of the Ethiopian's "black complexion" and "wooly hair." (17a) Snowden says, "That the Greeks regarded blackness as typical of the Ethiopian's color is apparent not only from descriptions of the Ethiopian's skin as the blackest in the world but the proverbial "to wash an Ethiopian white." (18)

Homer in an often quoted passage tells how the Greek gods used to go on their feast-days to Ethiopia to commune with their ancestors. Dionysius wrote:

"Upon the great Atlantic, near the isle

Of Erithrea, for its pastures famed,

The sacred race of Ethiopians dwell." (19)

14. Virenda Vandpopadhyaya. Dict. of Superstitions & Mythology (Great Britain) p. 177. 1927. Shakespeare said in Titus Andronicus, "The blacker, the fairer the Moor (IV, 2 71. 1593). W. P. Dabney, Cincinnati Union, Aug, 4, 1950, tells of white prostitutes in that town, who, on Saturday nights "used to pay an old black Negro to walk through each room to bring them good luck in patronage." For Negroes considered good-luck in present-day England see Sex and Race, Vol. 1, p. 217, 2nd ed.

15. Sex and Race, Vol. 3, p. 357. Index "Negro favorites." Others mentioned in this work.

16. Smith, Wm. Dict. of Greek and Roman Biography and Mythology. See AETHIOPS.

17. Herodotus, Book 2 Chap. 107. 17a. Book 15, Chap. I, 24. Trans. Hamilton and Boslock. 1857.

18. Negro in Ancient Greece American Anthrop. N. S. 50, 1948 p. 33.

19. Quoted by J. Bryant, Analy, of Anc. Mythol. Vol. 3, p. 185. 1776.

At the legendary siege of Troy black men and women fought with great courage. One of their kings was "black Memnon" of Ethiopia. The herald and companion of Ulysses, hero of Troy, was "black, wooly-haired Eurybiates." Zeus, Father of the Gods, is in love with Lamia, a black princess from Africa. Mylitta, Queen of the Gods, originally Assyrian, also worshipped in Greece, was black and associated with miscegenation. From her comes the word, Mulatto. (20)

Other black Venuses were Melainis, (21) from which is derived melanin, or the pigment in the Negro's skin; and Scota, or Scotia, Egyptian princess, married to a Greek, and from whom it is said, the name Scot-land, originated. She is believed to be the ancestress of the Scots.

Later, when Greek knowledge of Africa passed from the mythological to the geographical and Negroes arrived in numbers they were no longer defied, but were still well thought of. Herodotus said, "The Ethiopians are the tallest and handsomest men in the world," (22) and that the kings were chosen for their height and strength. In the Vulgate, or Greek edition of the Bible, of about 270 B. C. they are mentioned as "a nation, tall and of glossy skin . . . a people terrible from beginnings onwards. A nation that is sturdy and treadeth down." (23) In the Sybilline Books they are called "stout-hearted." Vol. 5, 1, 206.

Stephen of Byzantium wrote, "Ethiopia was the first established country on earth; and the people were the first, who introduced the worship of the Gods and who enacted laws. (24) "Lucian says that the first astronomers were Ethiopians. "It was the Ethiopians," he says, "that first delivered the doctrine of astrology to men." (25) Strabo says that geometry came to the Greeks from the Ethiopians.

20. Rawlinson, G. Herodotus Vol. 2, pp. 444-6. 1859. Weiner, L. says, "There can be little doubt that the name (mulatto) was derived by the Portuguese and Spaniards from the Berber, milati (Negress of the superior class) that is, a mulatto." (Mayan and Mexican Origins, p. 93. 1926). Century Dictionary errs in saying that it comes from the Spanish, mulatto —a young mule. Children born of Christian and Moslem parents were called muladi, regardless of race in Spain under Moslem rule.
21. This is from the Greek, melos-amos, black. Melainis was mother of Delphos, founder of the rites of Apollo. From her name also comes Melanesian, black peoples of the Pacific.
22. Herodotus, III, 20.
24. Bryant, Vol. 3, p. 185.
23. Isaiah, 18, 1.
25. Astrol. 3. Strabo XVI, 2, 24-5. (trans by H. Jonas. Vol. 7, p. 271). Fabre d'Olivet says, "The Black Race more ancient than the white was dominant upon the earth and held the sceptre of science and power; it possessed all Africa and the greater part of Asia." The White Race, he says, was still weak, savage and without laws, without cultivation of any

NEGROES FROM ANCIENT GREECE

1. Coins with Negro head. 2. Melainis, mother of Delphos, founder of the rites of Apollo. 3. Circe, sorceress in Homer's Odyssey. The others represent various subjects.

Greek artists and designers of smaller objects were clearly fascinated by Negroes. Grace Beardsley in her introduction to "The Negro in Greek and Roman Civilization" says. "The popularity of the type was tremendous, and is attested by a wealth of statuettes, vases, engraved gems, coins, lamps, weights, finger-rings, ear-rings, necklaces and masks from classical sites." Incidentally, she describes the Negro almost always as slaves. But since the ancients had such contempt for slaves would they have had them on their personal ornaments and on their coins?

Greek writers, too, spoke of the Negroes among them, Philostrates wrote. "Charming Ethiopians with their strange color." (25a) Menander said, "The man, whose natural bent is good, he, mother, though Ethiop is nobly born." (26) Aesclepiades, erotic poet of 270 B. C., praised a black woman thus, "With her charms, Didymee has ravished my heart. Alas, I melt as wax at the sight of her beauty. She is black, it is true but what matters? Coals, also are black but when alight they glow like rose-cups." (27) Alexander the Great's foremost general was a Negro, Clitus Melas, (28) that is Clitus the Black (in Latin, Clitus Niger). Greek legends tell of Negroes at the siege of Troy. They also appear on the monuments, especially in Crete. (29) There were Negro amazons, or female warriors, too.

Artemis, their goddess of chastity, who was identified with Dianna of the Ephesians, is sometimes shown with Negroid features.

sort, destitute of memories and too devoid of understanding even to conceive hope." He adds, "The black race then existed in all the pomp of social state. It covered entire Africa with powerful nations sprung from it; it possessed Arabia and had planted its colonies over all the meridional coasts of Asia and very far into the interior. An infinity of monuments which bear the African characters still exist in our day in all these latitudes and attest the grandeur of the peoples to which they belong. The enormous constructions of Mahabalipouram, the ramparts of the Caucasus, the pyramids of Memphis, the excavations of Thebes in Egypt and many other works which the astonished attributes to the giants prove the long existence of the Sudeen (Black Race) and the immense progress it made in the arts." Hermeneutic Interpretation, etc. pp. 6. 40. 1915. See Sex and Race, Vol. 1 p. 263-8. 2nd ed. 1940, for what other writers have said on this ancient power of the blacks.

26. Snowden. Op. cit. pp. 38. This work, which is so far the best done on the subject, gives sources and bibliography.

27. Deheque. Anthologie grecque, Vol. 1, p. 48. 1863.

28. Cummings, L. V. Alexander the Great. p. 50 Clitus Niger (Clitus the Black).

29. Evans, Sir A. Palace of Minos, Vol. 2, pt. 2, pp. 348, 755-7. 1928. On Negro amazons, see Rothery G. C. The Amazons, p. 8, 10. 1910 who mentions "a great Amazonia invasion coming from Ethiopia in the West . . . certain it is we have early evidence of bands of African women." See also Snowden. Op. Cit, p. 37.

NEGROES FROM ANCIENT GREECE

1. Artemis, Goddess of Chastity. 2. Negro Amazon. Left centre: Vase
with Negro and White Woman. Lower: Soldiers.

Circe, famed for her magical powers, is represented as a Negro woman. Some writers think the drawing grotesque because its features aren't Greek but it is "racially" correct. Circe, according to the legends, was the daughter of Aetes, king of Colchis, and Herodotus says Colchian were Negroes. Circe's sister was Medea, famous sorceress, associated with Jason and the Golden Fleece. She was honored as a goddess at Corinth, and figures much in the writings of Pindar, Euripides, and others.

Greeks and Ethiopians mated without prejudice. Lord Cromer, in an effort to learn the real attitude of the Greeks towards this, consulted four leading classical scholars — Ramsey, Haverfield, Bury and Evans. Cromer, a scholar, himself, said, "I cannot find anywhere any distinct indication that color antipathy considered by itself formed a bar to social intercourse and therefore to intermarriage . . . that color antipathy existed to any marked extent in the ancient world." He adds that neither the dominant Romans nor the intellectual Greeks seems to "have taken much account of whether the skins of their subjects or less intellectually advanced races were white, black, or brown." (30)

A. E. Zimmern says, "The Greeks thought Negroes very interesting looking people and were amused at their wooly hair but they show no trace of color prejudice." (31) Westermann is of the same opinion. (32) It is true that certain Greek statuettes and jewelry do show some Negroes as grotesque, that is they exaggerate size of lips and flatness of nose but that seems to have been flair for the bizarre and certainly not to prejudice since they wore such jewelry. Greek warriors, too had figures of Negroes on their shields. (33)

"Greeks of the classic period," says P. Perdrizet, "knew Negroes of diverse varieties from the most thick-lipped, wooly-

30. Ancient and Modern Imperialism, pp. 131-2. 1910.

31. The Greek Commonwealth, p. 323. 1931. See also pp. 320, 332, for Negroes in Greece. He adds, "The color-bar appears to be of comparatively recent origin and it has not spread to modern Greece."

32. Quar. Bull. Polish Instit. of Arts, Vol. 1, p. 346. 1943.

33. Harvard Studies in Class. Philology, vol. 13, p. 88. 1902. Shakespeare mentions a greek warrior with a black Ethiop on his shield reaching at the sun. Pericles II. 2.20.

For other pictures of Negroes in Ancient Greece and Rome see; Reinach, S. Repertoire des vases peints, Vol. 1, 48, 169, 244, 316, 518. Vol. 2, p. 104. 1922. Vol. 1, p. 169. Negro and mulatto soldiers of Busiris.

Reinach S. Repertoire de la Statuaire grecque et romaine, Vol. 2, pt. 2, p. 561, 562, 563, Vol. 1, p. 541. (Ethiopian child slave). Vol. 3, p. 273, 260 ; Vol. 4, p. 364, 353, 350. See Index "Negre" in Vol. 1910.

haired, flat-nosed sons of Ham to handsome, fine, elegant, pleasing Nubians — or to use their ancient name, Ethiopians." (33a)

Since Negroes were so well thought of there must have been
considerable mating of them with whites. But there is little mention of it. With no color prejudice there evidently wouldn't be any.
Such mention as we have is because when the white wife of a
white man bore a mulatto child it was clear proof of adultery
which was then punished with death. Had there been other
objections to race-crossing we would undoubtedly have known
of it. For instance, we know positively how the early colonists
of Massachusetts, Maryland and Virginia felt about miscegenation,
but from Greek and Roman literature which exceeds by far in
volume writings of the early colonists, we learn almost nothing
although Negroes were abundant, especially in Rome. Therefore,
if two thousand years hence one looks back on early colonial history as we are now looking on classical one, he would be justified
in saying that the Greeks and Romans in comparison were free
from color antipathy. The early American colonists had laws against
the mating of whites and blacks; the ancients, none.

The three cases of miscegenation so far found in the non-
mythological literature of Greece involve only adultery. Before I
mention them, however, it might be well to call attention to a fact
which, I am sure, will throw clearer light on the subject of the
mating of whites and blacks in Europe and the world over. It
is this: It is the foreign, or imported, males, regardless of color,
who coming into any land whatsoever as rulers, soldiers, sailors,
merchants, colonizers, slaves, are throughout history the pioneers
in race mixture. In the colonial expansion of Europe it was the
white man who went into Africa, India, Oceania, the New World
and in the absence of white women mated with the dark-skinned
women of those lands. (34) In the last two world wars, also,
American and other soldiers, white and Negro, mated with the
women of France, Germany, Italy, Britain, North and West Africa,
Egypt, Persia, India, Japan, China, Korea, the South Sea Islands,
West Indies and Latin-America. In a similar way, Negroes coming into Europe and leaving their women behind, have mated with
the white women there. In short, in the dark men's lands mating

33a. Collec. Fouquet, Bronzes Grec d'Egypte, p. 58. 1911. Lowenherz:
Die Ethiopien der Altclassichen Kunst. (Göttingen, 1861) gives a list of
Ethiopian statues and shows how well Negroes were known to Greeks.

34. Fabre d'Olivet thinks that white women were enamored of black
invaders. He says, "Some white women of whom the strangers had
taken possession and whose goodwill they strove to win, were not difficult
to seduce. They were to unhappy in their own country to have nourished

has been between white men and dark women; in white men's lands between dark men and white women; in white men's lands between dark men and white women. Negroes have been coming into Europe for nearly three thousand years, not to mention their being there in prehistoric times. And we shall see them there, too, in considerable numbers — a fact that leading historians have either not thought of or chose not to see.

The cases from Greece involved adultery, as was said. But the scientists of that time explained such births on atavism, that is, a throw back — that one of the parents had a Negro ancestor more or less distant.

Aristotle (B. C. 346-280) evidently favored this belief. He said, "In Sicily a woman who committed adultery with an Ethiopian brought forth a daughter that was white but this daughter had a son that was black." The dark skin here is thrown back to the grandfather. (34a)

The second case is from Plutarch, who lived three centuries later. He says, "A certain Greek woman, having borne a black child then being on trial for adultery discovered herself as being descended from an Ethiop in the fourth generation." The throwback here is to the great-great grandfather. (35)

The third is from Pliny (A. D. 23-79). It is "the famous boxer, Nicaeus, born at Istanbul (Constantinople) whose mother was the offspring of adultery with an Ethiopian and no different from her mother while Nicaeus was Ethiopian in color." (36) These instances, whatever they might or might not have proved, do show some miscegenation did occur.

any love of it. Returning to their caves they showed the brilliant necklaces, the pleasing and delicately shaded stuffs which they had received. Nothing more was needed for them to raise their heads above all others. A large number, profiting by the shadows of night, fled and joined the newcomers. Fathers and husbands thinking only of their resentment seized their feeble weapons and advanced to reclaim their daughters or wives. Their movement had been anticipated and was awaited. The result of the combat was not doubtful. Many were killed ; a great number taken prisoners. The rest fled." Hermeneutic Interpretation of the Origin of the Social State, p. 40. 1915.

34a. Generatione An. 1, 18, 722a. Hist. An. 7, 6 586a.

35. De sera numinis vindicta, 21. (Delay of the Divine Justice, p. 58. Peabody. 1885

36. Book VII, 12 ; 51.

A still earlier explanation is maternal impression, which is very ancient folklore. In fact, such a theory is attributed to Hippocrates of the fifth century B. C., called the Father of Medicine, who, it is said, explained the birth of a black baby to a white couple by saying that the wife while in intercourse with her husband saw the picture of a Negro cohabiting with a white woman, and thus the color of her baby. There seems to be no recorded proof of Hippocrates having said that (it might have been lost as so much of ancient writing is) but true or not the theory was to prove of much importance. It was used in ancient Rome; in France more than a thousand years later, (37) and was accepted and quoted by medical writers. (38)

In the Midrash Rabba, ancient Jewish legends, support is also given this theory of maternal impression .The Ethopian wife presents her black husband with a light-colored child. The husband tells the rabbi that the child is not his. The rabbi asks whether there was a picture of a man in the room at the moment of intercourse and being told there was, inquiries whether it was white or black. When told it was white, he answered, "This accounts for the color of your son." (39)

In the Ethiopian romance of Heliodorus, written in the third century, is a similar tale. Here Persina, Queen of Ethiopia, tries to convince her black husband, Hydaspes, that her child, much lighter in color than herself was due to a similar cause, that is, there was a white statue in the room at the moment of conception.

37. See story of the Black Nun, Daughter of Marie Therese, Queen of France, by a Negro (Sex and Race, Vol, 1, Chap. 21. 1940). I have run across many accounts of white women having black babies merely by looking at a black man. Le Cat, "Traite de la Couleur de la Peau Humaine" p. 21. 1765. tells of a German lady, who after seeing a Negro lackey among the servants of a German prince, had a Negro child.

In Vol. 2. Sex and Race. I've given instances of reports of such births in the United States. Also, it was once feared that women of the harems of the sultans of turkey with so many very dark Negroes about would be affected by sight of them and have black babies (History of the Serail Translated by Efl Grimeston). p. 61. See more of this in appendix, Chap. 7.

38. See, for instance, Gould & Pyle. Anomalies and Curiosities of Medicine, p. 81. 1937. "Hippocrates saved the honor of a princess accused of adultery with a Negro because she bore a black child."

39. Freeman and Simon. Midrash Rabbah. Genesis, p. 674. 1939. One suspects though that the narrator of this story tells it tongue in cheek.

(40) She did not succeed which proves that even at that time some had doubts on the subject. Medical science today rejects that theory. There are no nerves in the umblical cord which joins the child to the mother therefore her thoughts can have no effect on it.

The above incidents do show, however, that the ancients did give some thought to the crossing of whites and Negroes. Centuries later in Rome and under Islam we shall have more abundant and precise evidence of this. We shall also see a general absence of antipathy towards it.

4-. Underdowne. 1587. pp. 107.08 1895. See also Brome R. The English Moor, p. 67. first publ. 1658 ed. 1873.

There are educated whites who still believe that a white woman might have a black baby merely by looking at a Negro or that a white couple with a Negro strain, however distant, might have one. Science rejects both these beliefs. So do the courts. Even during slavery they refused to accept them. White women legally married to Negroes were bearing mulatto children and so were unmarried white women. It would have been useless for one of the latter to say that she was frightened by a black man or that the father of her child had some Negro strain.

NOTES ON THE BLACK MADONNA

The worship of a black woman as the mother of the human race goes back to the dimmest antiquity, it seems. Inman T. (Ancient Faiths Vol. 2 p. 267. 1868), says, "The vulva . . . the portal through which life passes in and emerges out into the world is black among all oriental nations. Its color, therefore, is appropriate to the female creator, the mother of Gods and men from whom all things spring. If we turn to the Hebrew we see that it supports me in the idea. We find the word, Shahar, or Shachar, which signifies 'to be black.'" In Vol. 1, p. 159, he mentions an "old black Venus" who was later worshipped as the Virgin of Amadou. See also p. 105 for Diana of the Ephesians, mentioned in the Bible. For picture of her and other Black Goddesses see, Sex and Race, Vol. 3 p. 142.

The earliest traditions of the "Saviors of Mankind," from the Buddhas to Jesus depict them as black, or dark-skinned (see Sex and Race, Vol. 1, 273-83. 2nd ed. 1940). Eisler R. says that Josephus, Jewish historian of the first century said that Christ "was a man of simple appearance mature age, dark skin, with little hair. About four and a half feet, 54 or 58 inches (tall), hunchbacked, with a long face . . . and undeveloped beard." He says this appears in the reconstructed original—Halosis, II, 174 et seq.) The early Christians, he says accepted that picture, including Tertullian and Augustine but that the Halosis underwent the usual "corrections at the hands of Christian copyists with a view to embellishment." The Christians had gained power, they had become mighty, Christ had become a King and it would no longer suit to portray him as unimpressive in appearance. The original text, says Eisler, "would give offense to believing Christians and their Hellenistic ideal of male beauty" therefore they changed the pen-picture of Christ to "ruddy, six feet high, well-grown, venerable, erect, handsome . . . blue eyes . . . beautiful mouth, copious beard." (Messiah Christ, pp. 411, 421-442.) See also F. Hertz: Race and Civilization, p. 183. 1928 on this.

A portrait of Christ, entirely apocryphal and with absolutely no foundation in truth, was conceived somewhere along the line by a European artist according to European ideals of beauty and that seems to have served as concept for thousands of pictures that since followed. Since the first one, or ones, were entirely the product of imagination, it follows that all the rest are. Their only value is artistic.

Peigot says, "There remains nothing authentic upon the exterior appearance of Christ." Recherches Hist. sur la personne de Jesus Christ." p. 2, 1829. He says also that neither St. Augustine nor Tertullian thought Jesus good-looking, pp. 116, 117, 118, 124, 129, 130. See also Stuart-Glennie. J. S. Isis and Osiris. "Out of Egypt have I called my son. Out of the Osiris myth have I called my Christ" pp. 417-432. 1878.

ADDITIONAL NOTES ON EGYPT AND THE NEAR EAST

Aeshylus Greek dramatist (525-456 B. C.) makes Danaus say in the "Supplices" that he knew the approaching ship was Egyptian because "the crew may be distinctly seen with their black limbs that appear from their white garments." (Collected Works. Trans. Blomfield, p. 272. 1840). Pindar, Solon and Herodotus, all of whom visited Egypt have said similarly.

A. Block on the origin of the Egyptians, says they were Negroes, especially as seen in the fullness of their lips. "This characteristic is nothing else but atavistic proof of the Negroid origin of the Egyptians and consequently of their African origin. It is the same with the enlarged base of the nose and its lesser height." He cites as further proof Lucian and Galen, who lived five years in Egypt. (Bull. et Mem. Soc. Anthrop. 1901, pp. 393-403.)

"The Egyptians, though healthy, large and robust were clumsy in their forms and coarse in their features. Like other African tribes they were wool-haired, flat-nosed, thick-lipped, and if not absolutely blacks, very nearly approaching to it in color." (Specimens of Ancient Sculpture Society of Dilettanti, Vol. 1.)

"On the sculptures of Egyptian monuments on the fact of the Sphinx, in the features of the most ancient mummies and in those of Egyptian and wooden and stone statues, I saw the Afro-Asiatic type as clearly as I see it in the faces of the fellaheen and nobles of the present day." Their color, he said was "dusky, dark, dark-skinned" and their hair "varying from coarse, straight, black to curly, crinkly, wooly." Henry M. Stanley, North Amer. Rev. Vol. 170, pp. 656 et seq. 1900.

Gurowski says that the artists, architects, merchants, mechanics operatives, sailors, agriculturists and shepherds of ancient Egypt were undoubtedly of Negro stock. (Slavery in History, p. 5. 1860).

Prince and Princess of Cheops Family. Amer. Jour. of Archaelogy, Oct.-Dec. VVol. 45. Dec. 1941.

GREECE

For Sir Arthur Evans on Negro connections in Greece see Crisis Maga. Oct., 1923, p. 268. Evans says also, "A Minoan chieftain is seen leading the first of a Negro troop at a run . . . the employment of Negro auxiliaries by Minoan commanders thus authenticated is, of itself, an historical fact of the greatest significance . . . At Knossos, as shown suggested above these black mercenairies may well have served as palace guards . . .

"It seems quite possible that the Minoan commanders made use of black regiments for their final conquest of a large part of the Pelopennese and Greece." Palace of Minos, Vol. 2, Pt. 2, pp. 348, 755-7. 1928.

A great number of Ethiopians, eastern and western, served with Xerxes in Greece. Herodotus (Rawlinson) vol. 4, p. 57. 1859. For more on Negro soldiers see Graindor P. Les Vases au Negre. Musee Belge. Vol. 12, pp. 25-33. 1908.

Graindor P. Tete de Negre du Musee de Berlin. Bull. de Corresp. Hellenique, Vol. 39, pp. 402-412. 1915.

Frichet. H. Fleshpots of Antiquity, p. 188. 1934.

Theophrastus. On the Vain Man. "He takes pains to be provided with a black servant who always attends him in public:" Characters Trans. by Howell, p. 61. 1824.

PERSIA

On the Aryano-Negroes of Persia, Dieulafoy says "The Greeks, themselves, seem to have known two Susian races. Have not their old poets given as direct decendants of the Susia, Memnon, legendary hero who peristed at Troy, a Negro—Tithon—and a white mountain woman, Kissia? Did they not make Memnon command black regiments and white regiments?" Acropole de suse, p. 44. Also pp. 9, 16, 26-29, 102-3. 1893.

"The Persian Gulf was called in antiquity the Ethiopian Sea. There the Cushites ruled over the whites and intermixed with them and the great Eastern founder of the first empire whom the dim Eastern and Persian legends call Zohack, was in all probability at the utmost a mulatto, Semiramide, his mother being of the white, then the subjugated stock . . . . A black eunuch, Bagoas put on the throne, Darius Codomannus." Gurowski, A. America and Europe, pp. 175-7, 5, 27. 1957.

CHAPTER FOUR

INTERMIXTURE OF WHITES AND BLACKS IN ANCIENT ROME

Rome was a melting pot second in variety only to the United States and Brazil. All the "races" of the Old World met and mingled there. Rome traded with China so there were probably Chinese, too. Droves of fair Britons, Celts, Gauls, Teutons, Slavs, Spaniards, Moors, Persians, Egyptians, Ethiopians, Sudanese and Nigritians, were brought to Rome. Martial (A. D. 40-102) mentions Thracians, Sarmatians, peoples "from the Nile at its sources," Arabs, Sabaens, Sicilians, Sicambrians (Germans) "with twisted" hair, and Ethiopians "with woolly hair" as among the peoples to be seen at the games. (1) Modern historians as Carcopino, (2) Frank, (3) Barrow (4) and Duruy (5) mention Rome's racial variety. "All the barbaric peoples, all the conquered were represented," says Duruy. Slaves were so numerous in Rome, says Pliny, "that we require the services of a nomenclator even to tell us the names of our servants."

The Negroes were brought principally from Greece, Carthage, Egypt, the Sudan and Morocco. Like the whites and near-whites from the East they were processed first through the great slave-market on the island of Delos and later through Corinth and Carthage. Rome, itself became still later the greatest slave-mart of antiquity. Strabo (B. C. 63-A. D. 21 says that as many as 10,000 slaves a day were sold in Rome alone. White and blacks were sold indiscriminately.

Slaves were employed at not only menial tasks as street-cleaners but as actors, tutors, secretaries, counsellors and physicians. Among occupations of Negroes, as named by Roman writers, were actors, dancers, acrobats, soldiers, gladiators, priests of Isis, outriders, litter-bearers, charioteers, bath-attendants, cooks,

1. On The Spectacles, III.
2. La Vie Quotidienne a Rome.
3. Race Mixture in the Roman Empire. American Hist. Rev. Vol. 21, p. 703 1916. The Roman masses, he says were "a conglomeration of Europeans, Asiatics and Africans."
4. Slavery in the Roman Empire, pp. 17-18. 1928. Also Chap. "The Slave Population" in Fowler, W. W. Social Life at Rome, pp. 204-236. 1929. Seneca, great legislator and thinker, had Negro slaves (see NEGRE) in Larousse. XIX siecle.
5. Histoire de Rome, Vol. 2, pp. 379-388; Vol. 3, pp. 560 et seq.; Vol. 4, pp. 88, 763. 1882.

waiters, domestics, divers, bootblacks and the like. (6) Others
were conductors of elephants, who sometimes were of high military rank. (6a). Some slaves rose to be rulers in all but name.
Such, says Carcopino, "were often gorged with wealth and honors as Narcissus and Uallas who held absolute authority in
Caesar's name over the wealth and life of his subjects." (7) Two
others mentioned by Juvenal were Licinius and Crispinius. The
latter, favorite of Domitian, was enormously rich. He was an
Egyptian. Juvenal called him "one of the dregs of the Nile."

The color of these powerful ex-slaves was not given but some
were undoubtedly Negroes. That they were dark-skinned is clear.
It was the custom to whiten with chalk the naked feet of newly-
arrived slaves exposed for sale. Such slaves, it appears from
Juvenal, where those from the East. Certainly the feet of those
already white, as blond ones from the north, would not be whitened.
Pliny mentions Pallas as coming "with whitened feet" (pedibus
albus) and Juvenal does so of Licinius and Crispinius. Pallas, freedman of Emperor Claudius, was lover of the Empress. Later, in
Greece and Turkey we shall see clearer proof of unmixed Negroes,
a long line of them, holding power as great or greater than these
Roman ex-slaves.

Whiteness of skin made it no easier for a slave. Fair British
slaves, according to Cicero, were the least desirable of all the barbarians brought to Rome. (8)

Human nature being what it is there were undoubtedly animosities which had color of skin as the outward sign but it could
not have been serious since the upper classes, unlike those of
Haiti, Venezuela, or the United States, did not encourage them.
In Rome and in all the ancient world a slave was a slave. In
fact the racial variety was so great that it was impossible to set
off any one group as in America where white indentured servant
was set against Negro one. In ancient Rome a slave was valued
according to his ability.

Roman literature, though abundant, has very little on color
prejudice, though Negroes were plentiful. In fact the chief passages used to prove color antipathy can be limited to three
from only one writer: Juvenal of the second century A. D. In
attacking Roman wives for general misconduct, one of which is

6. Snowden, F. M. Negro In Classical Italy. Amer. Jour. of Class.
Philol. July 1947, pp. 287-88. See also his Classical Addendum in Classical
Outlook, April 1948, p. 71-72.

6a. Seneca, Epistle 85; Martial Epigrams, I, 105; Armandi D. Hist.
Militaire des Elephants, pp. 252-5. 1893.

7. La Vie Quotidienne a Rome, 83, 1939. Pliny, Bk. 35. Chap. 58.
Juvenal. Sat I, 111; VII, 16; XIV, 305; IV 1.

8. Epist. Ad Atticum I, 4. Epist. 15, 1.

illicit sex relations with Negroes, he says that these matrons are likely to bear black children — offspring of a color that "one would rather not see of a morning." (9)

But this is not at all evidence of race prejudice. It was merely superstitious fear. The ancients were even stronger believers in omens than ourselves. The first thing they saw on arising in the morning was for many a sign of good or bad luck for the day. For instance, black was a sign of mourning for them, thus some associated a black skin with that pretty much as some persons today see even in black cats. Also, Romans thought certain days unlucky as we do Friday the 13th. They called such, dies atri, and marked them with charcoal on their calendars, hence "black" days, all of which, by chance, happened to be the color of the Negroes.

Juvenal says again, "Your cups will be handed you by . . . the bony hand of some Moor so black you'd rather not meet him at midnight." (10) This is clearly poetic extravagance. Romans had Negroes waiting on them by day why then be so afraid of their color at night when with their unlit streets "all cats were black" at midnight. In fact to have a number of Ethiopian slaves in one's service was a sign of great luxury in the imperial epoch, so much so says Babelon, (11) that they were brought "in droves" to Rome after the Egyptian conquest. It is clear that with so many Negroes about and their being of use too, the superstition against black, in their case must have amounted to no more than the belief about black cats amongst us.

Even in America where color prejudice was strong many whites not only used them as intimate servants but preferred them as wet-nurses. People who live together not only learn to overcome inculcated prejudices based on physique but in time may even defend such physical differences against strangers. Superstitions about human coloring, as say red hair, have never amounted to much. Besides, blacks fetched a higher price than whites, according to Blair. It is therefore clear that the above were not signs of "race" prejudice, such as we see them today. Even greater than the superstition about black was that about left-handed persons. They were considered wicked, designing, evil, so much so that from them came one of the words most suggestive of evil in

9. Sixth Satire, 596-600. Lombroso classes left handedness as "atavistic and pathological." Crime pp. 370-1. 1918.
10. Fifth Satire, 54-6 ; 59-62.
11. Les cabinets des antiques, p. 52. 1887. See also Larousse 19e siecle (NEGRE) on Seneca re Negroes in Rome. Blair, "Slavery Amongst the Romans, says, "The natives of some particular countries were purchased at high prices as personal attendants ; in this situation were Egyptians, Ethiopians and Asiatics." p. 150. 1833.

our language that is, "sinister," from the Latin, sinistra (left hand).
The belief lasted even into modern times. Lombroso, great crim-
inologist (1836-1909) listed left-handedness among the "criminal
traits."

The third passage from Juvenal reads, "Let the straight-
limbed mock the bandy-legged, the white man sneer at the Ethiop."
This passage does show some dislike for a black skin but the
satirist immediately follows it with something he considers worse,
namely, the conduct of one of Rome's noblest families, the Gracchi.
He adds, "But who could endure the Gracchi sneering at sedition."
(12)

Juvenal is also far more severe against Greeks than against
Negroes. He "avoids Greeks above all others" he says. He charged
them with corrupting Roman manners. Finally, it must be remembered that Juvenal was a satirist and satire to be effective must
exaggerate.

Cicero, also, is supposed to have called an Ethiopian "coarse,
dull, awkward" (cum hos an cum stipite Aethiope). (13) But the
authenticity of this is doubtful. This is omitted from the best editions.
On the other hand what he did say about white-skinned Britons
was definite. He said they were so dull-witted one could expect
from them "no fine hand in music, literature and the arts." (14)
tasks then expected of slaves. Of course, Britons were then further away from civilization than numbers of Negroes, who as
a result were more advanced. But it is safe to say that Britons of
the second or third generation born in Rome were no different from
the average Roman.

Another passage considered of much significance by certain
classical scholars is one scribbled on the walls of a brothel in
Pompeii. It reads, "Candide me docuit nigras odisse puellas."
The literal translation of this is, "A white girl taught me to hate
black girls." But another scribbler of that time wrote underneath
this, "Odero septero sed invitus amabo." This is generally translated as, "You may hate them but you will return to them." (15)

In short, it is the very fewness of anti-Negro statements that
give significance to those quoted. Certain classical scholars

12. 2, 23.
13. Red en Sen. Cited in Harper's Latin Dict. The passage is omitted
in the best Latin texts, says Snowden. Moreover, Cicero said also "There
is no difference in kind between man and man . . . In fact, there is no
human being of any race who cannot attain to virtue." (De legibus, 1, 10).
14. Epist. Ad Atticum, I, 4.
15. Gusman, P. Pompeii, pp. 56-7. 1900. Also Berkeley-Hill says
(Spectator, June 13, 1931, p. 934), "Seneca in his Letters to Lucilius
written in the first part of the first century A. D. mentions that numbers
of Negroes were introduced into Rome at that time for the purposes of
prostitution."

Left. Ethiopian (Janze Collec.) Upper right. Phallic deity from Nida, Germany. Lower. Negro musician.

anxious to prove that whites were always prejudiced against Negroes, have vastly exaggerated their importance.

Again, there is no record of any anti-Negro riot in Rome. Able Latin scholars as Snowden, have been able to find none. It is safe to conclude that in the great slave-revolts, as that under Spartacus, all the oppressed, regardless of color, made common cause. Upper-class whites and Negroes, did the same. As in Greece, prejudice was strongest amongst "barbarians" regardless of color.

In fact the passages used to prove general aversion for Negroes are nowhere as strong as those used by classical writers against non-Negroes. Aeschines condemned Demosthenes for his Scythian ancestry and the Scythians were white. He says, "By his mother he is a Scythian — one who assumes the language of Greece but whose abandoned principles betray his barbarous descent." (15a)

Cicero attacked Pison for his Gallic ancestry. His people reached Rome, said Cicero, on a sarraco, or Gallic cart. As for Cleopatra, whom many Nordics call white — one writer calls her golden-haired and blue-eyed (16) even if she were that was nothing at all in her favor. She was non-Roman — a Barbarian (that is, a babbler) one whose language a Roman couldn't understand. That she was one of the most highly educated persons of her time didn't count either. Cicero wrote, "Reginam odi," (I hate the Queen). (17) Virgil called her marriage to Anthony. "A fatal monstrosity," while Horace, himself of slave ancestry, was most denunciatory. After Caesar's death Cleopatra had to fly back to Egypt for her life.

There was also Berenice, Jewish queen. She was probably fairer in color than Cleopatra but Emperor Titus could not marry her because she was an alien.

Again, one finds greater dislike expressed for Greeks, Syrians and Jews in Roman literature than for Negroes, the Jews especially. The Roman writers who attacked the Jews are Molon, Cicero, Horace, Seneca, Martial, Juvenal, Persius, Quintilianus, Tacitus, Apuleius, Celsus, Ammianus, Claudianus and Rutilius Numantius. Cicero called them "a people born to slavery and

15a. Orations of Aeschines against Ctesiphon. Trans. by Thos. Leland. p. 147. 1831. Orations of Demonsthenes, pp. 88-175. Cicero said "Quum tibi tota conatio in sarraco advenatur. (Pis. Frag. ap. Quintilian 1, 1).
16. Wilkins, R. N. Eternal Lawyer, p. 170. 1947.
17. Ad Atticum, XV, 15, 1.

protected only by the contempt they inspire." Their religion, he said, was "a barbarous superstition." Seneca called them, "a most outrageous nation"; Celsus: "descendants of lepers and unclean persons": and Emperors Claudius and Tiberius expelled them from Rome and sent their young men to the provinces to be killed by war and hardships. (18)

If, therefore, there was similar strong dislike for Negroes would we not have known it, too? Dislike for Jews was not based on race. Coming from the East they were so dark that many Romans took them for Ethiopians. The objections were religious, economic and political.

Finally, as opposed to instances of color aversion are others showing none of it. Emperor Augustus used to relax from affairs of state by playing marbles with Moorish children. (19) (Moor was another name for Ethiop). Also, figures of Negroes appeared on cameos, bracelets and other ornaments and were born by the wealthy and were on the ointment-jars and other accessories on the dressing tables of grand dames. Pulzky mentions cameos which depicted "Negroes with all the elegance of the imperial epoch," and reproduces one such from his collection." (20) Imagine the like being done by American slavemasters and mistresses. Duruy cites "one Negro . . . cleverly sculptured in polychrome," now in the Louvre. (21) It is over life-size and of jet-black Negro in gorgeous robes with hair twisted in the Ethiopian style of that time. Babelon says there were many statuettes of Negroes in Rome and lists some of them. (22) Snowden, too, gives other instances of lack of color prejudice. (23a) Most important proof of all however is that the worship of a black goddess, Isis, was very popular in Rome. Arnobius Afer (that is, the African) of the third century, wrote, "Isis, burnt black by the Ethiopian suns." (23b)

19. Vita Aug. (Life of Augustus Caesar) Chap. 83.

20. Nott & Gliddon's Indigenous Races, p. 190. Revue de l'Art says "Representations of Negroes are frequent in Greek art at every epoch but especially in the Roman epochs, which consecrated to the honour of the Ethiopians, works of some importance. "Petit Negre de Bronze," p. 134. (Jan.-Mar. 1900).

21. Op. Cit. Vol. 2, p. 379. 1880.

22. Le Tresor du Cabinets des Antiques Vol. 2, p. 56. 1928. Vol. 3, pp. 37-8. 1929. There are reproductions of some of them.

23a. Op. cit. 287-88.

23b. Book 1, 36. 23c. Paganism to Christianity in the Roman Empire, p. 52. 1946. Platner & Ashby, Topographical Dict. of Ancient Rome, pp. 283-6. 1929.

W. W. Hyde says of Isis, "Soon there were shrines where-
ever Roman armies went. Traces of them have been found from
Africa to Britain and from Spain to the Black Sea . . .
Isis had influenced the Greek world for eight centuries from her first ap-
pearance in the Piraeus in the early fourth century B. C. and with
Serapis the Roman Empire for five." (23c)

Unions, licit and illicit, between whites and blacks were as
free in Rome as it is in Europe of our time. "Always and everywhere," says Tenney Frank, "a large part of the ore that furnished
the material for race mixture" was the Oriental. (24) A considerable part of the latter was Negro. Carcopino says, "Thus we
find in the best families a veritable cross-breeding like to that
which other slave-holding peoples have more recently submitted."
(25) Babelon says, "Lawful marriages took place between Romans and Ethiopians." (26) St. Jerome in his famous XXIInd
Epistle mentions the marriage of Romans to Ethiopians.

According to Juvenal and Martial adultery of Roman matrons
with Negroes was common. Juvenal advised the husbands not to
take abortive potions from their wives. "Grieve not at this, poor
wretch," he says, "and with thine own hand give thy wife the potion
whatever it be for did she choose to bear her leaping children in
her womb thou wouldst, perchance, become the sire of an Ethiop,
a blackamoor would soon be your sole heir." (27)

Martial, in attacking wifely misconduct, mentions a Roman
matron, who bore her husband seven children, none of which is
of his "race." He says, "One of them with wooly hair, like a
Moor seems to be the son of Santra, the cook. The second with
flat nose and thick lips is the image of Pannicus, the wrestler . . .
of two daughters, one is black . . . and belongs to Crotus, the
flute-player." (28)

24. Op. cit. p. 703. Gordon, M. L. says. "The most 'oriental' element
in the melting pot of races was composed of Syrians, Jews and Egyptians."
Jour. of Roman Studies, p. 95. Vol. 14. 1924.

25. La Vie Quotidienne a Rome, p. 127. 1939.

26. Les Cabinets des Antiques, etc. pp. 51-2, 151-4. 1887. He says,
"The licentiousness increased. It finished by smothering social prejudices
and lawful marriages took place between Romans and Ethiopians to the
great scandal of the moralists. St. Jerome did not hesitate to thrust
at Eustochia, 'Non est sponsus tuus arrogans non superbus: Ethiopissam
duxit uxorem." The Romans, he says, knew three kinds of Ethiopians:
the pigmies, the Moors, and the Nubians. See also p. 152 on Negro
statuettes. However, objection, as was said, was due not so much to
"race" as to difference of culture and of religion.

27. Satire VI, 596-600.

28. VI, 39.

Julius Caesar had a love affair with Eunoe, a Moorish (that is, Negro) queen, wife of King Bogudis of Morocco. (29) Cleopatra had a son for him and three children for Antony. There seems to be no proof of Cleopatra's real color but according to European tradition she was black. Shakespeare so describes her (30) and certain jewels of the Renaissance shows her as a Negro woman. (31) Robert Ripley who says he has proof of all his "Believe It Or Not's" says that she was "fat and black." (32) A reason for saying she was white, though an Egyptian, is that she was of "pure Greek" ancestry. The latter is not so. Her father, Ptolemy XIII (sometimes called Ptolemy XI) was known as "The Bastard." (33) His mother was a slave and his portrait does show Negro ancestry, particularly in the thickness of the lips. This is also true of Alexander II, also a Ptolemy.

Roman matrons who bore mulatto children charged it to maternal impression, a theory which Quintilian, famous orator, defended so strongly that one was freed on a charge of adultery. (34) Another school, however, held that maternal impression was a fraud. Calpurnius Flaccus, orator of the first century, discussed it pro and con. In his "De Natus Aethiops" (of Ethiopian Birth), he makes the white wife who has a mulatto child say, "Tell me then did I love a Negro?" She says she did not and asserts that "the element of chance may effect a great deal within the womb." Of the child's color, she says, "You see there skin scorched by an imperfection of the blood." (35) As was said the main issue in these trials was not race mixture, but adultery.

29. Suetonius. De Vita Caesarum (Divus Julius) Book 1, Chap. 52.
30. Antony and Cleopatra, Act. I, Sc. 5.
31. King, C. W. Antique Rings and Gems, p. 326. 1872.
32. Believe It or Not p. 83. 1934 (6th printing).
33. Rapoport, S., says, "The legitimate line of the Ptolemies came to an end on the death of young Alexander. The two natural sons of Soter II were then next in succession and as there were no other claimants the crown fell to the elder (Ptolemy XIII) who took the name of Neus Dionysius, or the young Osiris," (Vol. 1, p. 283. 1904) P. Elgood says, he was a son of a mistress of Ptolemy Lathymus (The Ptolemies of Egypt, p. 175. 1938) A portrait of him in Lepsius K. Denkmaler Abth. III, B1. 303, shows him with distinctly Negroid lips. He is called in some histories Ptolemy XI.
34. Liber Hebr. Quest. in Genesim. ed Migne: Lat. t. 23, p. 985. History repeated itself two thousand years later when Italian wives bore children for Negro soldiers during the American occupation of Italy. In Florence the Court of Appeals ruled that the birth of a mulatto child was not proof of a wife's adultery. The husband contended that the father of the child was an American Negro (Reported by Baltimore Afro-American).
35. Biblioteca Latina, Vol. 80.

In Africa, race mixture was taking place, too, but we find it more harshly criticized. Doubtless it was necessary to preserve there a fairer skin as a symbol of authority as it was in the American colonies and is in South Africa. Claudian (A. D. 365-408) raged against the race mixture that went on under Gildo the Moor, ruler of Africa, appointed by Emperor Valentinian. He says that Gildo, "when tired of each noblest matron hands her over to the Moors. These Sidonian mothers, married in Carthage city, must needs mate with barbarians. He thrusts upon me an Ethiopian as a son-in-law. The hideous hybrid affrights the cradle." (36) Among the fathers of these "hideous hybirds" he names the Berbers, who, according to modern ethnologists, were white Here, again, it is clearly a case of "barbarian-prejudice" rather than race-prejudice. Claudian, himself, was African but of the upper-class.

There is good reason to believe that certain Negroes and near-Negroes rose to be Roman emperors. Indications of this are in the surnames, which were often given then according to some physical characteristic. It is likely therefore that Roman families, or descendants of them, bearing names generally given Negroes, originated as such. (37) In Rome, Negroes were first called

36. De Bello Gildonico I, 189.

37. Snowden says, "That the Romans however, did not always mean a Negro by the use of these adjectives is clear from the frequent use of 'niger' and 'fuscus' to describe peoples of various racial origins who were dark-complexioned." (p. 274). But is it not clear that since these terms were very definitely used for unmixed Negroes that in time they could have extended to mulattoes, octoroons and those who by mixing had in time become indistinguishable from white. When one knows of the great number of Negroes in Rome and of the free intermixture with whites, it does not take much imagination to see this possible especially if one thinks of the types produced by mating of whites and blacks in the United States.

Surnames, at that time and much later, often came from physical characteristics and place of birth. People from the River Niger were called Niger, for instance, therefore is it not logical to assume that those with such names as Niger, Fuscus, Afer, terms used for Negroes, were passed on to their descendants when the latter by mixture had become white? I shall later give abundant evidence of white families bearing names as Moore, Blackamore, Saraceni, whose ancestors were indisputably Negro.

In fact, a Negroid element ran through all the peoples of Asia Minor —Palestine, Assyria, Arabia—and along the Indian Ocean as far as Malaya. Certain classical scholars stick to the statement of Herodotus that the Eastern Ethiopians were strait-haired. But this is only partly true. Some East Indians were. But India and all the East, including New Guinea, had then millions of wooly-haired blacks indistinguishable in features from the Eastern Ethiopians, whom Herodotus said were wooly-haired." One Roman name for black people was Indi (literally Indian). Undoubtedly many wooly-haired Indi came to Rome from Asia.

Ethiops. The Romans took that name from the Greeks who took it from the Africans. (38) Later "Moor" (39) seemed to have come into fashion. This too, was an African word imported into the Greek to describe black people, that is, mauros, black. The word, Mauretania, in Greek, meant "black" says Harper. Still later came "Niger" from the river of that name. It is likely that people from Nigritia (land of the Niger) now Nigeria, brought that word into the language of the Romans and since they were black-skinned "Niger" came to mean "black." Originally the Latin for black was "ater" but later the terms became interchangeable. This seems sure: Niger is not originally Latin. As Leake says in his dissertation on the Niger, "More than one celebrated writer have fallen into the error of supposing Niger a Latin word." (40) Two other terms were "Afer" from Africa (another African word, according to Gerald Massey and others) and "Fuscus." In the Moretum, the skin of one Negro woman is described, as "fusca colore." Are we to assume that the same word was used for brunette whites as for very dark Negroes. Incidentally if it did would it not nullify still more the contention of those who hold there was prejudice against blacks? It would be equivalent to calling the brunet whites, Negroes, today.

As regards "Afer" there is much dispute. Some hold it applies to white people. But with the vast number of Negroes in Rome what proof have we that "African" was not used the same as now? For instance, in the Moretum, which is ascribed to Virgil, "Afra" which is a form of "Afer" is used in the description of a Negro woman, which some modern racists hold, is typical of Negroes.

In fact as late as the 18th century, Negroes continued to arrive in Europe from India, three conspicuous examples being the painter, Higiemonte ; Zamor, favorite of Mme. du Barry ; and Sake Dean Mohammed, barber— surgeon to George IV and William IV of England.

38. Bryant, J. Analysis of Ancient Mythology, Vol. 3, 179. 1776. He says, "It is not a title of Grecian original . . . Ethiops is a title of Zeus." He adds it was a sacred title for the chief god of the Cushites from whom came the Ethiopians and that the Cushites later called themselves by the name of that god. Still later, the Greeks who got their religion from the Egyptians and Ethiopians used "Ethiops" as the title for their god, Zeus. See also Massey G. Book of the Beginnings, Vol. 2, Pt. 2, p. 588. 1881.

39. Harper's Dict. of Class. Literature. See Mauretania, p. 1017. 1923. Also Sir Wm. Smith. Dict. of Greek and Roman Geog. 1865. Atgier: Bull. et Mem. Soc. d'Anthrop. de Paris, 5 ser. IV, pp. 619-23. Bloch. Ibid. p. 576, 624-7. Massey G. Book of the Beginnings, Vol. 2, pt. 2, p. 590.

40. Jour. Royal Geog. Soc'y., Vol. 2, 21, 1832. Also, Donkine R. The Niger, pp. 16, 144. Massey G. A Book of the Beginnings, Vol. 2. pt. 2, p. 610. 1881. Smith, Sir. Wm. Dict. of Greek and Roman Geog., Vol. 2, p. 429. 1865.

Translated, it reads:

"Of African race, whose whole appearance
Bears witness to her native land, with
Wooly hair, thick-lipped, dark of hue . . ."

Now is it likely that after such a description "Afer" would also be used for white people?

Among "Moors" who rose to great power were Emperors Macrinus, (41) Firmus, (42) and Emilianus. (43) Lusius Quietus, foremost military figure of Trajan's reign and named by Trajan as his successor, was a Moor. (44) So was Gildo, (45) ruler of Africa under Emperor Valentinian. Among the "Nigers" are Emperor Pescennius Niger, Aquilius Niger, Brutidius Niger, Q. Caecilius Niger, Novius Niger, and a legal counsellor of the imperial family, named Niger, who accompanied the sister of Emperor Octavius Antony, who had deserted her for Cleopatra. Trebius Niger was a proconsul in Spain and a naturalist, mentioned by Pliny. A Niger was an authority on materia medica and is mentioned by Galen and Caelius Aurelianus. Among the noted Afers are Domitius Afer, orator; Terentius Afer, dramatist; Arnobius Afer, Christian writer; and Victorianus Afer, "a scholar of African birth" who taught rhetoric at Rome in the middle of the fourth century with so much reputation that his statue was erected in the forum of Trajan. For Fuscus, there were Aristus Fuscus and Cornelius Fuscus.

Finally, as regards racial amalgamation in Rome, this is certain: the vast hordes of slaves, foreign soldiers and captives — blond brunet, yellow, brown, black — brought into Rome from about 500 B. C. to about 350 A. D., or for over eight hundred years finally merged to form the Italian people of about the fifth century.

At about this latter period, too, great masses of white barbarians, Visigoths, Ostrogoths and Vandals from the north and east swept down on Italy there to mingle their blood with this already much mixed peopl.e Following these whites, we shall see in the next chapter, great numbers of Africans, mostly Negroid. came in the eighth century to add to this mixture.

41. Dio Cassio (A. D. 155-229) Roman Hist. Vol. 9, p. 361 (Cary).

42. Gibbon. Decline and Fall . . . Vol. 4, p. 273. 1781.

43. Rostovtzev M. Social and Econ. Hist. of the Roman Empire, p. 390. 1926.

44. See sources in Rogers, J. A. World's Great Men of Color, Vol. 2, p. 699. 1947. Graindor, "Tete de Negre, p. 412. Bull. de Corresp. Hell. Vol. 39. 1915.

45. Claudian. De Bello Gildonico. Duruy, Vol. 7, p. 496. 1885.

CHAPTER FIVE

RACIAL INTERMIXTURE IN SPAIN AND PORTUGAL

While white Vandals were pouring into Africa in the fourth and fifth centuries, Africans continued to arrive in Southern Europe, chiefly as slaves. But in 711 A. D. they came in as conquerors. (1) Crossing into Spain they captured Gibraltar, and defeated the Goths, white Germanic invaders of three centuries earlier. Their commander, Tarik, a Negro, gave his name to Gibraltar, formerly Calpe.

These Africans were Moors, sometimes called Arabs, because of their language. To the earlier Greeks, the Moors were "a black or dark people" (Mauros) and to the Romans, Maurus, a black wooly-haired people, known synonymously as Ethiops, Niger (Negro) and Afer (African). Even as late as the fifth century A. D. Procopius, Roman historian, calls the people of Morocco "black."

About the second century B. C. began invasions of white people into Morocco. The Romans, who called it Mauretania, came in and it is to be presumed that their soldiers mixed with Moorish women. Julius Caesar, himself, had a Moorish queen as sweetheart. Later came the Vandals, a white people, who were for a time allies with the Moors against Rome. Still later came Islamic invaders, whose ancestors for thirty centuries had been a mixture of white and black. Due to these invasions of lighter-colored peoples the Moors of the eighth century A. D. were probably about the color of the native population of Casablanca or Fez. In fact, if one goes by the description of white writers and painters the Moorish invaders were, on the whole, very black.

1. There were, however peoples of Negroid type in Spain many centuries before the Christian era. The Peninsula was once joined to Africa and there are abundant evidences of Africans, probably Bushman. As Freyre says "The Moorish and Berber invasion was not the first to inundate with Negro and Mulatto strains the extreme southern tip of Europe, and particularly Portugal, a region of easy transit by way of which the first and most vigorous waves of African exuberance might overflow the continent . . . Looked at in this way, the Arabs, Berbers and Mussulmans, in the course of their invasion, would simply have been taking possession of a region where the way had been prepared for them by an infusion of their own culture." Masters and Slaves, pp. 208 200-2 Ortiz also names Negroes among the other invaders. Phylon. 2nd Quar. 1943, p. 145.

In the Chanson of Roland written soon after they invaded France in 718 A. D. they are described (verses 145 and 146) as "blacker than ink with large noses and ears" and with "nothing white except the teeth." They are 50,000 strong and are led by Marganice, Emperor of Ethiopia and Carthage. Their most valiant figure is Abisme (that is, Abyssinian), who (verse 126) is described as "black as melted pitch." In this epic, the Moors are called Sarrazins, a term which was also used for Negroes.

Again, in the Romance of Morien" one of the King Arthur legends, Sir Morien (that is, Moor) is described as "all black, his head, his body and his hands were all black, saving only his teeth. . . . Moors are black as burnt brands. But in all that men would praise in a knight he was fair, after his kind. Though he were black what was he the worse? In him was naught unsightly; he was taller by half a foot than any knight who stood beside him." Also, "his teeth were as white as chalk, otherwise was he altogether black." Again, "Morien . . . blacker than any son of man whom Christian had ever beheld." (2)

One of the Knights of King Arthur who is also mentioned as black is Sir Palamedes, who was Moorish or Saracen. Morien and Palamedes represent Moors, who were converted to Christianity and joined in the fight against Islam. In Parsifal (that is, Percival) (3) the Moorish queen, Belakane, is beloved by the Scottish king, and is wedded by Gahmuret, a white knight.

Moors also appear by thousands in European heraldry and except in very rare instances are shown as coal black and with Negro hair. The earliest representations I have been able to find of any are in the arms of Aragon, which has four Moorish kings killed in battle by Pedro VIII, king of Aragon, on November 18, 1096. All are shown as jet-black. (4)

Moorish, (that is, Islamic) heraldry, on the other hand, has no human beings, and very rarely, an animate object. It was

2. Moriaen. Arthurian Romance No. 4, pp. 29, 39, 41, 103. 1907. Trans. by J. L. Watson.

Of the saying that there was nothing white about the Moors but their teeth and the whites of their eyes, I was strikingly reminded of this when at a meeting in London I saw an African who got up in the audience to speak. The room was rather dark and the man himself so very dark that his teeth and the whites of his eyes hardly made me conscious of the rest of his face. In America one rarely sees such jet-black Africans as he does in Europe.

3. Griffith R. H. Sir Percival of Galles p. 85-93. 1911. Hunt, R. Popular Romances of the West of England, p. 292.

4. Biblioteca de escritores aragoneses. Blancas. Comentarios de las cosas de Aragon. Seccion histor. 3, p. 110. 1878.

forbidden by Islam. In Mayer's Saracenic Heraldry, there is
seen now and then only a lion or an eagle. In the Hall of Judg-
ment in the Alhambra are murals with men supposed to represent
Moors but the faces are not only European but are alike as if
the artist used the same model for each one. In the Partal are
murals of Moors on horseback, now indistinct, but they, too, re-
semble one another. The Alhambra was built in the fourteenth
century and it is believed that the few human figures there were
the work of an Italian Christian artist. (4a). The great Mosque
of Cordova also has a few figures in the ceiling. Of course, there
were white Moors, especially after Moors had been living in
Europe for centuries and had been whitened by unrestricted mating
with Europeans. However, this is certain: To the Christians of
the eighth century and much later, the Moors were a jet-black
people, so much so that until Shakespeare's time, "Moor" was
used to signify an unmixed Negro. (5)

There is probably no mention of color in the earliest Moorish literature. In the fourteenth century, however, a Moorish
historian, Ali ibn Abd Allah, does mention it but with no more
intent than when a white historian describes a white ruler as blond

4a. Gomez Moreno, D. M. El Arte en Espana: Alhambra (no. 17), p.
12. Also Pictures de Moros en la Alhambra. 1916. Calvert, Moorish Remains
in Spain, Vol. 1, p. 42. Pietro Tacca in his monument to Ferdinand I
erected at Leghorn, 1620, has four Moors in chains, which are said to
have been modelled from originals, one of whom is distinctly Negro—
Raymond M. La Sculpture Florentine, XVIe siecle, pp. 182-3 1900.

5. So predominant was the black skin of the Moorish invaders of
Europe that blackamoor (black as a Moor) came to be used not only
for Moroccans but for other blacks as Ethiopians and Sudanese. As
Elliot Smith says, "Negro admixture is so evident among the Moorish
population that the word, Moor is often used to suggest Negro influence,
as we see it in 'blackamoor.'" (Human History, p. 124. 1919). The Oxford Dictionary also says it was commonly used for Negro in the Middle
Ages and as late as the 17th century. Hambly, a more recent writer,
says, "In physique a Moor may be a Berber or an Arab, or a mixture
of the two with Negro blood as well." (Source Book of Anthropology,
Vol. 1, p. 135, 935. 1937). But since many Arabs and Berbs are already
Negro. We can say simply that Moors range in color from unmixed
black to fair white with all the shades between.

Many American Negroes are indistinguishable from Arabs. The
New York Times (Feb. 2, 1045) reports of the meeting between President
Roosevelt and King Ibn Saud. "It was a matter of considerable aston-
ishment of the King's servants to discover American Negro cooks and
messboys and it was more than difficult to persuade them that these
were not also Arabs. The matter was never entirely cleared up."

My impression is that the general aspect of the Moroccan people,
especially towards the south, is that of any Negro district in America
with its few whites. Moors are, on the whole, darker than the average
American mulatto.

or brunet. Abd Allah describes some of the earlier Moorish sultans as blond, white, copper-colored, brown, reddish, dark, frizzly-haired, wooly-haired and the like. (6)

In the ninth century the Moors were to be aided greatly by other Islamic peoples as far east as Egypt and Arabia, whose armies from the days of the Pharaohs were predominantly black or dark mulatto. As for the Moslem empire, when it stretched from Bagdad to Portugal, on both shores of the Mediterranean, it was, as Keane rightly calls it, "Negroid." Of course, it had a large percentage of whites, too, but so great was the number of Zenghs, or unmixed Negroes, in the armies that in 870 A. D. when Islam was at the height of its power the blacks revolted and held Bagdad, capital of the world's then mightiest empire, for fourteen years. (7) In 871, their Negro general, Mohallabi, seized Basra, rich city, famous in the Arabian Nights, and made slaves and concubines of the white women and children. (7a) During the Crusades (1096-1270) so many Negroes were taken out of Ethiopia and the Sudan to fight the white Christian invader that in 1196, Negro troops in Egypt, "50,000 strong dominated the court and the armies." The Marshal of the Palace, a Negro enunch, the Moutamen Elkhelafe, their protector, was one of the most powerful men in the empire. Ibn Alatir, Moslem writer of the times, says the revolting Negroes made the streets of Cairo run blood for days. (8)

General Mangin, in an article on the role of Negro troops in Europe, tells of the important part they played in the conquest and development of Spain especially under Abderrahman I. (757-787), who founded the independent kingdom of Cordova. This calpihate flourished he said "until black contingents disappeared from the army." But a rival Moorish leader "brought from Africa a great number of Negroes from which he formed a redoubtable regiment of cavalry in 1016" (9) and restored it. Incidentally Franco repeated this with Moorish troops in 1936.

After the invasion of 711 came other waves of Moors, probably even darker. In 1086, Yusuf ben Tachfin, who is described

6. Aoudh el Kartas (trans. by Beaumier) pp. 25, 61, 190, 257, 288, 353, 355, 364, 367, 373 et seq. 1860. Mohammed ben Idriss is described as "blond" while Abou el-Hassan el Said had as mother "a Nubian slave . . . dark and of mixed blood." p. 367.

7. Hitti, P. K. Hist. of the Arabs, pp. 467-8. 1937. 7a Durant, Will. The Age of Faith, p. 210. 1950.

8. Reinaud, J. T. Extraits d'auteurs arabes relatif aux Croisades, pp. 142-3. Ibn Khaldoun. Histoire de Berberes (Chap. Rois des peuples Negres). Vol. 2, pp. 105-116, trans. by Baron de Slane. 1927.

9. Troupes noires. Revue de Paris, p. 62. July 1909 (pp. 61-80).

as "dark" and "wooly-haired," (10) and was probably a Nigerian, brought in an army composed largely of "pure Negroes" (11) and defeated a much superior white Christian force at Zalacca, Spain. Another, Yakub el-Mansur, definitely recorded as "the son of a Negro woman," (12) invaded the Peninsula in 1194 and made himself master of almost the whole of it. The guards of these Moorish kings were gigantic Negroes, jet-black and of immense strength, recruited from the Atlas, Tumbuctoo, and Nigeria. (13)

Moorish sultans, whose fathers might be of any hue from black to white, were sometimes the sons of white Christian mothers captured on the ships or the coasts of Western Europe, including the British Isles. Among such are Aby el-Ola, Mohammed abd el-Ouhad, and Abu Debbus. (14) Female slaves with faultless complexions and golden hair were imported from Sweden and Finland, and Greek and Circassian beauties as dancers, singers and wives. (15) For eight centuries shapely black women from Ethiopia and West Africa were brought in for the same purposes. White French slaves were also sold in numbers to the Moors by Jews with royal permission. They used Bordeaux as a slave port. (16) Arnold thinks that most of the Islamic slaves came from the Slavonic peoples. (17) It was not until 1560 when Moorish power waned that black women, by Christian edict, ceased to arrive in Spain for Moslem harems. The Christians, however, for two centuries later, continued the importation of blacks.

The favorite wife of Yusuf ibn Tachfin, already mentioned was a white Christian captive. Fadh-el-Hassen (Perfection of

10. Roudh el Kartas, p. 304.
11. Ency. Brit. Vol. 21 (See SPAIN—Almoravides). Ibn El-Athair. Op. cit. pp. 525 Also pp. 457-60, 462. Scott, S. P. Hist. of the Moorish Empire, p. 622. 1904.
12. Roudh el Kartas, p. 304.
13. Scott. S. P. History of the Moorish Empire, p. 668. 1904.
14. Roudh el Kartas, pp. 355, 364, 373.
15. Scott, S. P. p. 622 Sir Walter Scott in his ::Notes on Thomas the Rhymer," says that according to Spanish Chronicles the Christians had to pay tribute to the Moors in Christian maidens. Sir Tristrem, p. 206. 1883. Saco. J. A. Hist. de la esclavitud desde los tiempos mas remotos, vol. 3, p. 211. 1937. Also Saco's Historia Raza Africana Vol. 1, 192 Dozy, F. Spanish Islam (Stokes). p. 430. 1930. For more details on slavery of whites and Blacks, Christians and Moslems with prices paid for them see Revue Hispanique—L'esclavitud en Cataluna—t. 41, pp. 1-109, 1917. One Negro slave brought 672 francs ; a white slave, 650 ; and a Circassian white girl, 735 (p. 89). Also Verlinden, C. L'esclavage dans le monde iberique mediaeval (In Anuario de Historia del derecho espanol) Vol. 11, pp. 283-448. 1934.
16. Michel, E. Hist. de Commerce de la Navigation de Bordeaux, Vol. 2, pp. 409-410. 1870.
17. Arnold T. Legacy of Islam p. 101. 1931.

Beauty). (18) She was the mother of his frizzly-haired son and successor, Ali. Alphonso VI, white Christian king, who was so often beaen by Yusuf, took a Moorish wife, the lovely Zayda, who was the mother of his favorite son, Sancho. "Abdul-Aziz ibn Musa," says Freyre, "not only wedded the widow of king Roderico but took many Christian virgins for his concubines. On the other hand, Ramira II of Leon fascinated by the beauty of a Saracen maid of noble lineage — undoubtedly one of those who later became 'enchanted Moorish damsels' — slew his legitimate wife and married the exotic creature by whom he had numerous progeny." (19)

Sancho VIII, Christian king, wished to marry one of the daughters of Yakub el Mansour, whose mother, as was said, was a Negro but Yakub declined. Abu Hassan Ali, " "The Black Sultan" whose mother was also a Negro slave, had as his favorite wife, Shams-ed-Douha (The Morning Sun), a beautiful white captive. (20) Of the three Moorish kings killed in the battle of Alcazar in 1578, two were mulattoes and one, an unmixed Negro, Mulai Mohammed "the Negro." (21)

The whites thought marriage with the Moors an honor. Moors were then the foremost power in Europe. They were the conquerors and the whites the conquered. In such a case, says Roy Nash, "it would be an honor for the white to mate or marry with the governing class." (22)

The Moors, like the Greeks and Romans, had a very low opinion of the whites to the North. Had they not beaten them often on the battlefield and with inferior numbers. Aristotle, Cicero, Caesar, Tacitus, Constantine the Great and St. Jerome hadn't thought much of them and they hadn't probably advanced much in the ten centuries since. Said of Andalusia (1029-1071) thought Nordics no higher than the primitive blacks of the African interior. He wrote, they "are nearer animals than men . . . They are by nature unthinking and their manners crude. Their bellies protrude; their color is white and their hair is long. In sharpness and delicacy of spirit and in intellectual perspicacity, they are nil. Ignorance, lack of reasoning power and boorishness are

18. Roudh el Kartas, p. 224.
19. Masters and Slaves, p. 215.
20. Scott-O'Connor, V. C. Vision of Morocco, pp. 99-100. 1923.
21. Chenier L. Recherches Hist. sur les Maures, Vol. 3, p. 328. 1787. (Muley Mohamet qui fut surnomme' le Negre parce qu'il 'etait fils d'une Negresse). He is the king mentioned by Peele in the Tragical Battle of Alcazar.
22. Nash R. Conquest of Brazil, p. 37. 1926.

common among them." (23)

Of the Central African blacks he wrote, "They have hot tempers and excitable manners; their skin is blackened and their hair wooly. Turbulence, stupidity and ignorance are common among them."

Modern white historians agree with this Moorish writer. Michaud in his "History of the Crusades" describes the Prussians of the thirteenth century as being just a few grades above savagery. Draper says that the palaces of the then rulers of Germany, France and England were, in comparison with those of the Moorish rulers of Spain "scarcely better than the stables" of the Moors. Launcelot Hogben says, "The Moorish scholars of Toledo, Cordova, and Seville were writing treatises on spherical trigonomentry when the mathematical syllabus of the Nordic University of Oxford stopped abruptly at the fifth proposition of the book of Euclid." (24) Lane-Poole says, "Whatever makes a kingdom great, whatsoever tends to refinement and civilization was found in Moorish Spain." (25) The Alhambra and the Generalife in Granada and the Mosque at Cordova are testimony to this. Nothing more superb in architecture has ever been built. Blackness of skin was not the "disgrace" it was later to be in colonial America. Proud white knights thought Negroes such worthy foes they placed them in their family crests, (26) and welcomed those who became Christian as allies and social equals.

With the dark-skinned race in power miscegenation with the whites was as easy as that of whites with Indians and Negroes in the New World. Polygamy speeded up the process, too. "The constant intermingling of Spaniard and Moor meets us at every step," says Lea. (27) Freyre writes, "If the Moors did not mingle freely with the Portuguese population then I do not know what miscegenation is." (28) Scott thought that "the mingling of races and the resultant prevalence of crosses with the influence of climate "had much to do with the later high civilization reached by the Moors." He adds, "No greater contract in comparative ethnology" could be found than the variety of "races" then in Spain. (29)

23. Kitab Tabakat al Umam (Blachere R. p. 36. 1935). 23a. Michaud Hist. of the Crusades, Vol. 2, p. 223. 1853 (Trans. J. Robson). Draper. Intellec. Develop. of Europe, p. 348, 1863.

24. Genetic Principles in Medical and Social Science, p. 213, 1931.

25. Moorish Spain p. VIII. 1893. In Arnold's Legacy of Islam, a Moor, Sidi Hamete bin Engeli, is mentioned, as the originator of the Spanish classic, Don Quixote, p. 39. 1931.

26. See illustrations in this book.

27. Spanish Inquisition, Vol. 1, p. 53. 1922.

28. Scott, S. P. p. 672. See also Prieto y Vives A. Los Reyes de Tarifa, p. 39. 1926.

Among these peoples from eastern Europe were Slavs, who thanks
to the cosmopolitan spirit of the Moors, rose like the unmixed black
slaves, even to be rulers. "The African influence," says Freyre
"seething beneath the European gave a sharp relish to sexual
life, to alimentation and to religion; with Moorish or Negro blood
running through a great light-skinned population, when it is not
the predominant strain, in regions that to this day are inhabited
by a dark-skinned people. . . .

"The noble families in Portugal, as in Spain, that absorbed
the blood of the Arak or the Moor were innumerable. Some of
the knights who, in the wars of reconquest distinguished themselves most by the Moor-killing ardor of their Christianity had
such blood . . . Of the Count of Coimbra, Don Sesnado, the
chronicles tell us he was of mixed blood, of Christian and Moor,
and that he was a vizier among the Saracens . . . Another
mixed blood. Dom Fifes Serrasim, became a member of the
Christian nobility by marrying a Mendes de Braganza." (30)

Gandia says similarity, "As to the mixture of Moors and the
other inhabitants of the Iberian Peninsula it is useless to deny
its occurrence. Without going into the social life of the Christians
and Moslems, it may be mentioned in passing that the son of
Musa, married the widow of King Roderick and that the royal
family of Witza united with Moors of the purest stock." (31)

The color of the population of Southern Spain from about
the ninth to the sixteenth centuries was very likely similar to the
native quarter of Casablanca today or of Harley, and with about
the same proportion of whites. As for Portugal where Negro
slavery on a large scale was introduced in 1440 or 1442, the Negro
element was greater.

The Moors were finally thrust out of Spain in the seventeenth
century but they continued to be a maritime power. Moorish sea-
rovers raided the coasts of Western Europe and the British Isles
for slaves whom they sold in the great white market at Sallee.
Mulai Ismael, their greatest emperor since Yakub el Mansour,
had an army of captured white slaves and 25,000 other white
slaves of both sexes to build his colossal place and stables at
Meknes. Mulai Ismael, himself, was the son of the ugliest and
most wretched unmixed Negro female slave (32) in the empire
according to Abbe Busnot who went to him on a mission from
Louis XIV to free French slaves. There is no authentic portrait

30. Masters and Slaves, pp. 4, 216.
31. Del Origen de los Nombres y Apelidos. etc. p. 104. 1930.
32. Recit d'aventures au temps du Louis XIV, p. 51, reprint 1928.

of Mulai Ismael but there is one of his brother, Mulai Archid, by
the same mother and father and it is certainly that of an unmixed
Negro. (33)

Ismael's wife is described by Abbe Busnot as an unmixed
Negro woman — "black, of great height and enormous size." (34)
His second wife, he says, was a white Englishwoman, and his
third, another Negro, Lila Coneta, whose son, Mohammed Deby,
succeeded to the throne.

The present Sultan is a descendant of Mulai Ismael. In
Moorish, as in other North African harems, are still to be found
women of all colors. When Abdul Aziz, the last independent
Sultan, who was the son of a mulatto father and a white Circassian mother, went into exile about 1908 of his three hundred reported wives several were unmixed Negroes. Flournoy rightly
says of Moorish royalty, "Especially the aristocracy and the royal
family had Negro blood in their veins." (35)

The Jews also brought in much Negro strain. Some of the noblest of the Sephardic families, aristocrats of Jewry, were Negroes.
Isaac DaCosta mentions sons and grandsons of Don Jachia ben
Jaisch, who were royal treasurers, court physicians, astrologers,
and royal favorites at the Court of Castille and Portugal, one of
whom "was Don David Negro, who with another illustrious Israel-
ite, Don Juda, in the following year followed Dona Leonora, widow
of Dom Fernando, whose favorites they had been in Castille. His
name "Negro" is derived, according to the author of the Shalsheth
from "dos Negros," one of the three seignories which were given to
his progenitor by the King of Portugal.

"Certain it is that the House of Braganza with all descendants
in Europe of King John I of Portugal have Jewish blood in their
veins." (35a)

He mentions also another noble family, named Negro, "bearing the same arms as the Pretos." Preto was the name later used,
and still used in Portugal, for Negro. Pombal, in abolishing
slavery in Portugal, decreed that the term "Negro" should no
longer be used, says Wyndham. "In Portugal," says this writer,
"mulattoes frequently rose to high positions. They were deco-

33. See sketch of Mulai Ismal in Vol. 1, Rogers J. A. World's Great
Men of Color.

34. Busnot, p. 67.

35. British Policy Toward Morocco, p. 17. 1935. A Leared says,
"No social disadvantage is incurred by those who in any way betray their
alliance, whether more or less, to the Negro type. The late emperor of
Morocco showed evident traces of black blood." Morocco and the Moors.
p. 220. 1876.

35a. DaCosta, I. Noble Families Among the Sephardic Jews, pp. 149,
155, 307. 1936

Left. General Bassa of the armies of Mulai Ismael. Right: Mulai Archid, Emperor of Morocco (1631-1672) ; Moorish chess players of Spain (From the 13th Cent. Mss. of Alfonso le Sage) Note the white servant.

rated with the Order of Christ. They commanded Portuguese ships." (35b)

As regards Christian Spain and Portugal, Negroes were imported in droves from 1440 until the abolition of slavery in Portugal in 1773. "Already before the discovery of America," says Fernando Ortiz, "several thousands of Negro slaves had been expatriated from Senegal, Guinea and the Congo and were working in Lisbon and Algarves, in Seville and in all Andalusia. The Catholic sovereigns were dealers in Negro slaves. It was Christopher Columbus who went plundering in Negro slaves in Guinea before stealing Indian slaves in Cuba. Before the discovery of America the Negroes already were cutting sugar cane in Andalusia, and in Seville there was a municipal council of native Negroes with fraternal orders, kings and overseers. The Negro came first to the Indies from Spain, not from Africa. And as Euclides de Acunha said of Brazil, "The mulatto was not made in America, he came to us already made from the Mother Country." The African Negro slave trade was more abundant during the fifteenth and sixteenth centuries for the Peninsula than for America. In one city like Evora, Portugal, the Negroes undeniably exceeded the whites. Several thousands of Wolof, Mandingo, Guinea and Congo slaves entered Lisbon and Seville each year and were sold for the cities and fields of the south of Iberia. And without the bestial prejudices which afterwards were current in American societies of agrarian slave-holding economy, the Negroes and mulattoes were frequently emancipated and both rose to prominence by virtue of knowledge, art, valor or love." (36)

Negroes were adopted into royal families, given the royal surname, and accepted into marriage with the Nobility. Moreno Villa names several such, among them Don Alfonso Carlos de Bourbon, adopted son of Charles III and an architect. (37) Guzman

35b. The Atlantic and Slavery, pp. 9, 143. While there was little prejudice against color in the Peninsula there was much against religion. Severe laws were passed against Jews and Moors in 1412 and 1451. Neither could wear silk. E. H. Lindo in "History of the Jews of Spain and Portugal," gives the Seven Codes (Las Siete Partidas) against them. They could not buy Christians or slaves imported from Africa; could not marry or cohabit with a Christian under pain of death; and had always to be polite and respectful to them. The Moors were finally driven out. Many of the Jews went to Holland, Belgium, Germany and the New World in the sixteenth century. (pp. 92, 102, 320. 1848). See also, Wyndham, p. 245. If, however, the Jew or the Moor was accepted into the Christian faith, the stringencies against him ceased.
36. Negro in the Spanish Theatre, Phylon. 2nd Quar. 1943. pp. 145-6.
37. Villa Moreno, J. Locos, enanos, negros, pp. 21-2, 30, 49, 153-7. 1939.

de Alfarache, who had a Negro sweetheart, himself, mentions a "Negra" (Negro woman) who lived like "a great lady." (38) Goya (1746-1828) depicted the great Duchess de Alba holding her little black favorite tenderly and Queen Isabella, mother of Alphonso XIII, had a Negro favorite, Marie Marline, who was a clever guitarist.

Marie de Pachecho, Spanish Joan of Arc of 1520, had a Negro favorite to whom was attributed most of Marie's powers; (39) and at Salamanca, Chicava, a Negro girl from Guinea, adopted by Charles II, became an important figure in the religious life of Spain. (40)

Juan Latino, Negro ex-slave, was one of Europe's great Latin scholars and poets. From servitude in the household of the Duke de Sesa, he became tutor to children of the nobility and in 1565, a professor at the University of Granada. He married one of his pupils, Ana de Carjaval, by whom he had four children. A writer of the times said of his daughters, "Very beautiful, although mulattoes, elegant and dressed in the fashion of gentlewomen." (41) Two other noted mulattoes of that time were Cristobal de Menenes, a priest, son of a nobleman and a black woman; and Licentiate Orti born of a white father and a black mother. Cervantes in his preface to Don Quixote dedicates a poem to Latino.

Lazarillo de Tormes (1471-1510) tells of his mother's love affair with a Negro, named Tejares, near Salamanca, and of her child by him. (42) Illicit love affairs and marriages in high and lowly life were not uncommon, all without prejudice. "The Count de Salinas, Don Diego Sarmiento," says Gandia, "was the nephew of Pedro de Villandrando, Count Rivadeo and a Negro woman . . . The Countess of Rivadavia was the illegitimate daughter of Juan Pimentel, Senor de Miranda and a female slave." (43)

Race mixture was so common in Portugal that even the royal family was mulatto. John IV shows evident Negro strain and John VI was described as a dark mulatto by the French Duchess d' Abrantes, who was at his court. (44)

38. Aleman M. Guzman de Alfarache (1623), Vol. 4, 304-172. Trans. by James Mabbe. Ed. of 1924.
39. Sandoval. Vida y hechos del Emperador Carlos V. p. 418, 1614. Notes & Quer. 3 ser. Vol. 5, 1864, p. 149. Robertson W. Hist. of Emperor Charles V. Vol. 2, p. 33. 1876.
40. Enciel. Univ. Ilus. Vol. 53, pp. 136-7.
41. Spratlin, V. E. Juan Latino, pp. 5, 16. 1938. Woodson, C. G. Jour. of Negro Hist. Vol 20, 190-243. 1935. Encl. Univ, Ilus. Vol, 29. pp. 1022-3. 192.
42. Pleasant Hist. of Lazarillo de Tormes, p. 5.
43. Del Origen de los Nombres y Apelidos, etc., pp. 104, 107.
44. For John VI's Negro strain and that of certain of the Portuguese nobility see Abrantes: Memoires Vol. 6, p. 10, 39. Paris. 1935. 12 vols.

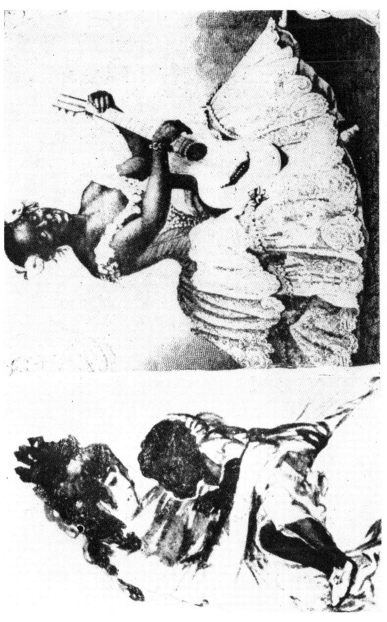

NEGROES IN SPAIN. Left. Duchess of Alba, with her Negro favorite, Maria de la Luz, by Goya (1746-1828). Right: Maria Marline, guitarist and singer, favorite of Queen Isabella in the 1850's.

67

Offspring of these Moors and West Africans were among the discoverers of the New World and the first builders of Latin America. As de Leeuw says, "In that century when the Portuguese acquired African possessions they had already much colored blood in their veins. At first the colored blood had come to Portugal in dribbles and later it actually became a flood. Some of the whites and many of the Iberian-Gothic-Arabian-Negro offspring were

The dark-eyed girls of Cadiz, their raven hair adorned with a single rose, of whom Byron wrote so ecstatically in Childe Harold's Pilgrimage, undoubtedly owed much of their beauty to their mixture of African "blood." Their compeers may be found in Latin America today. The dark skin softened the glare of the white one to produce a complexion of matchless beauty.

The most recent importation of Negroes into Spain are those in the army of General Franco. One of his prize cavalry battalions is made up of coal-black Moors. They find mates among the Spanish women, precisely as did the Moors of Tarik in 711.

45. Crossroads of the Buccaneers, p. 173. 1937.

For further details on Spain and Portugal see Sex and Race, Vol. 1, chap. 15. 1940. 2nd. ed. Also Stephens, N. M. Portugal, p. 162 ; Southy R, Life and Correspondence. Vol. 2, 69. 1850. "The Emperor of the Holy Ghost, he says, "had musicians, all Negroes." Napoleon had in his army small, black Portuguese, nicknamed "The Fleas." (N. Y. Times, July 1, 1940).

CHAPTER SIX

THE NEGRO AS "MOOR" — NEGRO ANCESTRY IN ARISTOCRATIC EUROPEAN FAMILIES

Seven years after the capture of Gibraltar the Moors invaded France; and conquered or overran most of its southern portion. They probably went as far east as Geneva. Switzerland was then a part of France. (1)

In 732, they reached Tours, two days' march from Paris but were beaten back by the Christians under Charles Martel. They remained in Southern France, however until 1140, principally in the Camarque on the western Riviera, which is still known as La Petite Afrique (Little Africa).

In 838, they took Marseilles and in 842, Arles. Aided by fellow-Moslems from the East they captured Sicily in 837 and took a million pieces of gold. In 846, they invaded Italy, seized Rome, plundered the Vatican and St. Peter's Cathedral and carried off immense wealth i ngold, jewelry, tapestry, and paintings. (3) Later, with the Jews as intermediary, they sold back much of this loot to the Pope.

In 982, they defeated the flower of Christendom under Otto II of Germany. Unmixed Negro troops, most of them from Ethiopia and the Sudan furnished a large part of the Moorish, or Saracen, troops. Thereafter they dominated most of Italy for years and parts of it until the thirteenth century when they were swamped by further white invasions from the north. Gradually they were absorbed into the Italian population even as the Africans brought in by the ancient Romans had been.

In Africa, the Moors continued to be a leading power, and to no little extent in India, also. They dominated the Mediterranean and the North Atlantic and plundered the coasts of Western Europe and the British Isles. They even conquered and ruled parts of Scotland. David MacRitchie, eminent British archaeologist, says, "So late as the tenth century three of these provinces were wholly black and the supreme ruler of them became for a time the paramount king of Transmarine Scotland. . . .

"We see one of the black people — the Moors of the Romans

1. Reinaud J. T. Invasions des Sarrazins en France, p. 1874. 1836. 19th Century, Vol. 58. July-Dec. 1905, p. 268.

Negro troops helped capture Sicily. (Ibn El-Athair, 1160-1223, mentions them in his Annales du Maghreb et de l'Espagne, pp. 498-503. Trans. by Fognan. 1901. Also Desmichels, M. Des Sarrazins en Provence et en Italie. Revue de Marseilles. 1831. Lavisse, Histoire de France, Vol. 2, Pt. 1, p. 381. 1911. Crawford M. Southern Italy, Vol. 1, p. 292.

3. Gregorovius F. Rome in the Middle Ages, Vol. 3 pp. 65, 87-9, 105. 1903. Trans by Hamilton.

— in the person of a king of Alban of the tenth century. History knows him as Kenneth, sometimes as Dubh, and as Niger. . . .

"We know as an historical fact that a Niger El Dubh has lived and reigned over certain black divisions of our islands — and probably white divisions also — and that a race known as "the sons of the Black" succeded him in history." (4) Welsh traditions, he says, tell also of these black people "and the legends and history of the Scottish Highlands are both witnesses to the existence of a purely black people" there.

With the then most powerful navy the Moors preyed upon shipping in the Atlantic, capturing the passengers and sailors and selling them into slavery in Africa and Islamic lands of the East. "A veritable terror reigned in the Mediterranean," says Georges Hardy, ". . . they ravaged the coasts of Portugal, Spain, Southern France and went as far as Britain." (5) In 1631, they attacked Baltimore Castle, Ireland, and their leader, "black Ali Krussa," carried off Mary, daughter of Sir Fineen O'Driscoll. Ali Krussa, native of Morocco, had been a slave of O'Driscoll. Escaping back to Morocco, he returned and surprised the castle. (6)

Chambers says, "Captivity among the Moors of Northern Africa was no uncommon fate for Scotch mariners." (7) He tells of a number of them sold at Sallee, Morocco, in 1636.

George I in his speech from the Throne, October 19, 1721, mentions "the great number of my subjects' delivery in slavery," (8) a result of his treaty with Mulai Ismael, emperor of Morocco. So many whites were being taken into slavery in Africa that in 1150, a religious order, the Trinitarians, was founded to free them by purchase. (9) For the next three centuries or more, collections were taken up in the churches for that purpose. (9) One of those freed was Cervantes.

There is reason to believe that there were Negroes in Britain before Julius Caesar. Irish folklore mentions a small black people, the Firbolg. These might have ben prehistoric Bushmen. Pygmy flint instruments, Negrito skulls (10) and Grimaldi relics have been found in Scotland. A very ancient British saying, according to

4. Ancient and Modern Britons, Hull, E. Hist. of Ireland, p. 32. 1926. Lancas. & Cheshire Antiq. Soc. Trans. Vol. 20, p. 229. 1902.

5. Les Grands Etapes de l'Hist. du Maroc, pp. 50-4. Other sources given in Rogers, J. A. 100 Amazing Facts About the Negro, p. 45.

6. Driscoll, C. B. Doubloons, pp. 297-304, 1930. Playfair, R. L. Scourge of Christendom, pp. 53-4. 1884.

7. Domestic Annals of Scotland, Vol. 1, p. 471. Vol. 2 p. 93.

8. Cobbett's Parliamentary Hist. of England, Vol. 7 (1714-1722) p. 912. 1811.

9. Larousse. (see Jean de Matha). Dan, P. Histoire de Barbarie, pp. 316-321, 452-498. 1649. Deslandres, P. L'ordre Franc des Trinitaires Vol 1, 1903. Calixte de Providence. Corsaires et redempteurs. 1834.

10. MacRitchie D. Ancient and Modern Britons, vol. 1, p. 45. 1884.

Burton Stevenson, is "Blac as a bloaman" (black as a blackamoor). Godfrey Higgins, (11) Gerald Massey and David MacRitchie, have written of these ancient British Negroes.

What we do know, also, is that the Phoenicians, a Negroid people, did mine tin in Cornwall and that Egyptians went to Britain before the Romans. Gerald Massey gives abundant proof, including Egyptian words, in ancient British languages. The Silures, or western Britons, mentioned by Tacitus (13) of the first century, as having dark skins and unusually curly hair, were very likely of Phoenician or Egyptian descent.

Ancient Welsh folk-tales certainly do mention black people, unmistakably Negroes. In the story of Peredur (14) in "The Mabinogion" the blacks mentioned therein might be Silures. Another ancient Welsh poem, Gwadd Llud y Mawr, tells of rivalry between white and black (Mawr or Moor). (15)

Rome had Negroes (Ethiopians) in her armies in Britain. (15a) And the worship of the black goddess, Isis, with her Egyptian Negro priests, followed the Roman armies there. Hyde was quoted to that effect in Chapter One. Oakesmith mentions also an African tribe at Moresby. (16) Indeed, with so many Negroes in her population there must certainly have been some in her occupation forces in France, Belgium, Germany and Holland. Here and there some Negro skulls have been found at Cologne. Also near the Roman city of Nida there a Negro phallic deity was found.

Septimius Severus, one of the leading conquerors of Britain was an African. How much, if any Negro strain he had, we do not know. In 668, Pope Vitalien appointed a Negro, Hadrian, Archbishop of Canterbury but he declined presumably because of age. Theodore, an Oriental, was named in his place and Hadrian went as his mentor. (17) Ireland had a Negro bishop, St. Diman the Black, who died in Ulster in 658. (18) Sir Walter Scott has six Negro trumpeters in Old Mortality, "in white dresses, richly laced and having massive silver collars and armlets." In one of his introductions to Ivanhoe he replied to his critics by

11 & 11a. Sources given in Sex and Race, Vol. 1, pp. 196-8. 2nd ed. 1940.

13. Agricola XI.

14. Trans. by Ellis and Lloyd, Vol. 2. See also Bulleid and Gray. Glastonbury Lake Village, Vol. 2, p. 1917.

15. Massey G. A Book of the Beginnings Vol. 1, p. 454. 1881.

15a. Beddoe J. Races of Britain, p. 31. 1885.

16. Race and Nationality, p. 96. 1919.

17. See sources in Sex and Race, Vol. 3, p. 4.

18. Cambrensis Eversus, Vol. 2, pp. 686-7. 1848. "S. Dimanum nigrum Episcopum Connorensem in Ultona. An Dom 658 vivera desiisse tradunt."

confirming that there were Negroes in Britain in the Middle Ages. (19)

"Moor" (the race) as it occurs in European heraldry always means Negro. "Moor's head," says Berry, "is the heraldic term for the head of a black or Negro man. (20) "Abbot says, "Moor's head — the head of a Negro." (21) Edmondson says similarly. (22)

And this definition is etymologically correct. The Greeks, as was said used "mauros," to mean black, or dark; and the Romans used it for Negroes. "Wooly hair like a Moor's," says Martial. (23) To Claudian, Moors, Ethiopians and Nigritians (that is Negroes), were one and the same. He speaks of the Moors "who dwell beside the waters of Gir, most famous of the rivers of Ethiopia that overflows its banks as if it had been another Nile." The Gir, referred to here is the Ni-Gir, or Ni-Ger, (Niger). (24)

Sir William Smith says the Moors were known in the Alexandrian dialect as "Blacks," and that "the Moors . . . must not be considered a different race from the Numidians." (25) Atgier says that to the Greeks, Romans and Gauls, the Moors were known as "the Black People." (26) He adds, "The word, Mauretania, inhabited by black populations and was later called Nigritia, or Negro-land. Moor, therefore, was the equivalent of Negro . . . The word, Moor or More, signifies a primitive black population." Since, therefore, the Romans invaded Britain, France, Belgium, Germany and other parts of Europe, they undoubtedly took the word "Moor," meaning a black people, with them.

In fact, so common was the use of "Moor" for Negroes that it is astonishing to find some writers calling Moors, a white race. MacRitchie, referring to a passage in Claudian:

Ille leves Mauros nec falso nomine Pictos
Edomuit . . ."

19. Notes & Queries. 7 ser. 8, July 13, 1889, p. 43. Doran J. Hist. of Cour Fools pp. 43-4 1852.

20. Encyc. Heraldica, vol. 3, pp. 68-9. 1913.

21. Heraldry Illus. p. 102, 1897.

22. Complete Body of Heraldry (see MOORE, MORE, etc. 1780. Also Glover's Ordinary of Arms, Vol. 1, p. 43.

23. Martial. Satire 6,600; and other passages from Roman writers quoted in Chap. 3, of this work.

24. De Bello Gildonico I 249-54; 189-93.

25. Smith, Sir Wm. Dict. of Greek and Roman Geog. pp. 294, 297. See also "Mauritania."

26. Bull. et Mem. Soc d'Anthrop. de Paris, Feb. 4, 1904, p. 110. Also 5 ser. Vol. 4, 1903. pp. 619-627. D'Avezac, M. L'Afrikue. p. 4, 1842. Also Bloch: 5 ser. Vol. 4 Nov. 1903, p. 576. Also Rogers, J. A. World's Great Men of Color, Vol. 1, p. 56. Also Procopius; Hist. of the Wars (The Vandalic War) II, 2, 8. Vol. 7, p. 491. 1940. The index says, "Moors, a black race of Africa."

says, "Now when Claudian wrote and for a long time after, 'Maurus' signified a great deal more than a native of Mauretania. Any Latin dictionary — any old one, at least, will tell you that 'maurus' is a Moor, a blackamoor, or a tawny-moor. And Shakespeare used the word 'Moor' as a synonym for Negro." (27)

The Roman "Maurus" occurs in the European languages as Moor, More, Mor, Mohr, Moro, Morian, Morien and scores of other forms. For instance, the Italian dictionary says, "Moro: Uomo nero d'etiope." (Black man of Ethiopia). (28) The Century Dictionary says, Moor means "blackamoor. Hence Morian, Moresque, Morisco, Morris." It is much the same in the Teutonic languages. The word, Moor, in German, says Stoll, was "exactly equivalent to Negro," in the time of Othello. (29)

"Moor" for Negro continued to be in general use in England until at least the eighteenth century. Nathaniel Bailey, compiler of the first English dictionary, (1736) has: "(Moor): more, (French); more (Italian and Spanish), or Black Moor, a native of Mauretania." Dr. Samuel Johnson (1755) has, "(Moor, Maurus, latin): A Negro blackamoor."

Mulattoes were called Tawny-Moors and sometimes Tanny-Moors, Tannimoors (30) Bailey says they were one born of parents of which one is a moor and the other of some other nation, or White." Albino Negroes were called "White Moors." This latter was also a nickname in Spain for usurers. (31)

"Niger," the ancient African word from which evolved "Negro" (niger, nigra, nigrum of the Romans) started to supplant Ethiop

27. Ancient and Modern Britons, Vol. 1, p. 46. 1884.

28. Boccardo: Neuva Encic. Ital. says, "Negri, Mori, Ethiopi, Melancici, are various names to describe that portion of the human race with black skins and who are descendants of Ham, son of Noah." (See NEGRI).

Among noted persons with such names are Andalo Mori, astronomer of Genoa, 1270. Encyc. Universelle names among others Francois Negro, or Negri (1500-1560) Philologist. There are an abundance of names of Negro origin in the encyclopedias.

29. Stoll, E. Othello. Univ. of Minnesota Studies, No. 2, p. 46.

30. Hopkins, J. T. This London, p. 179. 1929.

31. Aleman M. Guzman de Alfarache, Vol. 2, p. 178 (1623) trans. by James Mabbe, reprint 1924.

32. Eden. Decades. p. 384. ed. Arber. 1895. In a letter of 1581 in Archives Curieuses de l'Hist. de France, the Ethiopians are spoken of as "Moors, very black." (ser. 1, Vol. 9. 1836. (by governor of La Rochelle). Sir Thomas Browne (1663-1704 said, "The word, Ethiops, applies to the memorablest nations of Negroes, that is of a burnt and torrid countenance." Works, Vol. 3, p. 233. 1926. Also in Wm. Painter's "Palace of Pleasure" Africa is called "the land of black people such as the Spaniards call Negroes." (Novel XXXV, p. 697. 1813). Painter was a contemporary of Shakespeare. See also Sir John Mandeville, 14th century traveller. He wrote, "And men of Nubia (that is, Ethiopia) be Christian but they be as the Moors for the great heat of the sun." In chap. 17, he calls the Ethiopians "Moors."

and Moor about the middle of the sixteenth century Richard Eden in his "Decades" (1555), says "Ethiopes, which we now call Moors, Moorens, or Negroes." (32) Diego de Torres in a work printed in Spain in 1586 said of Mulai Mohammed, emperor of Morocco, "El qual es negro." (Who is a Negro). John Harrison of England in his play. "The Tragical Life and Death of Muley Abdallah Malek, late King of Barbarie" (that is, Morocco), printed in 1733, says he was "the son of Mulay Sidon by a negra (Negro woman) and so by complexion, a mulatto." (33)

George Peele in his "Tragical Battle of Alcazar" played in London in 1588 (or before Shakespeare is believed to have written his first play) used Moor and Negro interchangeably. One of his characters is Muley Mohamet, emperor of Morocco, who is mentioned in such passages as "And aids with Christian arms, the barbarous Moor, the Negro, Muley Mohamet," and "thunders for vengeance on this Negro Moor." (34)

Christopher Marlowe in "Lust's Dominion, Or the Lascivious Queen," (written before Shakespeare's Othello The Moor) also uses Negro and Moor interchangeably several times. This play deals with the illicit love of Eleazer, Prince of Fez, Morocco, with the Queen of Spain, who has a child by him.

". . . there goes the Moor.
He that makes a cuckold of the Spanish Queen
That's the black prince of devils."

He is also called, "The Negro king" and "the soft-skinned Negro." (35) Richard Brome in his "English Moor" (1659) used, Blackamore, Ethiop, and Negro, interchangeably on a single page. Ben Jonson (1602) in his "Masque of lackness" which deals with Ethiopia, says, "It was famous by the name of Niger; of which the people were called Nigritae, now Negroes, and are the blackest nation in the world."

It might be noted in passing that the subject of the queen, or other high-born white woman in love with a Negro has intrigued story-tellers from early times. We find it recurring in European literature. In the folk-lore of the Greek island of Lesbos, the daughter of a king is enamored of a Negro. (36 In Emile Le-

33. Malone Soc'y Reprints, p. 103. 1922 (W. W. Gregg) "To an Englishman a Moor was usually a blackamoor."

34. Works of George Peele, Vol. 2. 1828.

35. Act 1, & 2. Act 3, Sc. 1. (Dodsley's Old English Plays, Vol. 14. 1875).

36. Georgeakis and Pineau. Le Folk-Lore Lesbos, p. 107. 1894.

37. Recueil de Contes Populaires Grecques, pp. 27-37. 1881. The Queen tells her husband "How I love black raisins on a white plate!", the meaning of which I had better not give here. For a similar story see Hahn, J. G. Grieschische und Albanesische Marchen, No. 73. 1864. Also Benedetto Croce's notes on the Pentamerone, Vol. 1, pp. 12, 201-02. 1932.

grand's "La Reine et le Negre" (the Queen and the Negro) another ancient tale, it is a queen who is. (37) Von Hahn, in his folk-tales of Greece and Albania, gives another similar story. Also in the Arthurian legends, which are believed to be of Eastern origin, the beautiful Queen Isolde, is in love with the black Moorish knight, Sir Palamedes. Arabian erotic tales, notably the Perfumed Garden and The Thousand and One Nights tell of queens and noblewomen cohabiting with unmixed Negroes. (38) In two of the Novellinos of Masuccio of fifteenth century Italy, white mistresses are in love with Negro slaves. (39)

A verse of ancient English poetry reads:

The Moore so pleased the new-made empress' eye
That she consented to him secretly
For to abuse her husband's marriage bed
And so in time a Blackamoore she bred. (40)

In Shakespeare's time were at least four plays dealing with this theme, all of which were popular: Peele's Battle of Alcazar; Marlowe's Lust's Dominion; and Shakespeare's Titus Andronicus and Othello. In Titus Andronicus, Tamora, Queen of Goths, is paramour of the black, wooly-haired Aaron the Moor, and in Othello, the high-born Venetian lady Desdemona, is in love with Othello an ex-slave. (41)

Shakespeare uses "Negro" only once and uses it interchangeably with "Moor," in the case of a white man getting a Negro woman with child. "Moor" for "Negro" was just coming into use. But in 1623, seven years after Shakespeare's death, James Mabbe, in his translation of Aleman's Guzman de Alfarache, uses Negro almost always for Moor. (42)

It seems clear, therefore, from the foregoing that when Europeans placed Moors in their coats-of-arms, they had no other than what were later called Negroes in mind. The latter appear by thousands in heraldry. I counted 497 families in Rietstap's Armoriale Generale that had one or more Negroes in their coats-of-arms. Some had as many as six. Siebamcher's Wappenbuch of eighty-eight volumes had even more.

Families with Negro in their coats-of-arms range from Sicily to Finland. Of the 497 I counted in Ritstrap, France had 146,

38 & 39. See sources and excerpts in Sex and Race, vol. 1, pp. 103-05, 166. 2nd ed. 1940.

40. Percy, T. Reliques of Ancient English Poetry, Vol. 1, p. 243. 1823 (This poem is generally known as "The Lady and the Blackamoor." Some authorities think it was written after Titus Andronicus; others that is is much older.

41. In the Dutch version of this play Aaron is a Moorish general of the white Goths, beloved by Thamera (Tamora). See sources of Titus Andronicus. Publ. Modern Language Assn. Vol. 16, No. 1. (Fuller, H.).

42. Vol. 3, p. 260; Vol. 4, pp. 172, 304. 1924.

NEGROES IN COATS-OF-ARMS
OF NOBLE FAMILIES

BLACKMORE, 'Argent, a fesse between three *blackmoors'* heads erased, sable; those of

British Families. Top left: The Mores of Yorkshire, including Sir Thomas More, Chancellor of Henry VIII. (Yorkshire Genealogist, Vol. 2, p. 78). The others are from Fairbarn's Book of Crests; Fox-Davies' Armorial Families; and Elwen's Book of Crests.

77 NEGRO ANCESTRY IN THE WHITE RACE

Germany 126, Holland 53, Italy 24, Switzerland 18, Poland 14, Denmark 8, Sweden 3, inland 2. The 497 are not all, however. I might have missed some. Besides Rietstap gives few extinct families, some of whose descendants are no doubt now living. His works, too, deal principally with the Continent. Not many British families were named. Later with only little research I found 162 of the latter with one or more Negroes.

Who were these blacks? Wade, (43) Grandmaison (44) and some others say they represent Moors whom the Crusaders fought in Spain and Palestine. Some, as Gough says, represent trade and exploration, that is, of whites who adventured in black men's lands. For instance, Sir John Hawkins, father of the English slave-trade had a bound Negro in his coat-of-arms. Both these views are right only in a very small way because they do not explain why so many of these families with Negroes are named Moor, Blackamoor, and the like. McRitchie is correct when he says that families with the name of Moor, Moore, Morris, Morrison, and other derivatives of Moor, had Moors as their ancestors. He adds, "Nor can the Moors of heraldry be explained sufficiently on the theory that the founders of families bearing Moors as supporters and Moors' heads as crests had won their spurs in assisting Spaniards to expel the Moor. The bearing among ancient coats-of-arms is too common to admit this explanation. And the heraldic representation of a 'Moor,' or Negro man' does not suggest Granada. The features are ugly, irregular, and the hair though longer than that of a pure Negro, is wooly . . . The complexion is, of course, black." (45)

As proof he gives instances of Negroes in much later times who were brought to England, chiefly from Africa, being baptized into the church and given the surname, Moor, Moore, or More. He cites the case of Elen More, maid-of-honor to Queen Margaret of Scotland. "In 1504," he says, "two blackamoor girls arrived and were educated at the court, where they waited on the Queen. They were baptized Elen and Margaret. In June, 1507, a tournament was held in honour of the Queen's black lady, Elen More, which was conducted with great splendour." Her husband, King James, had Negro minstrels, the chief of which was "Peter the Moryen, or Moor." MacRitchie concludes, "The Elen More offers an unmistakable example of this surname 'More' having been given because the person it distinguished was a Moor, Morrow, or Murray. Peter the Moryen

43. Symbolisms of Heraldry, p. 144. 1898.
44. Dict. Heraldique, Vol. 1, p. 540. 1852.
45. Ancient and Modern Britons, Vol. 1, pp. 54-55. 1884. Vol. 2, pp. 328-9.

NEGROES IN COATS-OF-ARMS
OF NOBLE FAMILIES

English. Morison means "Son of the Moor."

is a kindred specimen; and it is probable that he ultimately became Peter organ (for this is apparently a form of that word). (46) The Negro minstrels at the Scottish court served as the climax to an evening of enjoyment. "To bring in the Moors," says MacRitchie, "was commonly used to denote their coming in to add the finishing touch to "an evening of gaiety."

MacRitchie adds that "the legends and the history of the Scottish Highlands are both witnesses to the existence of a purely black people there." Boswell and Dr. Johnson saw descendants of these black people when they visited Scotland. In his "Journey to the Hebrides, September 1, 1773," Boswell wrote of one clan, the McCraes, "Some were as black and wild in their appearance as any American savages, whatsoever." Martin who had visited these Western Islands eighty years before Boswell said of the people of Jura, "black of complexion," of Islay, "generally black"; and of Arran, "generally brown and some of a black complexion." (47) The use of "brown" for some shows very clearly that when he said "black" he meant black. Also Robert Knox, in 1850 mentions a small colony of mulattoes living at Minch Moor, Scotland, the offspring of Negroes and white women. (47a)

Another explanation for the surname, Moor, Moore, More, is that it comes from the Anglo-Saxon, mor, damp waste land. (48) This is true in some cases but it still does not explain the "Moores" with Moors within their coat-of-arms, especially since Continental families named Moor (or its equivalent) also have Moors in their heraldry. The Anglo-Saxon, mor, for instance, bears no resemblance to Moors, (human beings) in the Latin languages. Its equivalent in Latin is terra uliginosum, or palustria. In Italian it is brughiera; in Spanish, parano; in French bruyere and sometimes marecage, or marsh, from the Latin for sea. If there is any connection between the Anglo-Saxon, mor, or wasteland and the Latin, mare, (sea), on one hand, and the Greek and Latin Maros, Maurus (Moor) on the other it goes too far back in prehistory to be relevant. When the Greeks and Romans used that word they very definitely meant human beings.

Moreover since the Romans colonized Britain and were there fully five centuries before the Anglo-Saxons it is safe to say that Maurus (Moor) as a surname, was deposited in the English

46. MacRitchie, Vol. 2, p. 327. For other Negro jesters see pp. 328-9.

47. Races of Men, p. 106. 1850. Dr. Johnson's first guide on his visit to Scotland was a Negro, Gory—Boswell's Jour. to the Hebrides Aug. 21, 1773, pp. 139-40.

47a. Western Islands of Scotland, pp. 236, 268, 272. Reprint 1934 from ed. of 1703.

language before the Anglo-Saxon, mor. Again, in British heraldry even as there are "wild" men and women, that is, nude and in a savage state, there are Negro men and women of the same. Might not these black folk, like the whites, represent ancient Britons, such as the Silures and the Picts, who are said by MacRitchie to have been Negroes?

What shatters the theory that the English, Moore, comes only from mor, (wasteland) is that families with the name, Blackmoor and Blackamour, which comes from "blackamoor" have blackamoors in their coats-of-arms. (49) Lower, who has traced the origin of English surnames, says, "The most natural and the one which best united the name of the person is that giving a designation which relates to his most conspicuous qualities." Color of skin certainly came into this category. "Color and complexion," he adds, "have given rise certainly to such surnames as Black, Blackman . . ." (50) Some families named Black and Blackman also have Negroes. Grandmaison names a "Niger" with three Negroes in his coat-of-arms.

Negro proteges of the nobility — and there were a good many as we shall see later — were sometimes christened Blackamore, which, says Lower, comes from "blackamoor." He illustrated his point with three Negroes' heads. (51) It seems safe to say, therefore, that certain prominent Englishmen, as Sir Richard Blackamore (1650-1729), noted physician and writer, had a Negro ancestor somewhere. The British Museum catalogue contains a number of writers so named.

Burke in his "Encyclopedia of Heraldry" lists a number of Blackmores: "Blackmore, three Moors' heads . . . Blackmore (Devonshire) crest, a Moor's head . . . Blackmore (Rev. Richard Blackmore, the same . . . Blackmore (Milton Bank) the same . . . Blackmore (165) three Moors' heads . . . Blackmore (London) three Moors' heads . . ." (52)

Several "Moore" families in which "Negro" is used instead of "Moor" are also mentioned, as "Moore (Scotstoun, Scotland)

48. Anderson W. Genealogy of Surnames, pp. 127, 617. 1946.

49. C. W. Bardsley says, "John the Moor suggests to us at least the possibility that English heathlands did not enjoy the entire monopoly in the production of this familiar cognomen. The intensive Blackamoor, a mere compound of black and Moor seems to have existed early. A Beatrice Blackamore occurs in a London register of 1417." See also Riley's London with such names as Simon Blackamour and Richard Blackamore, pp. 525, 647. Hutching gives a Blackamore in Northumberland in 1601. Weekly says that Blackmoor is Blackamoor and cites Beatrix Blackamour as another spelling of that name.

50. Lower: English Surnames, Vol. 1, p. 140. Also, Nisbet A. System of Heraldry, p. 261. 1816.

51. Lower: English Surnames, Vol. 2, p. 114. 1849.

52. See Moore, Blackmore, etc. 1847.

three Negroes' heads . . . Moore, a blackamoor's head . . . More,
five Negroe heads . . ." Blacker has "three Moors' heads." Other
variations of Blackmore are Blackmuir, Blackmur, Blackmer.
Negro favorites were also christened Blackman and Blackie.
Blackness of skin was their chief physical characteristic and the chief attraction to those who adopted him.

Among families named Moore, or More, are some very distinguished ones as Sir Thomas More, great Lord Chancellor of
Henry VIII, and author of Utopian. (53) His coat-of-arms shows
a thick-lipped Moor, clearly of Negro ancestry. His arms are
also those of the Moors of Yorkshire. Another with the same is
Sir John Moore, hero of Corunna. (53a) Among other Moores with
Negro heads are those of London, Berkshire, Kent, Canterbury,
Wiltshire, Suffolk, Derbyshire, Ireland, and many others, including
some mentioned in Burke's Peerage as the Earls of Drogheda.

It is likely that some Negroes who reached England in the
fifteenth or sixteenth centuries and became prominent also took
Moors' heads in their coats-of-arms. One instance is probably
John Morison (son of the Moor), rich merchant of Edinburgh,
who founded that family in 1609. His arms are "three Moors'
heads and three Saracens' heads). The Saracens in his coat-
of-arms are white. (54)

It is highly possible that some Negro "blood" was also mixed
in with Norman one, which is the last word in British blue-blood.
Lower says of the Morrices, Fitz-Morices, and Mountmorrices (all
variations of Moor), "They are supposed to be of Moorish blood:
their progenitors having come from Africa by way of Spain into
various countries of Western Europe. It is a well-known fact that
the peculiar species of saltation called the morrice dance and several
branches of magic lore, were introduced into these centuries ago
by natives of Morocco. The professors of these arts, enriching
themselves by their trade, seem in some instances to have embraced Christianity and to have become founders of eminent
families. Certain it is that several magnates bearing the name
of Morice, Fitz-Morice and Mountmorris attended William the
Conqueror in his descent upon England and acquiring lands
settled in this country." (55)

In the Domesday Book, the great survey made in 1085-6 by
order of William the Conqueror, are to be found with the name
"More" or derivatives of Moor as Morinus, Moriton, Moretania
(that is, Mauretania or Morocco). The Earls and Dukes of Dorset
used to call their Negro valets John Morocco. There are also a

53. Yorkshire Genealogist vol. 2, p. 78.
53a. Berry W. Encyclopedia Heraldica, pp. 412, 413, 513, 514. 1909.
54. Nisbet A. Heraldic Plates, pp. 135-7. 1892.
55. English Surnames, Vol. 1, p. 54. 1849.

number of Blac's (Black) as Blackeman (Blackman) and Blackmer, another form of Blackmoor. (56) This is quite independent of the fact that Anglo-Saxon for black and white sounded much the same. They were spelt the same, blaec, meaning absence of color. White however was accented. I am dealing with families named "black" that had Negroes.

Another important fact: There is good reason to believe that families with names as Negro, Moor, and their derivatives but who do not have blacks in their coats-of-arms, had Negro ancestors. Also, still another proof of the presence of early Negroes in England is that the morris-dance, England's national dance, is of African origin. It might have been brought over by Moors with the Romans and it seems certainly by the Moors with William the Conqueror in 1066. Sir John Hawkins, an earlier authority on music, says, "It is indisputable that this dance was the invention of the Moor." (57) Tabourot, another authority, says the same. (58) Dr. Johnson's dictionary, (1755) says "Morris dance, that is, Moorish or Morrice dance."

Its Negro origin is further seen in that white dancers blackened their faces to dance it. "The Moresca," says Paul Nettl, "was originally a dance of the Negroes, or Moors and the pantomine of one or more Negroes in black face; then quite generally a masquerade or pantomine and in particular a play or song sketch in which Negroes tok part . . . In the seventeenth century any sort of masquerade was called "Mauresque" because the guise of the black man was the most important and popular, a phenomenon which points on the one hand to the significance of the black race for the esthetic life of the whites; on the other hand to the ancient habit of all Europeans to paint the face black on certain occasions of cult ritualism." He quotes Arbeau, French writer of the sixteenth century, who said that often in good society he would see "a youth with blackened face" do this dance. In the Italian madrigal literature of the Renaissance, he says, "real Negroes were introduced." (59)

Real Negro minstrels, as was said, were popular at the Scottish court and in London, at least later, they were as popular on the streets as Negroes were on those of Philadelphia in Franklin's time.

56. Ellis, A. Gen. Introd. to the Domesday Book, Vol. 1, p. 455. Vol. 2. pp. 49, 187, 356. 1833. Negro christened John Morockoe (Morocco). Noes & Queries, 11 ser. Vol. 6, p. 372. Nov. 9, 1912.

57. Hist. of the Science and Practice of Music p. 216. 1853.

58. Orchesographie p. XXXII. 1888. Welford E. Court Masques, pp. 28-30. 1927. Welford E. The Fool, pp. 28-30. 1927.

59. Phylon. 2nd Quar. 1944, pp. 105-113. See also Arnold, T. Legacy of Islam, p. 373. 1931, where is also mentioned the dyeing of faces "in imitation of Moors."

NEGROES IN COATS-OF-ARMS
OF NOBLE FAMILIES

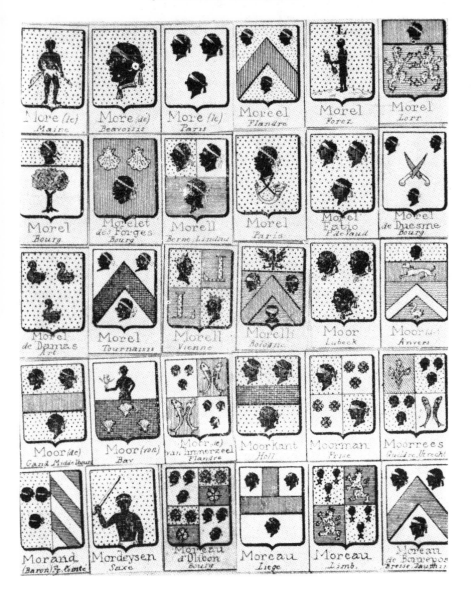

French, Dutch and Belgian Families with Names of Negro

NEGROES IN COATS-OF-ARMS
OF NOBLE FAMILIES

Names of these families, except three denote Negro ancestry.

NEGROES IN COATS-OF-ARMS
OF NOBLE FAMILIES

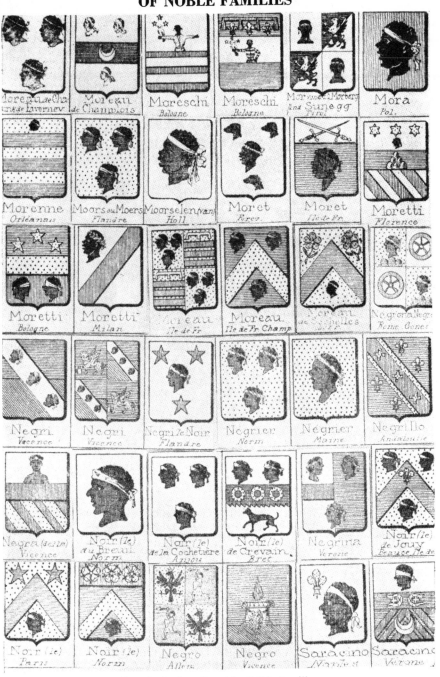

French, Italian, Spanish, Polish families.

NEGROES IN COATS-OF-ARMS
OF NOBLE FAMILIES

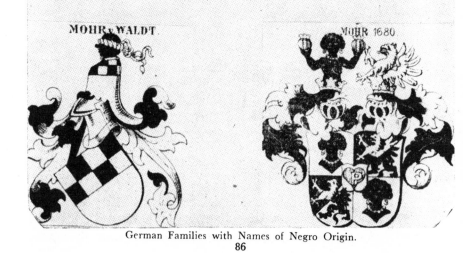

German Families with Names of Negro Origin.

White people blackened their faces not only for the morris-dance but because of attraction for a dark skin. MacRitchie says, "Many British peoples of fair complexion were accustomed to blacken their faces artificially 'that they might the better pass for Moors'." (60) To understand this fully one must divest himself of all notions of the American dogma of color superiority. However, one finds a clear relationship in this darkening of the skin, as that of the ancient Druids, with the tan many white now try to acquire either by sun, lotion, or electric lamp. At one of Ben Johnson's masques given at Whitehall, January 12, 1605, Queen Anne of England and her ladies blackened their faces and arms to the elbow. (61)

Moorish blood came into the English royal family, also. Elizabeth, daughter of Edward IV and mother of Henry VIII, had several Moors in her family among these Count More and Count Morienne. There is also an Almoravit (Almoravide), which says Turton, is distinctly Moorish. (62) The Almoravides were conquerors of Spain in 1086 A. D., and were "largely Negroes."

MOORS IN FRENCH, GERMAN, DUTCH AND OTHER EUROPEAN FAMILIES

Families on the Continent also have Negroes in considerable numbers in their coats-of-arms. There are fifty or more variations of the word, Moor, in the European languages. (63) One noted Dutch family is descended from "Jan the Moor" who is

60. MacRitchie, Vol. 2, p. 431. Burton A. Rush-bearing, p. 96. 1891.

61. Masque of Blackness. Works of Gifford, Vol. 7, 8. 1816.

62. Turton, W. H. Heiress of the Plantagenets, pp. 44, 78, 126 & Note 3.

63. Hoorebeke G. says "Morel, black man" . . . When we write de Moor (the Negro, or black man) "how clear, lucid and comprehensible it is" pp. 289, 411. 1876. De warte (the black man, one with color of a Negro)" p. 290. Chapuy P. Origine des noms patronimiques francais says "Negre, black." He gives this as a surname of mediaeval origin. p. 51. 1934.

Gottschald M. Deutsche Namenkinde, gives derivates of Moor as, "Mohr, der Mohr, Neger" also Morian, Morillo, Maurelius, Mohrentonih, Mohrenstecher. p. 97. 1932.

Berry W. (Encyc. Heraldica) gives as some derivations of Moor— Morand, Morel, Morican, Morlot, Mormand, Mauriac.

Larchey, Loredan Dictionnaire des Noms, pp. 326, 336, 337. 1880, gives the following derivatives of Moor—" Maure, of Moorish origin or with skin brown like that of a Moor, Murel, Maurice, Maurand, Maurant, Maury, Maurin, Mauritz, Moran, Morand, Morard, More, Moreau, Moreaux, Morellet, Moricaud, Morricard, Moricault, Morice, Moriceau, Moricet, Morillon, Morillot, Morize, Morland, Morot, Mory. Lemor, Lemorc.

As regards Negro, "Negre Nom d'homme a peau noire. S'ecrit d'abord Le Negre, Negrel, Negret." p. 343.

De Renesse, T. Dictionnaire de Figures Heraldiques, Vol. 2, pp. 164-182. 1895, gives many Moors in the different ways in Mores (Moors,

NEGROES IN COATS-OF-ARMS
OF NOBLE FAMILIES

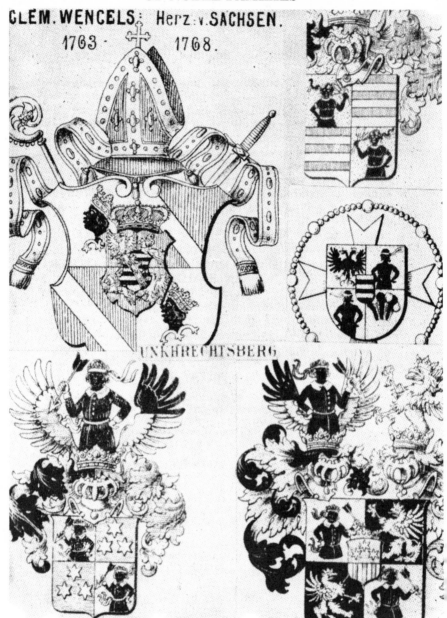

German Families. Note the Negroes (upper left) wearing crowns and the archbishop's mitre.

NEGROES IN COATS-OF-ARMS
OF NOBLE FAMILIES

ANSELM Fhr. REICHLIN v. MELDEGG.
Fürstabt von Kempten.
1728.

GERMAN

NEGROES IN COATS-OF-ARMS
OF NOBLE FAMILIES

RESICH

GAZA, II

BAROCZ·MELLETHE

KUEFSTEIN 1654

GEDELER

STOSSEL

BECK·TAVERNIER

CENTRAL EUROPE

NEGROES IN COATS-OF-ARMS
OF NOBLE FAMILIES

RUPERT v. BODMANN

1678.　　　1728

WERDEN, III.
(Cleve)

KUEFSTEIN, St.W.

1594.

CENTRAL EUROPE

shown as a Negro. In Holland and Germany where swart, swarte, schwartz, schwarzmann, that is black, there are families with such names with Negroes in their coats-of-arms. Belgium has several Moers, de Moors, a Moor von Immersel, and other "Moors" with Negroes. Some of these could have been Negroes in the army of Spain when the latter ruled the Netherlands.

Poland has a Mora with a Negro. France has many families as Moret, Morel, Moricaud, Morot, Moreau and many other derivatives of Moor (Maure) represented by Negroes. Le Noir, which is still used in France for "the black man" was one of the great French families with branches in Anjou, Normandy, Brittany and Beaune, has a Negro. The family, Negre, still used by the French for Negro, also has a Negro. Migne lists a Justine de Sorbier married to Jean de Negre and a Lady Marie d'Able. (64) Francois le Peloux, lord of Gourdan, and one of the courtiers of Charles V, was a mulatto. Brantome says, "he was handsome although mulatto (moricaut pourtant)" (65) The celebrated Chevalier de St. George, a Gaudeloupe Negro, was also called a "moricaut." (66)

Italian families with variations of "Moor" as Moretti, Morini, Morelli, with Negroes are many. The same is true of those with variations of Negro as Negrina, Negrona, Negra. "Saracen" an-

Negroes) have been spelt in heraldry.

La Chenaye de Des-Bois. Dictionnaire de la Noblesse. Vol. 14, pp. 505-620 gives list of noble families with Moor and derivatives of Moor beginning with Jacques de Moor in 1497 and his descendants (1869) Burke; Heraldic Illustrations, Vol. 2, p. Plate 75: (1853) see Meynell Family dating to 12th century with a Negro head. Plate 140, Vol. 3. Family of Richard Polwhele of Cornwall, Ancient family of Saxon origin with Negro, Vol. 2, Pl. 96. Moore of Stockwell descendant of Sir Thomas More.

Rolland. Armoire-generale de Rietstap. Suppl. Vol. 3, p. 254. Negre. Provence D'argent a trois tetés de Maure sables.

Fairbairn. Book of Crests. gives 45 families with figures described as 'Moors,' 'Negroes,' or 'blackamoors' in their coat-of-arms. All were named Moore, or derivatives of Moor, as Moore, Moorhead, Morison.

A French proverb is, "A laver la tete d'un More on perd sa lessive." which is the equivalent of the English, "To wash a blackamoor white." Maure, More, in French is exactly equivalent to Negro, at least it was then.

For a list of the derivatives of the English Moor see Marshall's Genealogist's Guide, Vol. 2, p. 560-66. 1903. For American descendants of "Moor" see "Index to American Genealogies, Vol. 2, 1900.

For coat-of-arms with Negroes due to trade see Gough: Glossary of Terms Used In Heraldry, p. 117. 1891; and coat-of-arms of Sir John Hawkins, slave-trader.

64. Migne Nobiliare Universel de France. Vol. 7. Art. on Fleury-Blachefort, p. 4. 1861. Also Vol. 2, p. 38.

65. Vol. 1, p. 98. 1864.

66. Larousse, Vol. 14, p. 68. See ST. GEORGES.

other term for Negro, have families as Saraceni and Saraceno with Negroes. In the story of "The Three Citrons" in the Pentamerone by Basile (1595-1632) the black slave wife of Prince Taddeo is called a "Saracina). (67) Wade says also, "Moors or "Moors' are supposed generally to refer to Saracens." (68)

In Continental heraldry, as in British one, Negroes are shown as "wild" or "woodsmen," that is savages, just as are some of the whites. Negroes, like whites, also wear crowns and coronets. Among the Negroes are Mohr von Stoessel, Sartorius of Schwanenfeld, and Werl of Germany; Pernet of Switzerland; Thommendorf of Poland; and Cornier de Perney and Dibart de Villetanet of France. Colerthure of Germany is a Negro woman wearing a crown; with Vogtmann, Schorer, and Vendelhoe of Germany the same. Moringer (a derivative of Moor) of Germany is a Negro holding a cross. Hylmair is a Negro woman with wings; Lampfuzheim is a Negro man with wings; and Dedinger of France is robed like a dignitary of the Church. Some of the Negroes are shown as loaded with jewels, signifying that whatever interpretation might be placed on them they were considered important.

Siebmacher's Wappenbuch of eighty-eight volumes, already mentioned, has a great number of Negroes, some of them with crowns and others as cardinals and archbishops. With these Negroes in German nobility, the evident Negro strain in Queen Charlotte Sophia consort of George III of England, who was a German princess, might be explained (see her portrait). Negroes, some with crowns, also appear in the coats-of-arms of German and other European cities and provinces. Alt-Otting of Bavaria has a Black Madonna; Coburg has the Negro saint, Maurice, and Kammersburg, Marktflechen, Austria, a jet-black Negro as St. Peter, holding the "Keys of the kingdom." In the text, he is called "a Mohr," that is, German then for Negro. Other Negroes

67. Basile says:
"Cuoco de la cocina.
Che fa lo Rre co la Saracina." (Le Tre Cetre, Trattenmiento IX, Vol. 2, p. 206. Napoli. 1787 (2 vols.)
In the translation of this work by Benedetto Croce (Vol. 1, pp. 6, 7, 12) Prince Taddeo marries a Negro woman, who is very dark, in the palace with feasts and illuminations. In the Fourth Day (Vol. 2. The White Prince and the Black Princess) is another description. In the Three Citrons, the parents of the Prince "although they saw the folly of their son who had sought the whole world for his white dove and had brought back a black slave they felt they could do no less than give up their crown to the bride and bridegroom and placed the Tripod of gold on the coal-black head." p. 156.
In the introduction the woman is called "black and hideous Negro slave." In the Fourth Diversion the youth is changed into a blackamoor slave."
68. Symbols of Heraldry, p. 144. 1898.

AN ANCESTRESS OF GEORGE VI
OF ENGLAND

Queen Charlotte Sophia, Consort of George III, and grandmother of
Queen Victoria from a portrait by Thomas Frye (1719-1762). She was
a German princess. (See text, and Sex and Race, Vol. 1, p. 288 2nd ed).

NEGROES IN COATS-OF-ARMS
OF NOBLE FAMILIES

WOLFGANG v. GRUNENSTEIN.
Fürstabt v. Kempten.
1536 - 1557.

German Family. Note the Bishop's Mitre.

NEGROES IN COATS-OF-ARMS
OF NOBLE FAMILIES

DON PIGNATELLI de MONTELEON=GRAF v BORELL
1650.

NICODEMUS · DELLA SCALA · HERMANN v CILLY.
1421 · 1443. · 1412 -1421.

German. Note the Negroes (lower) with crowns and the Bishop's mitres.

NEGROES IN COATS-OF-ARMS
OF NOBLE FAMILIES

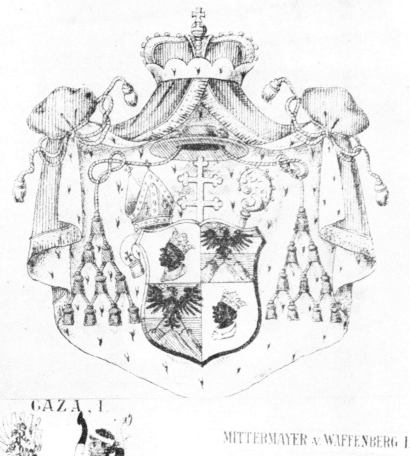

CENTRAL EUROPEAN

NEGROES IN COATS-OF-ARMS
OF NOBLE FAMILIES

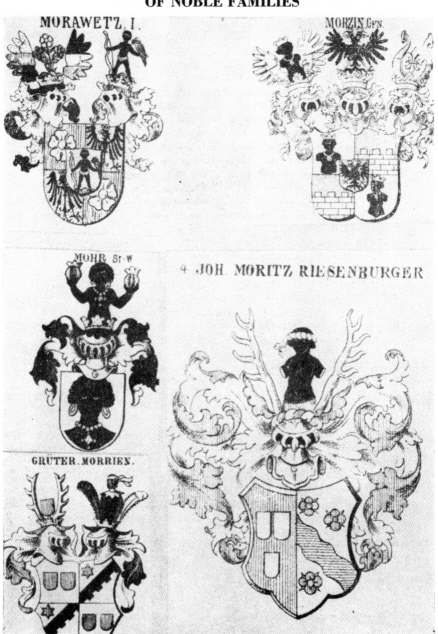

German Families With Names of Negro Origin.

in the coats-of-arms of cities are in Spain and Italy. (69)

Some of these Negroes are undoubtedly the Moors, (or descendants of them), who settled in Hamburg after their expulsion from Spain in the fifteenth century, some of whom were wealthy. Another important fact as regards to these coats-of-arms. To be jet-black and primitive in appearance, unlike our times, was considered desirable, therefore Negroes, or those who could trace ancestry to them, had Negroes in their family crests. Again, "Moor" was once a symbol of power in all Europe. At a time when prowess in battle ranked first, the Moors had a reputation second to none. In England, says MacRitchie, "the blacks were not always a servile race." And the Oxford Dictionary says, "Blackamoor" now a nickname was formerly without depreciatory force."

As was said, Negroes, men and women, wearing crowns and coronets appear in British heraldry. And on the Continent, some Negroes who were not only favorites of royalty but bore the family name of their kingly patrons, became founders of noble families. In Portugal two such families were Mina and Azambuja (See their coats-of-arms). Mina was an African tribe especially noted for the beauty and shapeliness of its women.

It is likely also that "nott-pated" (knotty-head) as used by Prince Henry in Henry V, refers to Negro hair. Chaucer, centuries before Shakespeare used it in connection with color. Describing a yeoman he says "A nott-head had he with a brown visage." Andrew Boorde, a century or so after Chaucer (1490-1549), also uses it in connection with Negroes. He says, "There be many Moors brought into Christendom into great cities and towns to be sold . . . They have great lips and notty hair, black and curled; their skin is soft and there is nothing white but their teeth and the white of the eye." (70) That is, "notty" for Negro hair preceded the use of the Danish, "kink" or kinky, the term now in use in the United States. However, "notty" still survives in the West Indies for the hair of Negroes.

To sum up why many families with Negroes in their coats-of-arms, and especially those with names which are a derivative of Moor, Negro, and Blackamoor are of Negro ancestry: First, they were of that old British stock which opposed invaders, as the Romans, Danes, and Saxons and distiguished themselves in so doing; second, they were Negroes in the Roman armies, who later founded families (Africans and Orientals were encamped in Germany at that time, says Hertz) ; third, Christianized Moors.

69. Siebmacher's Wappenbuch. 1 (4). Stadtewappen. Text, p. 100. 1885. For St. Peter as a Negro, see: 1 (4) Text. p. 100. 1885.

70. First Book of the Introd. of Knowledge (Dietary of Health) Republications. Early English Text Soc'y. Extra Ser. 10, p. 212. 1870.

NEGROES IN COATS-OF-ARMS
OF NOBLE FAMILIES

German. Note the Crowns and the Archbishop's Mitres

NEGROES IN COATS-OF-ARMS
OF NOBLE FAMILIES

WAFFENBERG IV.

STRASSOLDO. III

KUEFSTEIN. 1860

INTIMA CANDENT

CENTRAL EUROPEAN

NEGROES IN COATS-OF-ARMS
OF NOBLE FAMILIES

GRZYMAŁA.

WISSE v GERBEVILLER

BOBEST v ZITHAVIA

TAVERNIER Baron

GRAF KORYTOWSKI.

PRO REGE ET PATRIA

NEGROES IN COATS-OF-ARMS
OF NOBLE FAMILIES

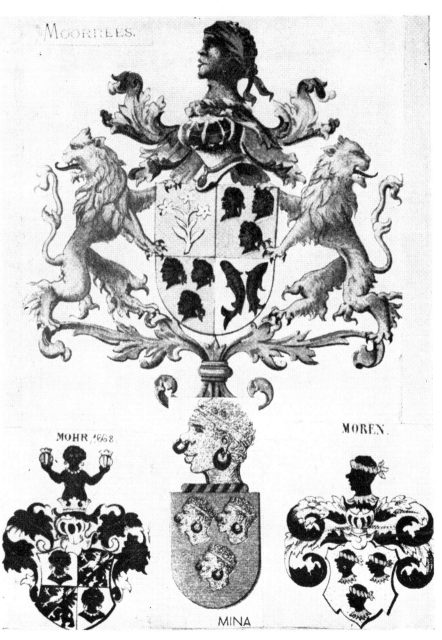

Families with Names of Negro Origin. Upper: Holland. Centre, middle:
Portuguese. The other: German.

103

GERMANY

JOHANN THEODOR HERZOG v BAYERN
CARDINAL BISCHOF
v.Freising, Regensburg u.Luttich.

Coats-of-Arms of a German Cardinal. Note the crown on the Negro's Head.

NEGROES IN COATS-OF-ARMS

Germany and Portugal

NEGROES IN COATS-OF-ARMS
OF EUROPEAN CITIES

Centre left: Arms of Aragon, Spain. Centre right: Arms of Kammersburg, Austria, Austria. St. Peter, foremost saint and founder of the Catholic Church, is shown as jet-black Negro.

NEGROES IN COATS-OF-ARMS
OF EUROPEAN CITIES

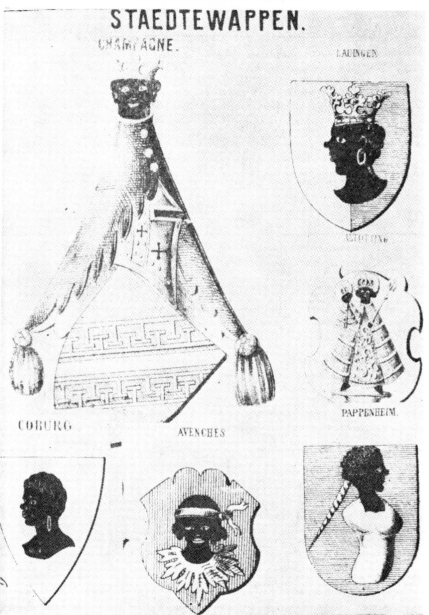

STAEDTEWAPPEN.

CHAMPAGNE.

LAUINGEN

COBURG

AVENCHES

PAPPENHEIM.

Centre; right. The Black Madonna and Christ of Alt-Otting, Bavaria.
Lowest, left. St. Maurice in the coast-of-arms of Coburg, Germany.

who joined with the English, French, Germans and other Crusaders in Spain and Palestine, as well as slaves, mistresses and even wives, brought from Spain and the Near East — Negroes even then were common in the homes of great lords, having them was "fashionable" (70a) — and fourth, African blacks of the Middle Ages or of the later slave period who found royal favor, or who rose to some prominence through ability or trade. For instance, there were Negro members of the Hanseatic League, great mercantile guild of the 14th and 15th centuries. The patron saint of the guild was St. Maurice, a Negro, foremost Catholic saint of Germany. The ornate building of the guild with its Negro heads still stand in Riga and Revel, Esthonia. (71) As was shown some of these Negroes with Negroes in their coats-of-arms took names, signifying their origin but others when adopted into families took the names of the latter, or even other names. Thus might be explained the presence of Negroes in coat-of-arms of hundreds of others families.

70a. Pedro de Carvalho. Das Origines da Escravidao em Portugal, p. 41. 1877.

71. Seth, D. Esthonian Journey, p. 28, 1939. Davis, E. C., a Wayfarer in Esthonia, pp. 11, 14, 105. Berejkov. Du Commerce de la Russie avec la Hanse jusqu'a la fin du XV siecle. 1879. Winckler. Die deutschen Hanse in Russland. Berlin 1886. Reau, L. L'art russe, p. 118. 1921. On the House of the Black or Negro heads in Riga and Reval.

NOTES ON OTHELLO

Othello's "race" since the days of Edmund Kean (1787-1833) has been in dispute. Here are some facts to be remembered as regards this. Shakespeare lifted his plot largely from the Hecatommithi (Novela VII, 1608) by Cinthio, an Italian romancer. Cinthio only called his character. "The Moor" and spoke of his "negrezza" or blackness of skin. To "The Moor" Shakespeare gave a name, Othello, which is said to be of German origin.

As I said before the union of a white woman of high birth and a black man has been a popular theme since very early times. On the Continent there was little or no prejudice to so-called mixed marriages but in England, then engaged in capturing Negroes and seling them in the Americas, color prejudice began to develop. There are clear evidences of this in certain of Shakespeare's contemporaries as George Herbert's "A Fair Nymph Scorning A Black Boy Courting Her"; John Cleveland's "The Blackamoor and Her Loves"; Christopher Marlowe's Lust's

Dominion," Peele's "Tragical Battle of Alcazar," and in Shakespeare's own Merchant of Venice, where Portia dismisses her dark-skinned suitor, the Prince of Morocco, with, "Let all of his complexion choose me so." Act II, Sc. VI). It must be remembered that while the scene of Othello is Venetian, its psychology is English.

Now I take it that Shakespeare, seeing the union of Negroes and white women and also the growing prejudice against Negroes made Othello a Negro for dramatic effect. Moreover, as I said, the subject of the black man and the white woman had not only been an alluring one long before him but that two of his contemporaries, Peele and Marlowe, had already written succesful miscegenation plays.

Shakespeare describes Othello's color and "race" so clearly that it is only those who read present conditions into those of centuries ago could say that he would not be guilty of so great an artistic error as to make him a Negro.

E. M. Stoll says, "Black he certainly is and a Negro" (Univ. of Minnesota Studies in anguage and Literature. No. 2, p. 45). Baldensperger, who goes thoroughly into the subject, says, "Othello is a Negro and a Christian." (Harvard Univ. Studies in Philology. Vol. 9-20, p. 7). S. A. Tannenbaum, "Shakespeare's description of Aaron the Moor, in Titus Andronicus, his use of 'Negro' and 'Moor' as synonymous terms in the Merchant of Venice (III, V. 42, 43) and Iago's insistence on the unnaturalness of Desdemona's choice, combined with the many references to Othello's blackness (as well as his sooty bosom and thick lips) . . . must compel the conviction that the poet, with true artistry intends us to think of 'black Othello' as a Negro." (Shakespeare's Othello. A Concise Bibliography, p. VII. 1934).

D. J. Snyder says, "A question has been raised concerning the degree of Othello's Africanism about which extreme opinions have been held in both directions. But he was not a Hottentot on the one hand, nor a Caucasian on the other; he was, however, born in Africa and his physiognomy is thoroughly African. The point which the Poet emphasizes so often and so strongly is the difference of race between him and Desdemona. He is her equal in rank, for he comes of royal lineage; he is the peer of her family in honor and fame for he is the most distinguished man in Venice. The sole difference which is selected as the ground of collision is race." (System of Shakespeare's Dramas, pp. 105-05. 1877.

For further background see Winstanley, L., Othello as the Tragedy of Italy (1924) and such earlier works as The Touchstone of Politics by Boccalius (1610) and the New Found Politics where the Spaniards are described as a black people ruling a white one. Finally, Burckhardt gives what I consider a clinching argument. In his "Civilization of the Renaissance in Italy," he mentions a noted Negro who lived in Venice and thinks he might have been the original of Othello. See the next chapter in the part on Italy.

NOTES ON NEGROES IN ROMAN BRITAIN

"The Notitia Dignitatum in partibus Occidentis" compiled by copyists of the Middle Ages from accounts of the Roman Empire up to the 4th Century A. D. has this in the part dealing with Britain." "In Britain he (Emperor Septimius Severus) was proceeding to the next resting place . . . a certain Ethiopian of the military class, famous among the clowns, and noted for his jokes, came up to him with a crown made of cypress." (Vol. 2, p. 888. 1853 — Bocking). "Military class" here undoubtedly infers the presence not only of Negro soldiers but of Negroes in other occupations.

CHAPTER SEVEN

MIXTURES OF WHITES AND BLACKS IN GREECE, TURKEY, ITALY AND CENTRAL EUROPE

The Byzantine, or Eastern Romane Empire, like the Western, was a great melting pot. Greeks, Armenians, Arabs, Jews, Negroes, Nordics met and mingled in disregard of "race." (1) Byzantium was closely linked with Ethiopia. Byzantine rulers took their title, Basileus, from Ethiopia. Such prejudices as existed were tribal, national and religious, principally the latter after Christianity came to power. "There was, "says Spengler," not the slightest difficulty about an Irishman in Constantinople marrying a Negro woman if both were Christians." (2) Justinian II married his Negro cook to a noble Roman lady. Nicephorous Phocas, greatest of the Byzantine rulers, was an Arab and from the description given of him by Luidprand, Bishop of Cremona, who saw him, a Negro.

Such prejudices as existed against "race" in the matter of marriage were directed chiefly against the fair whites to the north because they were considered heathen. Constantine the Great issued strict orders against even the marriage of their princes with with his people.

Negro soldiers who had been coming into Greece from about the tenth century B. C., continued to arrive until the War of Greek Independence in 1830 and later. The pirate who plundered the Temple of Neptune was, Sanno, a Negro. (3) In 904, Leon the African invaded Southern Greece with 54 ships and 10,800 Negroes and ruled it for years. (4) Negroes were an important part of the Turkish army that captured Greec in 1453. It was a gigantic Negro, Hasson, who was the first to mount the walls of Constantinople during its siege.

The Turks ruled Greece for the next four centuries. Under them blacks and mulattoes held high positions in the army and the navy, and had harems of white women and black. There was no color prejudice. Now and than an unmixed black man rose to be ruler in all but name. He was generally a eunuch — the Kislar Aghassi, or head of the harem. He was a Prince of

1. See sources in Sex and Race, Vol. 1, pp. 116-18. 2nd ed. 1940. Vol. 3, pp. 3-5.
2. Decline of the West, Vol. 2, p. 69. 1932.
3. Gilbert H. Boys' Book of Pirates, p. 11. 1916.
4. Schlumberger. Un Empereur Byzantin . . . p. 34. 1911.

Detail from "The Slave Market" by J. L. Gerome (1824-1904). Negroes and Whites being sold together.

TURKISH EMPIRE

Turkish Sultan with his Negro Favorite and Confidante. Known as Kizlar
Aghassis, the Blackers were exceeded in authority only by the Sultan
(Les Anciens Costumes de l'Empire Ottoman by Arif Pasha, 1864).

the Empire (5) and governor of the sacred cities of Mecca and Medina, and "by tradition a Negro." The Kizlar held power for seven centuries.

A French writer of 1635 says there were 500 Negroes for the 300 women in the Sultan's harem. He describes them as having "flat noses, thick lips, hair curled like wool, and face, fearfully black so there is no white to be seen but their eyes." (5a) Some of these blacks taught the women dancing and deportment.

Turkish power extended beyond Greece into Bulgaria, Roumania, Servia, Albania, and almost to the gates of Vienna. Large numbers of the soldiers used in that conquest were Negro levies from Egypt and the Sudan. They left traces of their blood in the whites of all that region. In 1840 Egypt sent 30,000 Negro soldiers to ravage Southern Greece. (6) Millingen tells of the large number of Negroes of both sexes he saw in Stamboul, alone. He says, "From the white Caucasian to the black Negro all the intervening tints and complexions are to be seen within the precincts of this metropolis . . . Among these various races the African stands conspicuous on account of both the tint and the number of its members." No distinction whatsoever, he says was drawn "between a white and a black face." He estimated that in the Greco-Turkish region had been brought in over the centuries 100,000 Negroes by each generation, most of whom died from overwork. Among the mulattoes holding high office he named General Mehemet Pasha. (7) Blacks were seldom permitted to marry among their own people.

White and Negroes were put up indiscriminately for sale in the Turkish markets. Patrick wrote, "In the time of Sultan

5. Porter, Sir J. Turkey, Vol. 2, p. 274. 1854. See also his "Observations sur la Religion . . . des Turcs, pp. 52, 141, 142, 167-174. Pt. 2, p. 6. Bull. et Mem. Paris Soc. d'Anthrop. March 14, 1901, pp. 234-40. Also Sex and Race, Vol. 1, pp. 286-7. 2nd ed. 1940. (5a) History of the Serail (trans. by E. Grimeston). The original is by a French writer of 1635 who tells of the great number of unmixed black in the Sultan's harem. He mentions the Kislar Aghassi, or head of the harem, and says that the Negroes were teachers of the women of the harem. He adds that there was a belief that the white women in th harem, seeing so many blacks about them would be frightened into having black babies but that "I never heard that any Sultana hath been delivered of a Moor although I know this may be done. History furnishes us with examples of such accidents. Women have borne children like unto pictures that were in the chambers" (p.61). Some of these Negroes who were virtual rulers of the Empire were Sunbullu, Bashir, Solyman, Bekir, Djevher, and Nadir, the last two being under Abdul Hamid, last Sultan in 1907.

6. Madden, R. R. Egypt and Mohammed Ali, pp. 67, 115. 1841. For Negroes in Greek Revolution see its history by T. Gordon, Vol. 2, p. 51. 1844.

7. Jour. Anthrop. Soc'y Rev. Vol. 8, pp. 1 xxxv-cviii. 1870.

Detail of Turkish Harem Scene by J. L. Gerome, 1824-1904.

Aziz there were slave markets which were open to the public. According to the Mohammedan religion all races are equal before God and the boys and girls sold in this way were sometimes fair Circassians and sometimes blacks." (8) Mrs. Mackintosh wrote, "Not only poor black Nubians are sold in Damascus but white slaves, beautiful Circassian women." (9) J. L. Stephens, an American diplomat, and a strong believer in white racial superiority, wrote of the slave market in Constantinople in 1835, "To my surprise I found there twenty or thirty white women. Bad, horrible as this traffic is under any circumstances to my habits and feelings it loses a shade of its horrors when confined to blacks but here whites and blacks were exposed together in the same bazaar. The women were from Circassia and the regions of the Caucasus, that country so renowned for beauty of its women. . . .

"One thing particularly struck me, though perhaps as an American, I ought not to have been so sensitive. A large number of men were at work in the fields and they were all slaves. Such is the force of education and habit that I have seen hundreds of black slaves without a sensation; but it struck rudely upon me to see white men slaves, an American and he one whose father had been a soldier in the Revolution and had fought to sustain the great principle that all men are by nature free and equal."

In other words in the Near East under both Christianity and Islam a pronounced difference of color as that between white and black counted for no more than say that between brunets and blondes in northern Europe. Stephens makes this clear in his impression of Russia. He was "forcibly struck," he says, "with the parallel between the white serfs of the north of Europe and Africa bondsmen" in America. He found the Russian slaves "not less degraded in intellect, character and personal bearing" than the Negroes on the American plantations. He added that when he compared these whites with "Africans of intelligence and capacity, standing upon a footing of equality as soldiers and officers in the Greek army and the Sultan's" he was "insensibly compelled to abandon certain theories not uncommon among my countrymen at home in regard to the intrinsic superiority of the white race." (10)

8. Under Five Sultans, p. 69. 1929.
9. Damascus and Its People, p. 78. 1883. For more on slavery of white and black see, Millingen, Jour. Anthrop. Soc. Rev. Vol. 8, pp. cix-cxx; Porter, Sir J. Turkey, Vol. 2, p. 87. 1854. Madden, R. R. Egypt and Mohammed Ali, pp. 127-155. 1844. Riya Salima: Harems et Musulmanes, says, "War in the Morea brought a crowd of young Greeks to the Egyptian harems and pirates brought Circassians." p. 200. 1902.
10. Incidents of Travel in Greece, Turkey, Russia etc. pp. 40, 237-9; 265-6 1839. For adventures of a Negro in Turkey and his mate, a white Scotchwoman see Dorr. D. F. Round the world, p. 138 et seq. 1858.

Much Negro strain also came into Greece and Turkey through Arabia, whose people for many centuries have been much more mulatto than white. The same is true of Egypt and other parts of North Africa which were once under Turkish rule. Sir Richard Burton, Lawrence of Arabia, and others tell of the absence of color prejudice among the Arabs and of leaders who were "coal-black." (10a)

The inflow of Negroes into Italy which had taken place under the Romans and the Moors continued into the seventeenth century. The slavery of the whites and blacks extended from Constantinople to Rome. (11) The Venetians, and Genoese, great slave-traders, brought Negroes in numbers to Italy where they were used as soldiers, slaves, wrestlers, divers, swimming-masters, musicians, jailers, hatchet-men, executioners, (12) pages and pets for noble ladies. Three of the latter were Lucrecia Borgia, Isabella of Mantua and Queen Isabella of Aragon. The latter wrote her agent in Venice asking him to send her a Negro "blacker in color" than the previous one. Unmixed Negroes were generally preferred in the courts and households of the rich to those with a white strain.

In Sicily, most of the slaves brought in were unmixed Negroes, accounting in part for the present dark color of its population. Livi, in an article on "Domestic Slavery in the Middle Ages and its Importance in Anthropology," says the Negroes

10a. Lawrence. T. E. says that one of his sponsors in Arabia was Sherif Abd el Krim "a coal-black Negro of pure Abyssinian type." Seven Pillars of Wisdom, p. 178. 1935.

Among the Arabs he says there "were no distinguishing traditions, natural or otherwise except the unconscious power given a famous sheikh by virtue of his accomplishment." p. 157.

"In Turkey, Persia and India, the Negro has played an important part in the sexual life of the inhabitants of these countries." O. Berkeley-Hill, Spectator, London, June 13, 1931, p. 394.

Burton, Sir R. Pilgrimage to Mecca, Vol. 2, p. 233 (1893) "Most Meccans are black and as has been said the appearance of the Sharif is almost that of a Negro . . . Abd al-Mottalib bin Ghalib is a dark, beardless old man with African features derived from his mother. "Vol. 2, p. 150.

"The Negro slaves in Egypt are far better off than in Christian countries . . . Manumission is common and the manumitted Negro has no prejudice against his color to encounter; he finds no distinction made in any society he has the means to enter into." Madden, R. R. Egypt and Mohammed Ali, p. 117. 1841.

11. Saco, J. A. Historia de la esclavitud, etc. Vol. 3, pp. 185-6; 197, 224. 1877 & Book XXI. 1937. Pirenne, H. Histoire du Moyen Age, Vol. 8, p. 20, 31, 116. 1944. Rodocanachi F. Les esclaves en Italie, XIII au XVIe, siecles, in Rev. des ques. hist. Vol. 79-80, p. 397. 1906. Livi R. L'esclavage domestique au moyen age etc. Bull. et Mem. Soc. d'Anthrop. de Paris: 5 ser. Vol. 10, pp. 441-4; 438-447. 1909. Also ser. 5, Vol. 9, pp.

12. Burckhardt J. Civilization of the Renaissance in Italy, pp. 296-

Left: Negro page of Venice by Bonafacio. Right: Gondolier by Carpaccio (1450-1522).

Lucrecia Borgia, daughter of Pope Alexander VI, with her favorite
(Attributed to Titian, 1477-1576)

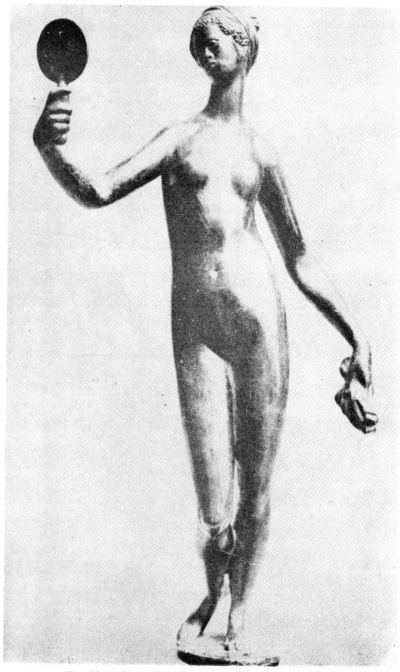

The Black Venus by Alessandro Vittoria (1525-1608).

came from Bornu and were therefore of the "purest African strain." Along with these blacks were Saracens, who might have been of any color from black to white. White Circassian slaves were common, too.

Negro soldiers served beside white ones. It was a Negro, who killed Marquis de Pescaire, French commander, at Castel Novo, Italy in 1496. De Pescaire had bribed the Negro to let him enter the castle but the latter tricked him. (13) In Venice Negroes were gondoliers. (14) Caldani mentions a Negro shoemaker there. (15) The famous printer, Aldo Manuzio, had a Negro in his printshop from whom came the phrase, "printer's devil." (16) One Negro slave gave to the physician of the Queen of Bohemia a cure for snake-bite; (17) and a herb shop, one of the most remarkable of its time, had on its sign the head of an Ethiopian. Burckhardt, using the Latin text of Benedictus, a writer of the times as authority, mentions, "A Negro (Ethiops) as superior officer at Venice by which we are justified in thinking of Othello as a Negro." Benedictus gives his name as Johannis, and says that because of the service he had rendered the state, the Venetian Senate had given his widow a pension and a mansion in perpetuity. (18).

White slaves were sold along with black ones. In 1649 Scotsmen captured by Cromwell were sold in Venice. (19) White women were exposed nude for sale. Brantome tells of one beautiful captive who was examined openly for virginity in the marketplace. He tells also of seeing Negro slaves and chambermaids, presumably white, dancing at Malta. (20)

Negroes became favorites and jesters at the Italian courts. Brantome mentions one at the court of Alphonso I, king of Naples and Aragon in 1450. (21) King Rene of Sicily had several. These blacks were sometimes crowned kings in jest at court festivals. (22)

7n. 1892. Welsford E. The Fool; his Social and Literary History. "Italian despots with blackmoors," p. 135. 1935.

13. Brantome, Vol. 1, 182. 1864 (Lalanne)
14. Molmenti P. Venice. Vol. 4, pt. 2, p. 240. 1907.
15. Prichard, J. C. Natural Hist. of Man, p. 86. 1845.
16. Brewers' Dict. of Phase & Fable, p. 348.
17. Thorndike L. Hist. of Magic and Experimental Science, Vol. 5, p. 225. 1941.
18. Eckhart, J. B. Corpus Historicum Medii Evi. Vil. 2, Col. 1608. (Al Benedictus de rebus Caroli VIII. Reg. Gall.)
19. Whitelock B. Memorials of the English Affairs, 1625-1660, Sept. 1648, pp. 329-30. 1632. For sale of other white slaves see Burckhardt, p. 267n.
20. Vol. 6, p. 79.
21. Vol. 1, p. 183.
22. Bull. et Mem. Soc. D'Anthrop. de Paris. Les Mores de Roi Rene. Oct. 18, 1906. For pictures of some of these Negro favorites of European rulers see Sex and Race, Vol, p. 167. 2nd ed.

White princes had Negro women as mistresses and their children were accepted into the nobility. Alfonso I of Naples had a daughter by a Negro woman. (23) She married the great Leonello. Cardinal dei Medici (later Pope Clement VII) had a son by Anna, slave or servant of his aunt. This son, Alessandro dei Medici, became the first ruler of Florence and married the daughter of Emperor Charles V. His children married persons of high rank. (24) Casanova, most famous lover of history, probably came of this Negro stock. He had "an African complexion." In his coat-of-arms are two Negroes. (25)

As a result of the importation of Negroes many southern Italians and Greeks in the eighteenth century were so dark that when Napoleon ran short of Negroes for his black brigades he used them. Sicilians were then much darker than now.

A more recent instance of Negro strain in a distinguished Italian family is that of the Garibaldis. Guiseppi Garibaldi, famous patriot, married a Brazilian mulatto woman. (26) His favorite aide in the Italian campaigns was an Uruguyan Negro, Andrea Aguyar, who had a white wife. American Negro soldiers in the second world war had a number of children by Italian women.

Austria, Germany, Holland, Belgium

The Negroid strain in the peoples of Northern Europe was already discussed in Volume One of Sex and Race. To this the following facts may be added. Most of the Negro strain in Northern Europe and Russia was taken in by the Jews, who, in spite of the religious prejudice against them, intermarried with Christians as Maurice Fishberg in his comprehensive study, "The Jew" has shown; and, says Hertz, "Innumerable aristocrats have married Jewesses."

As was already said, the ancient Jews who left Egypt must have been quite Negroid (27) after mating with Egyptians and Ethiopians for centuries. They were probably even originally Negroid. Abraham, according to the Bible, came from Ur of the Chaldees. Chaldea was the seat of Sumerian civilization, which was long considered to be white Aryan. But, it was Negroid says

23. Burckhardt, p. 21.
24. Hamilton, A. Rome in the Middle Ages, p. 666. 1912, says Alessandro's "mother had been an African slave and from her he had inherited the voluptuous nature and coloring and features of the mulatto." See his portrait by Bronzino in Sex and Race, vol. 1, p. 163. 2nd ed. Also sketch of his life in World's Great Men of Color, Vol. 2.
25. See sources in Sex and Race, Vol. 1, p. 168. 2nd ed. Also 299.
26. Sex and Race, vol. 2, pp. 57-8.
27. Sex and Race Vol. 1, Chap. 9.

Spearing in "The Childhood of Art." "The discovery," he says, "was very disconcerting to literary historians and philologists for that race was proved to be . . . not a branch of the civilizing Aryans, nor of the gifted Semites but of a Negroid people having affinities with Mongols." (27a) Dieulafoy, also, in his researches, says that the Elamites, who once dominated in that region were Negroes. One of their kings is mentioned in connection with Abraham in Genesis 14.

Strabo (30 B. C.) says the people of western Judea were of part Egyptian ancestry. "But," he says, "although the inhabitants are mixed up thus the most prevalent of the accredited reports in regard to the temple at Jerusalem represents the ancestors of the present Judeans, as they are called, Egyptians." (28) Tacitus of about 90 A. D. says "Many assert that the Jews are an Ethiopian race." (29) For Romans to have taken them for Ethiopians is clear indication of their color since the Ethiopians were definitely black to the Romans. Ancient Jewish legends, themselves recognize a Negro strain among the Jews. Genesis Rabba. 18, reads "When the Jews returned from Babylon their wives had become brown almost during the years of captivity and a large number of men divorced their wives. The divorced women probably married black men which would to some extent account for the existence of black Jews." (30) Solomon loved a black. Shulamite and his Song of Songs was written to her. She was "black but comely," and burnt by the sun.

Waitz says, "An interesting gradation of all shades down to the black is exhibited by the Jews." (31) Especially dark were the Jews of Spain and Portugal. The Portuguese Jews were "very dark," says Prichard. (31) The Duchess d'Abrantes, wife of Napoleon's ambassador to Portugal, said that "the Jew, the Negro and the Portuguese could be seen in a single person." (32)

So dark were the Jews, especially of Portugal and Southern Spain that many whites thought all Jews were black or dark. This belief, said Barbot, shows "what an error most people are in" since, he says, "the German Jews, as for example those of Prague, are as white as most of their German countrymen." (33) Many of the Jews who were banished from Portugal by John II

27a. Spearing. H. G. p. 255. 1912.
28. Geography, XVI, 2, 34, trans. by H. L. Jones (Vol. 7, p. 281).
29. Book 5. See also Whiston's comment on this in Sex and Race Vol. 1, Chap. 9.
30. Rapoport S. Tales and Maxims from the Midrash, p. 71. 1907.
31. Prichard, J. C. Natural Hist. of Man, p. 145. 1845. Waitz, T. Introd to Anthropology, pp. 47-8. 1863.
32. Memoires, Vol. 5. Chap. 26. 1835 (12 vols.).
33. Description of Guinea, p. 9, 1746.

GERMANY

Upper: Ferdinand Lassalle, founder of Socialism. Lower left: Higiemonte, 17th century, Austrian artist. Lower right: Dr. Ernest Schweninger, professor University of Berlin and physician to Prince Bismarck.

17th CENTURY HOLLAND

Negro Drummers, probably of the Spanish armies in Holland and Belgium
by Rembrandt, about 1637 (British Museum).

Left: Upper and lower: Mulattoes by Albrecht Durer, (1471-1528).
Right: Balthasar by Bernard van Orley (1490-1540).

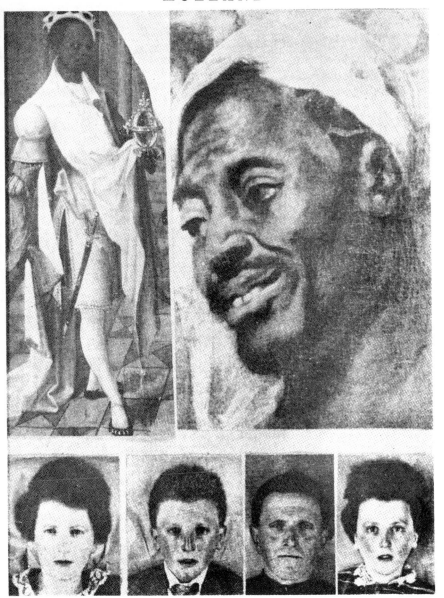

Upper left: Balthasar. Upper right: Negro by Van Dyck (1599-1641).
Lower: Europeans with wooly hair (Jour. of Heredity).

ПЕТРЪ ПЕРВЫЙ ИМПЕРАТОРЪ
ПРИСНО ПРИБЛАЖЕННЫЙ ЦАРЬ
ИСАМОДЕРЖЕЦ ВСЕРОССІИ

Peter the Great with one of his Negro Favorites by Schoenrich.

RUSSIA Left: Catherine the Great and her Negro page by Lampi. Right: Countess Julia Samilov by Karl Brulov.

129

settled in the West Indies. John Bigelow, who visited Jamaica in 1850, saw the descendants of these Jews and says they were Nogroid. (34)

The Eastern Jews who settled in Austria, Poland and Russia were Negroid, too. Count Adam Gurowski of Poland who visited the United States in 1857 said the Jews of his country strongly resembled American mulattoes. "Numbers of Jews," he said, "have the greatest resemblance to the American mulattoes. Sallow complexion, thick lips, crisped black hair. Of all the Jewish population scattered over the glove one-fourth dwells in Poland. I am, therefore, well acquainted with their features. On my arrival in this country, (America) I took every light-colored mulatto for a Jew." (35) Considerable Negro strain was found, too among the Polish Jews in London. (36) For years, two New York white dailies, the News and the Mirror, have been advertising "Kinky Hair . . . Straightened permanently in one Treatment." The service is for whites, only. The customers are probably Jews. A Negro hairdresser in Harlem once had many of them among her customers.

Karl Marx, who bore a strong resemblance to Frederick Douglass, undoubtedly came of this Negroid stock. His nose was broad, his hair frizzly and his color so dark he was called "The Moor." (37 Negro strain was even more evident in Ferdinand Lassalle, aristocratic founder of Socialism. Marx, his rival, called him "a Jewish nigger, a greasy Jew from Breslau who was always concealing his wooly hair with all kinds of hair-oil and make-up." In a letter to Engels, March 7, 1856, he said of Lasalle, "It is perfectly obvious from the shape of his head and the way his hair grows that he is descended from Negroes. . . ." (38)

Another source of considerable Negro strain in the white stock were the black pages who were common in the families of the nobility and the rich throughout Europe as far north as Russia. These blacks were so used for many centuries and as late as the first world war. They usually married into white families and are undoubtedly some of the Schwartz, Schwarzmann, Mohrs and others in European coats-of-arms. The park at San Souci, residence of the Prussian rulers, has busts of some of these Negro favorites.

In fact, Negro ancestry crops up in some of the unexpected

34. Jamaica in 1850, pp. 15-22. 1851.
35. America and Europe, p. 177. 1857.
36. Man, Vols. 5-6. No. 55, p. 93.
37. Schwarzchild L. The Red Prussian, pp. 9-25. 1947.
38. Schwarzchild, pp. 250, 277. Turner, J. K. says that "the favorite name of Marx and Engels" for Lassalle was 'Ikey.' or 'The Jewish Nigger.' (Challenge to Karl Marx, p. 227. 1941).

places as in the Swedish royal family. Bernadotte, its founder, had a slight Negro strain inherited in Southern France and Gustavus IV had considerably more as I have shown in Volume One of Sex and Race. Portraits of Gustavus IV, especially one of him on horseback by Lafrensen the Younger, and now in the private collection of Baron Ramel, leave no doubt of this.

In short, Germans are not the "pure" whites many assert they are. Several German writers agree on that among them Frederick Hertz, Brunold Springer and Rudolf Rocker. Beethoven, for instance, is named by all three as showing Negro "blood." Springer names among others, Dr. Ernest Schweninger (1850-1924), of Italian-Negro ancestry who was professor of dermatology at the University of Berlin (1884-1905) and was private physician to the great German Chancellor, Bismarck. Rocker includes Martin Luther and Goethe. He says, "We need but think of Luther, Goethe, Beethoven, who lacked almost completely the external marks of the 'Nordic' race and whom even the most outstanding exponents of the race theory characterize as hybrids with Oriental, Levantese and Negro-Malayan strains in them." (39)

The first world war brought considerable mixing principally between French Negro soldiers and German women on the Rhine, as was discussed in Volume One of Sex and Race. The offspring of these are gradually disappearing into the white population.

German women, (who from what I've seen and read of them, are very fond of ccolored men), welcomed American Negro soldiers with open arms in 1945. Mrs. Alice B. Shaw, U. S. Army Club director, who was stationed in Bremen and in Bavaria, said (Pittsburgh Courier, July 6, 1947) "I have been in Italy and France and have seen the success of the colored soldier (with women) but never in my life have I seen women trail our boys as the Germans . . . the French and Italians showed a little reserve but

39. Nationalism and Culture, p. 319. 1937. Springer B. Die Blutmischung als Grundgesetz des Lebens. He names Beethoven and others as being of part Negro ancestry and says, "Ein sondbares Elten paar das diesen dunkelaugigen, wahrscheinlich Africanisch malaischen Mischling, am besten getroffen auf dem prachtigen Bild Sleilers der Welt Gegeben het." p. 523. For abundant testimony on the Negro strain in Beethoven, see Sex and Race, Vol. 3, pp. 306-09. 1944. On Thomas Mann. pp. 301-3. On Rejane, p. 500. (Springer).

A present day instance of how Negroid strain disappears in the white on in Europe is the case of Maria Bertha Hertog, 13 years old bride of a Moslem school-teacher, whose taking away from her husband caused great riots in Singapore in December, 1950. The impression given was that Maria is an unmixed European but she was born in Malaya of a half-Malayan mother. Bertha is to all appearances white. She was taken to Holland and will in time probably marry white.

not the Germans." William Gardner Smith in his novel "Last of the Conquerors" has given an account of the German woman and the Negro soldiers in the second world war that is almost documentary.

Ollie Stewart (Baltimore Afro-American, July 3, 1943) estimated that there were 3000 children born in Germany to Negro fathers, with an additional 1000 yearly. He gives the approximate number for those born in such towns as Nurnberg, Giessen, Frankfurt, Mannheim, Munich. He wrote, "I visited one orphan home where children are cared for until they are five years old. Out of the fifty-five children there, nineteen are colored. . . . To their eternal credit, the German girls have loved and cared for their brown babies . . . for the most part in the face of the most brutal treatment . . . I have had girls tell me they've received nothing, from the father for their child. All they want is the child and work enough to care for it."

The Reich, he says, can no longer be looked upon "as a white country. Throughout our lifetime and long after there will be colored people in Germany." The first world war, as was said, brought thousands of mulatto children, offspring of Senegalese and white women, especially in the Rhineland. I have seen a number of German mulattoes, offspring of Negro soldiers in both these wars. The Nazis once had an exhibit of pictures of them at Dusseldorf.

John Welch, who lived in Germany for over thirty years tells "Twelve Years Under Hitler," of the mulattoes and octoroons he knew in Germany, and of an African, named Foli, who taught African languages at the University of Berlin. In fact, Hitler had some thirty Negroes teaching in the German colleges. He had hoped to conquer Africa and was preparing his young men to be able to speak the African tongues. (40) In Volume One of Sex and Race, I have also mentioned Negroes in Germany prior to Hitler. (40a) According to an estimate made by the German authorities, Sept. 19, 1949, there were 13,000 illegitimate children born to American fathers in the American zones of which 8.5

40 Pittsburgh Courier, May 6, 1944. Welch says "Before Hitler came into power, the Negro was treated exceptionally well. But even today, just as in any other European country unless things changed radically after my internment, the Negro may get a room in any of the best hotels ; he may attend the theatres and cinemas and be seated in any part of the house ; he may go into any shop, visit any restaurant, cafe or night club and be waited on courteously and attend the schools and universities. In short, he may do anything he is big enough to do as long as he carries himself respectable and has the money and means to do it with."

40a. As reported in New York Daily News, Jan. 15, 1950. The report includes only those cases reported by mothers to the German authorities. It said also that the Negro fathers cared better for their children than the white G. I's.

GERMANY

Offspring of Negro Fathers and White Mothers. Upper right: Of Moroccan Father, World War I (Afro-American photos).

Children of Negro soldiers by White Mothers (Afro-American photos).

per cent were Negroes. (40a) The estimate does not include legitimate births or births not reported to the authorities. On my visit to Germany in 1950 I saw much association of Negro soldiers and German women. Some of the girls were not only quite good-looking but had an air of culture. Some of the mothers were quite young. One I saw was only fourteen. She had a mulatto child of which she was very proud.

One much talked-of marriage was that of Arthur Semonu, son of an African chief and a German woman, to a German woman. Their son is almost white.

In Norway, Anne Brown, opera singer of New York, was married to Thorleif Schjelderup, son of a Supreme Court Justice, and his country's leading skier, on May 11, 1948. The groom's father was present at the ceremony. Among mixed marriages in Denmark was that of Chauncey Ellington, clarinetist and war veteran, to a Danish girl of good family. (41)

One family of Negro ancestry living in Oslo are grandchildren of General Mikhail Egypteos, Russian naval architect and shipbuilder, who was himself the son of a Negro artist and a Russian noblewoman. (42)

RUSSIA

Russia, in addition to her native Negroes, had many imported ones, who were used as servants and slaves, and who sometimes married into the nobility. Some masters, says Albert Parry, "were notoriously good to the black slaves." (43) Several American Negroes have reared families by white women in Russia. One was George Thomas, wealthy amusement parkowner, with many friends among the Russian nobility and a confidential agent of the Czar; (44) and "Professor" John Gordon of the Smolny Institute, who was a figure of more than a little importance in the Russian Revolution. A doorman at the American Embassy, he went over to the Bolsheviks and became a member of the Central Government. He is mentioned in two United States Senate reports. (45) He married an Esthonian woman.

41. As reported in the American Press, white and Negro, of about that date.
42. See sources in Rogers, J. A. World's Great Men of Color, Vol. 2, p. 702. See also Sex and Race, Vol. 1, Chap. 16.
43. Abbott's Monthly, April 1931, p. 13-14.
44. Jack Johnson, who met him in Russia, mentions him in his autobiography, "In the Ring and Out," pp. 92-3. 1927 (5th ed). I also met several Negro entertainers who met him in Russia.
45. Overman Report, 1919. and in the U. S. Congress Documents Vol. 4, p. 115, 66th Congress, 1919, testimony of Rev. George Simons, who married him. Also Marcosson mentions having met him in Russia (World's Work, Oct. 1918, 621).

Eugene Robinson of America, choreographer, and Gurl Lysell in an interpretative dance. (Photo by George S. Schuyler).

Eugene Robinson of the United States, Choreographer, in Oslo, Norway, and his dancing partner, Gurl Lyselle (Photo by George S. Schuyler).

NORWAY Eugene Robinson, choreographer of Oslo, and his cast at command performance for King Haakon of Norway.

Anne Brown, American-born soprano, and her Norwegian husband, Thorlief Schelderup (Afro-American photo).

HOLLAND

George Schuyler on his visit to Holland in 1951, wrote, "Here are Negroes too, mostly from Surinam — seamen, musicians, dockers, businessmen, students, nurses. About 3,000 in Holland; 1,000 in Amsterdam. Many men and women are married to whites, doing well in this land of no color discrimination. One Negro heads a public school wherein all teachers and pupils are white." Copenhagen, also, has an unmixed Negro, Victor Cornelis, as an inspector of schools.

Additional Notes on the Eunuchs.

Penzer, N. M. The Harem. 1872. In the chapter on Black Eunuchs says their chief, Kislar Aghassi, was ruler of the holy cities of Mecca and Medina, was a pasha of the highest rank, and had as many as 300 horses for his personal use. He, alone, "could approach the Sultan at all times of the day and night," and was "the most illustrious of the officers who approach the August Person and worthy of the confidence of monarchs and of sovereigns. He was also the most feared and consequently the most bribed official in the Ottoman Empire. Naturally he was a member of the Privy Council and in consultation with the Sultan and made appointments to vacant posts not only in the Seraglio but outside." pp. 125-151.

Zambaco. Les Eunuques d'Aujourdhui et Ceux Jadis, p. 44. 1911, says "this grand personnage was loaded with honors and decorations. He possessed the great decorations with diamond plaques. Next to the Sultan, he discussed the most delicate matters concerning the ruler and the state."

The black eunuchs also had their harems, with women, some of whom were white Circassians. Penzer tells of one who bought a white slave added her to his harem "which useless though it was pride and tradition made him support." He had bought her as a virgin but she soon proved to be with child. Sultan Ibrahim adopted the child "preferring it to his own." p. 190.

Zambaco says, "What is least comprehensible to us is that the eunuchs can marry the women they buy, even white ones, and in conformity with the law and Islamic rites.

"In the time of Sultan Aziz under whose reign I arrived in Constantinople, the grand eunuch of the palace, Sorour Agha, had a legitimate wife, very beautiful." (pp. 90-1). See also Malek Hanum. Thirty Years In the Harem, p. 98. 1872.

The eunuchs had their way of contriving coition. Sir Richard Burton, who described it, says certain of them were much prized in the zenana because of the long performance of the deed of kind and for abortive non opus. Martial and Juvenal, ancient Roman writers, tell how eunuchs were preferred by some women because there would be no children. Martial (VI, 67) said, "Do you ask, Pannicus, why your Celia consorts only with eunuchs? Celia wants the flowers of marriage, not the fruits." See also Juvenal, VI, 365-8.

Fazil Bey tells of the different kinds of women in the harem in Zenan-Nameh, written about 1810. See pp. 43-4, 94-5. 1879. Trans. by J. A. Decourdemanche. 1879.

Arif Pacha. Anciens Costumes de l'Empire Ottoman. Fig. 5. for Negro Chief Eunuch.

NEGRO FAVORITES

Left: The Prophet of St. Paul's by A. E. Chalon, R. A. (1789-1860). Right Princess Marie de Bourbon of France with her Negro favorite and her servants.

Additional Notes on Negro Strain in Jews.

Fishberg, M. (The Jew, p. 1911) says, "The Negroid type of Jew is yet to be mentioned. One occasionally meets with a Jew whose skin is very dark and the hair black and wooly, the head long with a prominent occiput. The face is prognathous, the two jaws are projecting in the form of a muzzle. The lips are thick and upturned so that the nostrils can be seen in profile. The Negroid type can be singled out in any large assembly of Jews. They are often mistaken for mulattoes and the author knows of one who had considerable difficulty to get along in the Southern States of America."

He says that certain Biblical scholars are inclined to attribute the origin of the Negroid type of Jews to intermarriage with Cushites of Biblical times and adds that type is to be met with among Jews of Eastern Europe who have not come in contact with Negroes for centuries. The Negro appearance of many Arabian and African Jews can be readily explained on the mixture with Negroes in those regions but that of the European type "no such explanation is tenable unless it be attributed to immigration from Southern Europe and North Africa. In fact many Jews driven from Spain and Portugal and settled among the European Jews may have had some Negroid elements which they obtained by intermarriage with the Moors who are known to have a considerable infusion of Negro blood."

He also says, Amer. Anthrop. Memoirs, Vol. 1, pp. 135-6, 1905-07: "The Cushites according to Biblical and other evidences were Negroes . . . The ancient Hebrews patriarchs and the aristocracy of Israel have freely indulged in intermarriage with those and other non-Jewish races and is can be safely assumed that the common people followed the example . . . . May the Negroid traits such as dark skin, thick lips, prognathism, wooly hair etc., which are often met with among the modern Jews, not be cases of atavism." See also Amer. Anthrop. n. s. Vol. 5. p. 89, on Physical Anthrop. of the Jews.

Max Radin (Life in Biblical Times, pp. 119-20. 1929) explaining why the Shulamite woman beloved by Solomon is described as "black but comely," says, "Between this dark skin and 'black' as we understand it there was a sharp contrast. The Ethiopians, for example, were black and there were a number of Ethiopians in Palestine."

He adds, "They were sharply marked out in color from the rest of the population. The famous phrase of Jeremiah shows that: Can the Ethiopian change his skin or the leopard his spots. The swartness or blackness of the lover in Canticles, therefore, must be a color quite different from that of the Ethiopians and not merely a slightly lighter hue."

The reference to the lover's dark color would scarcely be repeated he says, unless that color was supposed to be something "particularly beautiful."

The blacks need not to have been "sharply marked out" according to thinking, say in America where mixed bloods are classed with very dark Negroes. In the East some of these Negroes are so very dark (I've seen some in Europe, too) that a Negro who is only one-fourth white is quite fair in comparison. I have seen in Ethiopia similar contrasts between mixed-bloods, who are at least helf-Negro and the Chankalla blacks. These mixed-bloods look down on the blacks call the latter "Negro" and say they, the mixed-bloods, aren't Negroes (see Chap. 2, note 6.)

Hirschfeld, M. "We also found Hamitic, Negroid, Moorish and Mongolian strain among the Jews." Racism, p. 61. 1938.

CHAPTER EIGHT

NEGRO ANCESTRY IN THE FRENCH

The Moors, as was seen invaded France in the eighth century and remained there until the twelfth, when they were absorbed into the population. Five centuries later (in 1609) this stock was reinforced by the entry of about a million more who came in on the invitation of Henry IV on their final expulsion from Spain.

They settled in Auvergne where their strain is still evident in the general population. "There is a strong Negroid strain in many Auvergnese," says John Gunther. (1) Among those of Moorish stock were such noted figures as Bertrand du Guesclin; Charles Bernadotte, Napoleonic marshall and king of Sweden; Joachim Murat, Napoleon's brother-in-law and king of Naples; and Pierre Laval, twice Premier of France. Laval was an Auvergnat and rather Negroid in appearance.

In addition to the Moors were the Negro slaves and Negroid Levantines brought in by the Christians in the thirteenth century and earlier. "Ethiopians, Moors, Turks and Greeks furnished chiefly the crowd of slaves in the homes of the wealthy," says Mathorez. Later when modern Negro slavery started in Portugal about 1440 the number of Negro slaves as well as free Negroes increased in France.

The principal slave-ports were Bordeaux and Nantes. Mathorez says, "Dating from Henry IV (1553-1610) the arrival of Negroes multiplied in France." They came in "droves" to fill the gaps left in the population by the wars of Louis XIV. He adds, "The maritime ports are not the only places we find mention of them. We find also records of baptisms of Negroes born in Africa in the registers of parishes of the interior. The ship-captains, ambassadors, and admirals brought them to France and used them for various purposes. In Orleans there was a college for these blacks and a street was named in their honor . . . During the seventeenth century they were numerous in Paris." (2)

Most of the female slaves were white, says Lavisse. They were brought chiefly from the region of the Black Sea in Southern Russia.

Nantes and Bordeaux had many Negroes. In the Caveau de St. Michel at Bordeaux I saw the mummified bodies of two or three, one of them La Negresse for whom a small town was named, and has a railroad station with that name. In Toulouse, Anselme

1. Inside Europe, p. 104. 1936.
2. Les Etrangers en France etc. Vol. 1, pp. 156-170, 366, 403. 1919. Lavisse. Histoire de France, Vol. 4, Pt. 2, p. 163. 1911.

FRANCE

Princess de Conti of France and her Negro favorite.

d'Isalguier, a nobleman married Casais, a Negro, whose descendants married into some of the leading families of the city. (3)

Mulatto descendants of Zenon, a Negro, still live in the town of Bonny-sur-Loire. Some are old men others children. Most of them are a whitish-yellow, their Negro strain showing most in their hair, nose and lips. Zenon, who came from Ile de Bourbon, Africa, passed for rich and had many children by the white girls of the village. (3a)

The Negroes were well-received especially in military circles. Marshal Saxe (Prince Maurice of Saxony, 1696-1750) had a brigade of jet-black Africans, commanded by Jean Hitton, a Negro, which served as his bodyguard. Mounted on white horses and colorfuly uniformed these blacks were one of the great sights of Paris and Versailles. They served with distinction in the Flanders War. (4)

Count d'Avaux, French ambassador, had a bodyguard of 140 Negroes, picturesquely dressed, as his bodyguard. (5) In 1644, when he went to Germany to help write the Peace of Munster, he took them with him, creating a sensation when they accompanied him into the cathedral to worship. Napoleon, also had many Negroes, some of whom fought in Russia. They had such names as "Black Pioneers" and "Royal Africans." The latter, a cavalry regiment, served in Italy under General Hugo, father of Victor Hugo, and helped capture Fra Diavolo. (5a) After Napoleon's conquest of Egypt, Negroes were brought in numbers to France and served under Marshal Kleber. (6) Negro women were also imported from there at the same time for the brothers. (7) Napoleon had at least twelve Negro and mulatto generals. One of the most renowned of his earlier officers was Joseph Damingue, an unmixed Negro, called by Napoleon "Hercules," because of his size and strength. (8)

French Negroes rose to other high positions. One, Aben

3. See sources, Sex and Race, Vol. 1, p. 239. (2nd ed.)
3a. Bull. et Mem. Soc. d'Anthrop. de Paris, June 21, 1906, p. 275.
4. Fieffe E. Hist. des Troupes Etrangeres, Vol. 2, pp. 49, 54, 281. 1854. Revue de Paris, Vol. 16, pp. 193-210. 1916. Revue des Etudes Hist. No. 2, avril-juin. 1917. Revue de Mois, VVol. 16, pp. 193-210. 1906.
5. Les 140 Negres de M. d'Avaux. Bull. et Mem. Soc. d'Anthrop. de Paris, June 21, 1906, pp. 271-3. Ronciere, C. Negres et Negriers, p. 20. 1933.
5a. Georges Girard has a fairly long article on Napoleon's Negro soldiers in "Noir et Blanc," of Paris (date missing). He says (as did Mme. Abrantes) that when Murat ran short of blacks for his Africans he recruited them from Greeks and Turks "Who were of the same color as the natives of St. Domingue (Haiti)." Abrantes includes Italians.
6. Fieffe, pp. 49, 54.
7. Bloch, I. Sexual Life of our Times, p. 614. 1937.
8. See sketch of him in Rogers, "Worlds Great Men of Color," p. 703.

FRANCE

Left: Types of Negro soldiers of Napoleon. Right; a "Black Pioneer."

Ali, was private physician to Charles VII. Another, Antoine de Neyne, attended Louis XI. There is record of the generous fee paid him by the king for having cured him. (10) Still another physician, Francois Fournier de Pescay (1771-1833), was private physician to Ferdinand VII of Spain, when the latter was in exile in France. De Pescay, born in France of part Haitian parentage, was also a professor of pathology; a regimental surgeon-major; chief surgeon of the Paris police; and chief health officer of France. He compiled a medical dictionary, also."

Others became favorites of royalty and nobility. Aniaba, an ex-slave, was adopted by Louis XIV, baptized into the Christian faith by the celebrated Bishop Bosuet with the King in attendance, and given the royal surname. (12) Marie Antoinette had a young Negro favorite whom she christened Hamilcar (after the father of Hannibal of Carthage) in a ceremony in the royal chapel at Versailles. (13) Madame du Barry had a Negro favorite, Zamor, who was governor of her chateau, and was so spoiled that Louis XV not only deferred to him but was complaisant in sharing DuBarry's favors with him. (13a) A painting by Moreau le Jeune, "Fete a Louveciennes," shows Zamor being fed candy by a grand dame.

Zaga, another Negro, was one of the great imposters of history. Born of humble parents in East Africa, he convinced Catholic missionaries that he was the rightful heir to the throne of Ethiopia. On his father's death, he said he had been driven out by a usurper. The missionaries gave him letters to the Pope and he arrived in Rome, calling himself Zaga-Christ. Urban VIII installed him in a palace and later sent him to the great Cardinal Richelieu, who presented him to Louis, who lodged him in royal style. Jet-black, handsome, fascinating and dressed in costliest Oriental robes, he was a favorite with the ladies. He died in 1638 at the age of twenty-eight and was buried beside the Prince of Portugal. (14)

Negro men and women mated with royalty. Robert d'Eppes, son of William III, married a Sudanese princess, Ismeria, who attained such fame that a shrine was built to her and she became

9. Ronciere, p. 11.
10. Mathorez gives as the sources: Mss. 32511. Bound Vol. 685. Folio 399. Bibliotheque Nationale.
11. Biographie Universelle, Vol. 14, pp. 556-7. 1856.
12. Cole, C. W. French Merchantilism (1683-1700), p. 104. 1943. Revue de l'Hist. de Versailles, p. 519. 1913. Rev. des Etudes Hist. No. 2. avril-juin, 1917. Ronciere, p. 40.
13. Revue de l'hist. de Versailles, p. 519. 1913.
13a. Bailly. Mysteres de Vieux chateaux, Vol. 6, p. 210. See also Sex and Race, Vol. 1, p. 243, 249. (2nd ed).
14. Ricoles, J. B. Les Imposteurs insignes, pp. 390-2. 1693.

FRANCE

The celebrated Hottentot Venus. Brought from South Africa and exhibited nude in Europe, she was a sensation. She had several white lovers and her projecting buttocks set a fashion among white women, who, in imitation wore a bustle, or a large pad over their hips. (Cunnington, C. W. Why Women Wear Clothes, p. 96. 1941). This figure of her was modelled from life and is in the Musee de l'Homme, Paris. Her labia minoria (not shown here) were a sensation, too. For what they were like see **Sex and Race, Vol. 1, p. 27. 2nd ed. figure right.**

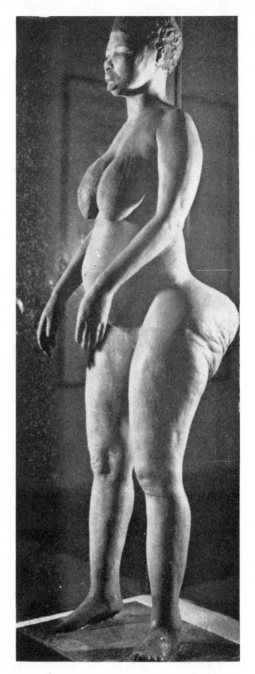

a Black Madonna. (15) Francois de Vendome, Duke de Chartres, cousin of the King and commander-in-chief of the French army, left his wife and the beauties of the court for a Negro woman; (16) Francis I had a Negro mistress. (17) The first mistress of Louis XIV was a Negro woman in the household of his mother, Anne of Austria. (18) Louis XV, according to police reports, had a Negro son. If this is so his mother might have been, Madame de St. Helene, a West Indian concubine of the king. (19) Marie Therese, wife of Louis XIV, undoubtedly had a daughter by her Negro favorite, Nabo, (21) though neither she nor her husband, Henry II, show Negro strain at least in their portraits. Alencon was so Negroid, so different in appearance from his royal parents that he was hidden as a child, like another royal duke. Alessandro dei Medici, of whose Negro ancestry we are certain. Queen Elizabeth of England was in love with Alencon and cried because she couldn't marry him. (22)

Marshal Junot of Napoleonic fame, had a son, Othello, by a Negro girl of whom he was enamored (23) and Mme. de Solms of the court of Napolean III was reported as being "especially fond of Negro males." (24)

Louis Sebastian Mercier (1740-1814) tells in his "Picture of Paris" how Negro favorites were kissed and caressed by their noble mistresses (25) and Jacques Delacroix of the same period tells how they were pampered. "When he cries everybody runs to him," he said. "Happy child, thy father groans, perhaps, under the blows of the whips . . . You are on the knees of Beauty; your hand rests upon a breast moved by pleasure, a soft, caressing hand moves over thy cheeks." (26) When these Negroes grew up they married white women, sometimes of good family. This explains, in part, the number of French families with Negroes

15. Calixte, R. P. Les Plus Illustres Captifs, pp. 93-101. 1892. Drochon. Les Pelerinages Francais, pp. 67-94. 1900. Costello, S. Pilgrimage to Auvergne, pp. 64-73.

16. Brantome. Vol. 6, p. 123. 1873.

17. Hackett, F. Francis I, p. 319. 1935.

18. Mathorez. Vol. 1, 396.

19. Bourdon E. Le Parc au Cerf, p. 95. 1790. Her maiden name was Fontenelle and her married one St. Helene.

20. See account in Sex and Race, Vol. 1, Chap. 21.

21. See sources in Sex and Race, Vol 3, pp. 224-24. Brantome says, however, that Henry II was "un peu moricaut." (mulatto).

22. See sources in Sex and Race, Vol. 3, p. 225.

23. Abrantes. Vol. 2, p. 192. 1835 (12 vols.)

24. Bloch, Iwan. Odoratus Sexualis, p. 170. 1935.

25. For translation from original see Sex and Race, Vol. 3, pp. 199-200.

26. "Sur le Gout de Femmes pour les Petits Negres" in "Peinture des Moeurs de Siecle, Vol. 1, p. 146. 1777.

in their coats-of-arms, named Maure (Moor) Negre, Noir and the like.

Empress Josephine, consort of Napoleon, might have had some Negro "blood." She was a West Indian, probably of the color of Lena Horne or Josephine Baker. Mme. de Remusat, friend of the Empress, said, "Her complexion was rather dark but she hid it very skilfully with red and white paint in the use of which she was an expert." (27)

Napoleon, himself, is said to have had as one of his mistresses, Fortunee Hamelin, of St. Domingue (Haiti)), of evident Negro ancestry, and with skin so dark and lips so thick, she was called "The Black Belzi." Intelligent, witty, a wonderful dancer, a splendid horsewoman, and of exceptional personality, she was called "la bele aide" (the beautiful ugly woman). She was Napoleon's chief female confidante and was a figure of more than minor importance in the French Revolution. When Napoleon was leaving for St. Helena, he gave her 300,000 gold francs, an immense sum even now. Later she was an intimate friend of Count de Chateaubriand, famous literary figure. (28)

Sophie Arnould (1740-1802), French actress, and one of the wittiest women in history, undoubtedly had a Negro strain. She was described in police reports of the time as having a skin "extrement noire." (very dark). (28a) Another great actress, Gabrielle Rejane, had Negroid features and is described by Brunold Springer as being "of the blond Negro type." One noted opera singer of our times is the daughter of a West Indian colored deputy. She sings (or used to sing) in the Paris opera.

The number of Negroes from the time of the Moors to Josephine Baker who have left some impress on French life is considerable. Jean Louis, (29) a Haitian Negro, was France's greatest swordsman (and probably the world's also). His descendants by his white wife still live in Montpellier, France.

Two Negroes of Napoleon III's time were Vries, "The Black Doctor" (30) of Surinam, and Tokou of Haussaland, called Le Prince Noir (The Black Prince). An escaped slave, he joined the French army and was decorated for valor in the Crimean War.

27. Memoires, Vol. 1, p. 1339. 1881.

28. La Grande Revue, Vol. 4, pp. 177-195. 1900. Les Annales Romantiques, Vol. 6. pp. 1-36. 1908-09. La Nouvelle Revue, 3 ser. Vol. 4, 289-304 ; 445 ; Vol. 5, pp. 17-28. Fortunee was so dark that it was said of her, "couchee dans ses draps blancs elle semblait a une mouche dans du lait. "(Lying among white she looked like a fly in milk.)"

28a. L'Espion Anglais, I, 1. (1809) Quoted in Goncourt De, E. & J. Sophie Arnould, p. 33. 1877. Douglas, R. B. Sophie Arnould, p. 27, 1898.

29. See sketch of him in World's Great Men of Color, Vol. 2, pp. 340-44. (Rogers).

30. Intermediare des Chercheurs et de Curieux, Vol. 37. p. 414. 1892.

Benjamin Constant, most noted painter of that time, thought him the most perfectly proportioned man he had ever seen. Noel used him as the model for the statue of the gladiator in the City Hall of Paris and Constant as Mohammed II in the picture "Entry of Mohammed II into Constantinople." Crowds followed him on the streets. He was a favorite with the women and had a number of children by them. (31)

One African woman, Saat Jee, who was called "hideous" had a considerable number of white lovers. She is the famous Hottentot Venus, whose massive breasts, protruding buttocks, and elongated genital lips — a prehistoric Hottentot inheritance — were a sensation when she was exhibited in England and France. (32)

An American mulatto, Pascal B. Randolph, had considerable prestige in France also. A graduate in medicine and the then foremost figure in occultism, he was a friend of Napoleon III and welcomed at his court. Randolph was Supreme Master of the Rosicrucians of the World. (33)

The last two world wars brought a great number of Negroes to France, some of them from Algeria, Tunis and Morocco, light-colored. Negro woman are rather few in France thus these blacks have mated with white ones. Negro regiments were (or are) garrisoned in Verdun, Perpignan, Toulon, Marseilles and other towns where there are almost no Negro women. I saw much of this race crossing between Africans and West Indians with Frenchwomen during the years I spent in France. In short, Negroes have been living in France from prehistoric times and infused a great deal of their strain into the French people even though it is today almost non-apparent. However, Negro strain may still be found sometimes where least expected. For instance, Colette, France's foremost female author, who was elected presidnt of the Goncourt Academy in 1949, is the great -granddaughter of a Belgian mulatto, (34) according to herself.

Among the mixed marriages of the second world war was that of Norman Ashton, American Negro war veteran, to Jeanine Bayard of Coucy-leChateau. The marriage for some reason was opposed and the Catholic priest of the neighborhood refused to marry them. They appealed to the Pope, received his special permission and were married before a large audience in the Cathdral of Aisne.

31. Bull. et Mem. Soc. d'Anthrop. de Paris Dec. 20, 1906., p. 86.
32. Encyc. Franc. Vol. VII, 60:7. Cuvier, G. Discours sur la Revolution du Globe, pp. 211-22. 1864. Bull. de la Soc. Philomanthique, pp. 183-190. 1914-16.
33. Clymer, R. S. Rosicrucian Fraternity in America, Vol. 1, p. 426. 1935. Also his introduction in Guide to Seership, vii. 1930.
34. See sources in Sex and Race, Vol 3, p. viii.

FRANCE   Right: Gaston Monnerville, President of the Council of the Republic, which post is equivalent to President of the United States Senate.

One of the most remarkable cases of fascination of white women for black men I've ever seen, or heard of, occurred in Paris in 1928 at the trial of two Negro dancers who had robbed and murdered an aged women for her money and government bonds.

The two men were French West Indians, Guillaume La Fortune and Lionel Julian, gigolos in a Montmartre cabaret, where their tall, athletic figures, clever dancing and flashy clothes won them great popularity among a certain feminine element.

From their crime they got about $200 in cash. When they tried to sell the bonds they were caught. Women with whom they had danced flocked to the trial, some elderly and well-to-do, others young, pretty, fashionable. Some did not hesitate to make known where their sympathies lay. Two were especially conspicuous. One, a rich Englishwoman of fifty, to whom La Fortune had given dancing lessons, got him one of the best lawyers and during his stay in jail showered on him, as one paper said, "A thousand sweets." She was a character witness. When she heard the verdict of death, she wept and was so overcome she had to be carried out.

The other, French, young, elegant, beautiful, said on the stand, "Never will I believe him capable of such a crime. He is a perfect gentleman." During the year he spent in prison she sent him money and expensive cigarettes. LaFortune asked his lawyer to get her husband, a rich chocolate manufacturer, to give permission to her to accept "my fine dress suit and elegant pumps." When she heard it, she wept. "My poor brown pet."

Clement Vautel, columnist of the Paris Le Journal, said of this case: Montmartre, which, after becoming the centre of attraction for the world, has become a colony founded by the sons of Ham among men, and especially among white women.

"It is impossible to count any longer the number of curious ones, the 'originals,' and the seekers of sensation who are devoted to the Negro. This black snobbishness among white people is increasing in all walks of life, and thus it was, that at the trial of these two dark brutes, a woman of the middle-class, wife of an honorable merchant, came to witness in favor of her lover, Firman LaFortune, today promised to the guillotine.

"One of our fellow-journalists relates the scene as follows:

'To the bar with firm step came a woman, thin, tall and supple, with finely-chiselled features and still pretty (for she is no longer very young) with great black eyes, with two large pearls in her ears, false perhaps. Very elegant in her tailored costume of blue, with white blouse, a fur scarf over her left arm, and a coquettish hat over her black hair.

'She enters the box, looks long and fixedly at the Negro, and smiles to him sympathetically. She declares: "Never have I believed him capable of such a crime!"

'Then, fine, pretty, elegant, unabashed, folding with care her fur over her left arm, she left the room not without having looked longingly again at her ex-dancer, who followed her with his eyes, intensely.'

"Let us be just, there is courage in the act of this woman who comes before all the world, without thinking of the scandal her act would cause, to save her miserable gigolo.

"She at least, does not hide the desire she has had for a handsome black. This up-to-date middle-class woman makes a public avowal, and is not the least troubled by the severe look of men with reddened faces.

"Evidently she still loves this Negro who spun her around in the Montmartre cabarets to the sound of savage music and even an odor more noticeable than is the custom. She has guarded the souvenirs, the regret without doubt, of all that.

"Such is the Madame Bovary, model of 1929. That of Flaubert seems to us, today, of faded sentimentality with his fine young man, his blond Rudolph. . . . Tell us now, of a lively young woman, who frolics with a robust Negro, seller of cocaine, stealer of jewels, and strangler of old women!

"Evidently, the woman of this type who consorts with Negroes is the exception. But anyway those white men who are trying to imitate Don Juan, De Lauzan, and the Marquis de Priola ought to take into still stronger account the charmer with the nut-brown skin and the wooly hair."

The Paris edition of the London Daily Mail said:

"It seemed incredible that this elegant lady could have anything in common with the broad-shouldered, elaborately dressed Negro in the dock.

"The answer may be found in a Montmartre cabaret. He had been her dancing partner and for him she had conceived the sudden, inexplicable sympathy which women seem sometimes to conceive for Negro dancers.

"It is a tale that has been often told since the end of the war when the music of the American Negro was introduced into the dancing halls of Paris.

"Even the story of the murder to which she listened did not shake this woman's faith in the Negro and to the judge's question she calmly answered 'I could never believe him capable of such a crime. He was a perfect gentleman.' "

Much color prejudice was brought into France by American troops in 1917 but it didn't change the French much. A survey made in various regions of France as to how Negroes would be accepted in hotels and other public places in 1928 showed this. (35) In 1950, I saw a greater number of Negroes in Paris than before and with probably even less prejudice. There were more Negroes in Parliament, with one being president of the Senate. Whites and Negroes intermarried and danced together in the cafes.

35. Social Forces. Sept. 1928, pp. 102-111. There are, of course, instances of color prejudice in France (see FRANCE, Sex and Race, vol. 1,) Also when Cora Pearl, celebrated English beauty, accompanied the dark-skinned Shah of Persia to the Opera and was fondling against her. One Frenchman wrote in indignant protest against her "making an open parade of her black lover" before the wives and daughters of Frenchmen. Anti-English feeling as well as the fact that Cora Pearl was, or had been the mistress of their Emperor, Napoleon III, undoubtedly had much to do with this. (Barry P. Sinners Down the Centuries, p. 192-272.)

In this respect the following from Briffault's Europa is interesting: "What if he is a nigger, anyhow," the woman in citron cried:

"Niggers is all right. They taught us how to dance. They've taught us how to sculp.

"Niggers, that's what we're becoming. Women fawn upon them because they're not castrated by religion and sex dogma and the French fawn upon them because their main hope of combining military power with contraception lies in the million potential black soldiers." p. 3. 1935.

Notes: Encyc. Universelle mentions a town called Negreville (Negro town) in Bourg de France, Manche.

There was a Mauritius, evidently a Moor, who was Bishop of Paris. (Wanley: Wonders of the Little World, p. 568. He gives his sources.)

For additional information on France see Sex and Race, Vol. 1, Chap. 19-22.

CHAPTER NINE

NEGRO ANCESTRY IN THE ANGLO-SAXON "RACE"

As was said there is evidence that Negroes, or Negroids, lived in the British Isles in prehistoric times and in the Middle Ages. From the fifteenth century onwards there is abundant evidence of them. Negro slavery was introduced in England about that time and lasted until 1773, and probably even to 1834 when there was a general emancipation in the British Empire.

How many blacks came in during those centuries will probably never be known. There must have been hundreds of thousands, however. They were enough, at least, to cause considerable mention in English literature, plays, and pictures. Eva B. Dykes, "The Negro In English Romantic Thought"; Sypher's "Guinea Captive Kings," Notes and Queries, and the drawings of Gainborough, Kent, Zoffany, Hogarth, Smith, Cruikshank, and Rowlandson are some of the many sources that show their presence.

Bristol and Liverpool were the chief slave-ports. Negroes were sold in batches there. (1) Newspapers carried advertisements of their sale. In 1769, the Czarina of Russia sent to England to buy some. (2) Catterall gives several lawsuits in England involving slaves, one of them over a shipment of one hundred. (2a)

Uffenbach, writing in 1710, said, "There are, in fact, such a quantity of Moors of both sexes in England that I have not seen so many before. The females wore European dress and there is nothing more diverting than to see them in mobs, or caps of stuff, with their black bosoms uncovered." (3) In 1731 there were enough Negroes in London to affect the labor situation and the town council passed a law forbidding trades to be taught them. (3a)

In October, 1764, the Gentleman's Magazine reported there were nearly 20,000 Negro servants in London alone and that their number is said to be "a grievance that requires a remedy yet more are being brought in." (4) These with the free Negroes and the mulattoes of English birth must have constituted a fairly large proportion of the city's population.

As in ancient Greece and Rome and as it was then in Italy.

1. Botsford, J. B. English Society in the 18th Century, p. 333. 1924.
2. Notes and Queries, Vol. 6, Oct. 30, 1852, p. 411. 2a. Judicial Cases Concerning American Slavery and the Negro, pp. 9-15. 1926.
3. London in 1710, p. 88. 1943 (trans. by W. H. Quarrel). 3a. Notes and Queries, vol. 161, p. 272. London Journal. Oct 16, 1731 The Negro women went with breasts exposed as in Africa.
4. Vol. 34, p. 493. 1764.

France, Germany, Austria, Russia and elsewhere coal-black youths as pages and favorites were in great demand. They became a fashion. As one writer says, a Negro page was "indispensable to the English lady in her daily walks . . . the collar known to the Roman slave was fastened around his neck with name and residence of his mistress engraved thereon." Goldsmiths of the time advertised collars for Negro pages and dogs. C. L. Lamb says, "There was always a market for little black boys, who dressed in Oriental trousers and turban and girt with a scimitar were frequent attendants on ladies of fashion carrying a cup of chocolate or bearing a prayer book. We read advertisements as the following: "Wanted Immediately a Negro boy must be of full black complexion . . . not above fifteen or sixteen years of age." (5) Brown says, "A favorite black boy to keep and dress." (6) A London book of 1680 says of "the Town Miss": "She hath always two necessary Implements about her; a Blackamoor and a little dog." (7) Harper says, "Black pages were almost as common as pet dogs and were advertised in much the same way." (8) Hogarth in his "Taste In High Life," shows a young Negro being dressed with great care by his aristocratic mistress. The black skins and wooly pates of the Africans fascinated English ladies as much as they did the French, German, Spanish, and others. Blacks became so common in England that the second Duke of Dorset, whose ancestors for nearly two centuries had had a Negro page in the family, decided to change to a Chinese since "everybody had a black one" and it was "more original." (9)

Professor Silliman of Yale University who visited England in 1805 wrote, "A black footman is considered a great acquisition and consequently Negro servants are sought for and caressed. An ill-dressed or starving Negro is never seen in England." (10)

Some were, of course, poor and ill-dressed. Many, known as St. Giles Blackbirds, were beggars. But most blacks were highly thought of. Before Shakespeare's time and certainly during his, a jet-black Negro, known as "King of the Moors," mounted on a

5. Story of Liverpool, p. 35. 1937. Hackwood, F. W. Good Old Times, pp. 356-63. 1911. Notes and Queries, Vol. 154, p. 173 ; Vol. 160, p. 20 ;12 ser. Vol. 3, Feb. 24. 1917. Chambers' Jour Vol. 68, Jan. 31, 1891, pp. 65-7 ; For baptism of adult Negroes, 1759-1764, Notes and Queries, Vol. 160, p. 80. Malcolm, Anecdotes of Manners and Customs of London, Vol. 1, p. 369. 1811.

6. Brown, B. C. Elizabeth Chudleigh, p. 24. 1927.

7. Hindley, C. Old Book Sollector's Miscell. Vol. 3, p. 7. 1873. Doran, J. History of Cour Fools, p. 42. 1858.

8. The Bath Road, p. 257. 1899.

9. Sackville-West, V. Knole and the Sackvilles, p. 191. 1923.

10. Jour. of Travels, Vol. 1, p. 272. 3rd. ed. 1820.

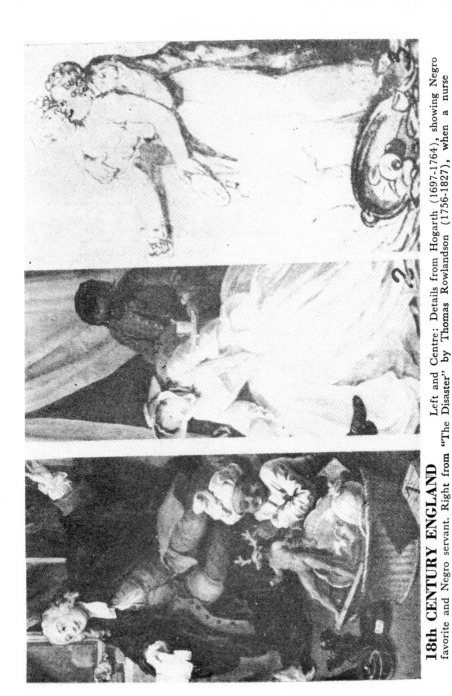

18th CENTURY ENGLAND   Left and Centre: Details from Hogarth (1697-1764), showing Negro favorite and Negro servant. Right from "The Disaster" by Thomas Rowlandson (1756-1827), when a nurse

Detail from "Taste In High Life" by Hogarth (1697-1764), illustrating how Negroes were pampered and dressed.

Detail from "Four Times of the Day" (Noon) By Hogarth (1697-1764).

"lion" and preceded by other Negroes bearing bars of gold, led the Lord Mayor's Show.

Of that of 1680, we read, "On the Lion is mounted a young Negro Prince attired in very righ habit . . . with a gold hilt in a scarf of gold by his side. With one hand he holds a Golden Bridle; in the other St. Georges Banner and representeth power." (11) There are records and other illustrations of Negroes with this, the greatest of all the city's pageants.

Dunster wrote:

> Sometimes at their head
> Index of Rank or opulence Supreme
> A sable youth from Aethopia's climes
> In milk-white turban precedes the Train."

British royalty, like royalty of Italy, France, Spain, Portugal, Germany, Austria, Denmark and Russia, set the example. Henry VIII had a Negro among his trumpeters. Queen Margaret of Scotland had two Negro ladies-in-waiting and she gave a tournament in honor of one of them. Her husband King James had Negro minstrels. Queen Elizabeth (12) had at least one Negro page not to mention her love for the mulatto Duke d'Alencon. (12a) Negroes took part in the "Masque of Blackness" a pageant of Ethiopia, staged by Ben Jonson in 1605, in which Queens Anne, wife of James I, played and in which the ladies blackened their faces. (13) Charles II (4) bought a Negro page for fifty pounds sterling, a large sum at that time; William III had a Negro page of whom there is a bust at Hampton Court; (15) George I had two, Mustapha and Mohamet to whom he gave preference over many dukes and lords; (16) William IV's barber-surgeon was Sake Deen Mahomed, an East Indian of Negro ancestry. He also

11. Sayle, R. T. D. Lord Mayor Pageants (Show of 1680 p. 8; No. 12, p. 15.) 1931.

12. Welsford E. The Fool, p. 170. 1935. 12a. See Sex and Race Vol. 3. p. 225. For more on D'Alencon's color see, Hume, M. A. Courtships of Elizabeth, p. 158, 211-12. 1896. Revue d'Anjou. ser. 2, Vol. 2, p. 133. 1857-8, where Turenne describes him as "noir" (black). Tommaseo, N. Relations des Ambassadeurs Venetiens, Vol. 2, p. 624. 1838, where Lippomani said he had "la faccia bruna." (dark-faced).

13. Masque of Blackness. Works of Gifford, Vol. 7, p. 8. 1816.

14. Secret Services of Charles II and James II. Roy. Hist. Soc'y. Publ. Vol. 52, p. 58. 1851.

15. Chambers Jour. Vol. 68, pp. 65-7 (On Negro slavery in England).

16. Thackeray's Works (The Four Georges) Vol. 23, p. 30. 1885. Mohamet was charitable. He freed 300 debtors by paying their debts. Malcolm, J. P. Anecdotes and Manners of London, Vol. 1, p. 27. 1810. Faulkner, Thos. History of Kensington says Mustapha and Mohamet saved George's life at the siege of Vienna in 1685. Mohamet left a family by a Hanoverian lady. Mustapha continued in the service of George II. pp. 358-9. 1820.

ENGLAND

Upper: Prince Sessakaroo, wealthy London dandy of the 1750's. Lower Left; William Davidson, leader of the Cato Street Conspiracy. Right: Alum-Ahiyou, Ethiopian prince, adopted by Queen Victoria.

served George IV. (16a) William IV, too when Duke of Clarence, had much contact with Negro women; once getting royally drunk in a Barbados brothel he created a scene. (17) A mixed-blood family in South Africa claims descent from George IV's affair with a Negro woman. (18) Prince George of Cambridge, son of George III, was taught boxing by Bill Richmond, a New York Negro. (18a) Queens Victoria reared a Negro girl, (19) whom she took into high society and adopted an Ethiopian boy, (20) whom she sent to Eton. Further search would, I am sure, reveal other favorites of British royalty.

The nobility had its Negroes, too. The immensely rich and dashing young Duke of Wharton had a Negro groom, Scipio, who rode nearly always with him. The Earls and Dukes of Dorset, as was said, had Negro pages for nearly two centuries. The Duke of York, son of George III, and commander-in-chief of the army, had several Negro favorites. In 1783, he brought from Germany a military band with Negroes for the bass drums, cymbals, and triangles. (21) They were probably some of the Negroes taken there by General Riedesel, (22) commander of George III's Hessian troops in the Revolutionary War in America. Englishmen returning to England after that war also took a number of Negroes with them, among them Bill Richmond, famous boxer.

As a result of the Duke of York's action, Negroes became a feature of British military bands. Leigh Hunt wrote of his walk on the Mall, London. "The blacks toss up their cymbals in the sun." (23) At the coronation of Queens Victoria in 1838 there was a Negro drummer in the Grenadier Guards that played at Buckingham Palace. (24) The most celebrated of the black drummers was Fraser of the Scots Guards. The custom ended

16a. Erredge, J. A. History of Brighthelmston (Brighton). pp. 235-237. 1862.

17. See account, Sex and Race. Vol. 2, p. 136. R. Fulford says, "grinning at Jamaican Negresses." (The Wicked Uncles. p. 102. 1933). But the Barbados affair showed he did more than grin. "The cultivation of wild oats was a life's work," for him, he says.

18. Sex and Race, Vol. 1, p. 140. 2nd ed. 1940.

18a. Egan, P. Art of Self-Defense, p. 12, 1845.

19. Anthrop. Rev. Vol. 1. p. 389. 1863. She was presented to the Queen by Capt Forbes-Smith. She was carefully educated, was proficient in music and mingled in good society.

20. Action, R. The Abyssinian Expedition, pp. 68, 77. 1868. Encyc. Britannica, Vol. 1, p. 76n. 1942. The boy was Alum-ahiyou, son of Theodore, usurping king of Ethiopia.

21. Notes & Queries 12 ser. Vol. 2, Oct. 14, 1916, p. 303. Carleton. J. W. History of the Hawk, p. 48. 1848.

22. Pennsyl. Maga. Vol. 15, p. 224. 1891.

23. Wishing Cap Papers, p. 72. 1873.

24. Notes and Queries 12 ser. Vol. 2, Nov. 4, 1916, p. 378.

Upper: Tambourinist of the Scots Guards, 1750. Lower Drummer.

in 1841 but Negroes were again admitted to British bands in the
first world war. In 1926, Edmund T. Jenkins, an unmixed Negro,
was instructor in a British military musical college.

Negroes in other occupations were not uncommon. They
were clerks, students at universities, acrobats, entertainers, street-
singers, cooks, maids. Samuel Pepys (1633-1703) tells of "Mr.
Cook" a clerk in the Admiralty at Whitehall. He mentions also
his "cookmaid" a "blackmore . . . Doll, who dresses our meat
mighty well and we are mightily pleased with her." He mentions several times Mingo, valet of Sir W. Batten. (25)

Notes and Queries tells of a Negro woman who played Jul-
iet in Scotland. (26) In 1788, Astley's London's leading musical
hall, (mentioned by Thackeray in The Newcomes) billed a troupe
of Negroes in its Ethiopian Festival. Macomo, a West African,
was one of England's greatest lion-tamers. He was succeeded by his mulatto son, Pablo Panque (1796-1871), real name
William Derby, who was the star of Astley's in 1847 with his
rope-dancing and his trained horse, Plege. Later he became a
circus manager and owner. (27)

Negro street-singers were so popular that whites blackened
their faces, learnt plantation talk, and imitated them on the streets.
Mayhew reported fifty such whites. (28) Negro crossing-sweep-
ers, street-entertainers and beggars grew rich. Ribton-Turner tells
of one who made so much money singing and dancing in Dept-
ford that he lived sumptuously and took his "country journey
with two women and makes plenty of money to pay all their
expenses." Another street Negro made a fortune estimated at
fifteen hundred sterling (a large sum at that time) and retired
to the West Indies. (29) Two figures very popular in London
around 1815 were Charles M'Gee and Joseph Johnson. The
first, having lost an eye in the Napoleonic War, took to sweeping
at the Obelisk near Ludgate Hill. His native wit and cheery
greetings brought him much coin from the rich folk who used
that thoroughfare. Joseph Johnson, another veteran, made a
model of the ship, "Nelson," wore it on his head and went about
singing and dancing to give the ship motion. J. T. Smith made
sketches of both and mentions other Negroes in his "Vagabondiana." (30) Mayhew gives the story of another Negro beggar,

25. Diary, Apr. 6, 1669. 25b. March 27, 1661. Jan. 21, 1659 (1660).
26. Notes and Queries, Aug. 31, 1889 cites Jackson's History of the
Scottish Stage.
27. Frost, T. Circus and Circus Life, pp. 20, 133-4, 262-4. 360-1. Also,
31, 97, 99, 117, 192. 1875.
28. London Labour, Vol. 3, pp. 200-04. 1864.
29. Hist of Vagrants and Vagrancy, p. 247. 1864.
30. Vagabondiana, pp. 14, 15, 23, 24. Pl. 11 & 12. 1874. Smeeton, G.
Doings in London, p. 124. 18—.

Sake Deen Mahomed (1749-1851), barber-surgeon to George IV and William IV of England. Expert on cholera and muscular ailments From two of his three portraits in the Brighton Pavilion. Courtesy of the Brighton Public Library).

Edward Albert, who had lost both legs and seems to have done well by selling a short sketch of his life. Unlike most of the other Negroes, he had a Negro wife, born in England. (31)

Jonathan Wild (1682-1725) England's greatest "gangster" was very likely of Negro ancestry, also. His color and features showed it. (32) Wild, who had the title of "Thief-Taker General of Great Britain and Ireland" used his office to organize one of the most formidable bands of burglars, pickpockets and highwaymen in history. He was very rich and was probably the original of Fagin in Oliver Twist.

Some Negroes also cut a considerable figure in London society. Soubise, son of a Negro slave from St. Kitts, West Indies, an unmixed Negro, was protege of the rich Duchess of Queensbury and one of the leading swordsmen and violinists of his time. Henry Angelo, great fencing-master who knew him well, says he was "one of the most conspicuous dandies of London. He frequented the Opera, sported a fine horse and groom, became a member of fashionable clubs and generally cut a figure." Gainsborough and Zoffany made portraits of him. Another Negro of that time in high society was the celebrated Chevalier de St. George of France, also a great swordsman and composer, who was companion of the Prince of Wales, later George IV. (33) Two other Negro friends of that king were Prince Saunders of Boston, Massachusetts, and George Bridgetower, celebrated violinist and accompanyist of Beethoven. One social lion was Prince Sessakaroo, son of the king of Annamboe, West Africa, who sent him to England to be educated. (33a)

Other Negroes in high society were the sons and daughters of rich West Indian planters and officials who were sent to be educated in the most expensive schools.

Among the Negro scholars were Job Ben Solomon, an ex-slave of Maryland. Taken to England he became one of the leading Arabic translators of his time. He worked with Sir Hans Sloane, whose collection started the British Museum in 1759; also Gustavus Vasa, writer, naturalist, physician and poet. Born in Africa, 1754, and sold into slavery in Barbados, he finally reached London, where he was educated and later became one of the greatest of the anti-slavery agitators. His son was librarian for Sir Joseph Banks, celebrated scholar. Another scholar was Ignatius Sancho (1729-1780), born on a slave-ship while on the way to South America. Reaching England, he was befriended by the Duke of Montague, who took him into his service and educated him.

31. Mayhew. Vol. 1, p. 56-9.
32. Lyons. F. J. Jonathan Wild, Prince of Robbers, p. 17. 1936.
33. Angelo, H. Reminiscences, Vol. 1, pp. 446-52. 1828.
33a. Gentleman's Maga. Vol. 21, p. 33. 1751.

Lady Jane Ellenborough. Inset: Second wife of Ira Aldridge.

Sancho, a writer of ability, was much beloved by Londoners, and made considerable money from his writings. And in 1765 a Negro was ordained into the ministry by the Bishop of Exeter before a large congregation. (34)

Boxing was represented principally by Bill Richmond, who was born on Staten Island, New York, in 1773 and was taken to England by the Duke of Northumberland; and Thomas Molineaux of Virginia. Richmond was heavyweight champion of England and taught boxing to Lord Byron, the poet. Molineaux, who had considered success at first, knocked himself out by falling backwards in a fight with Tom Cribb for the championship in 1810. (35) A fairly large number of noted Negroes who made their home in nineteenth century England could be named as Ira Aldridge, tragedian, and Duncanson the painter, friend of Lord Tennyson.

A Negro woman is said to have started the famous "Black Doll" shops of England. Brought there for sale but with no purchaser, she was given to a ragman who reared her. She finally acquired his business, using a black doll as a trademark. Her children carried on the business and in time had fifty shops in Britain. (36)

With Negroes in such favor with royalty and the nobility there was little or no restrictions against them, as a group. Hester Piozzi wrote of London in 1802. "Men of colour in the rank of gentlemen; a black Lady covered with finery in the Pit at the Opera and tawny children playing in the Squares — the garden of the Squares I mean — with their nurses." (37)

Pierce Egan found a similar lack of prejudice among the lower classes. He says of his visit to All-Max Cafe in 1812, "Colour and country considered no obstacle . . . Lascars, blacks, jacktars, women of colour, old and young and a sprinkling of the remnants of once fine girls." (38)

Of course there was some aversion for a black skin. But it was based solely on non-acquaintance and had no economic motive as it then was, (and is) in the Americas. That is, it was

34. Gentleman's Maga. vol. 35, 1765, p. 145.
35. Miles. Pugilistica, pp. 282, 289, 290, 301. 1906.
36. F. W. Hackwood says that antiquarians doubt this was the origin of the great rag trade (Good Old Times, p. 402). Another belief is that the black dolls are symbolic of the Black Virgin Mary (Notes and Queries, Vol. 2, p. 510). The earliest Madonnas of Britain, like those of Rome, were black. Cruikshank's illustrations, Vol. 3, Pl. 73. 1820 (6 vols.) has a drawing of the black dolls.
37. Intimate Letters, p. 243. 1914. 37a. Gentleman't Maga. Vol. 29, p. 240. 1759
38. Life in London, pp. 227, 273-4. 1904.

as purely psychological as fear of the blacks for the color of the first whites they saw, as reported by Livingstone and others. (39) Blackness of skin was also allied in "white" mind with man's primitive fear of night. Thus English mothers instead of using the blackness of night to frighten their children would use black men, or blackened white men, as chimney-sweeps. Mothers would say, "Be good or the black man will come down the chimney and get you."

Black men were used to create fear in literature, also. In Stephen Hawes, "Palace of Pleasure" written in 1509, one reads, "Out of the dragon's mouth there flew right black and tedious a foul Ethiop." (40) Aversion for a black skin is also found in the writings of Shakespeare and in some of his contemporaries, as George Herbert's "The Blackamoor and Her Loves," and John Cleveland's "A Fair Nymph Scorning A Black Boy Courting Her." In The Merchant of Venice, Portia, in rejecting the Prince of Morocco, says, "A gentle riddance . . . Let all of his complexion choose me so." In Othello the mention of blackness and thickness of lips by Iago, Brabantio and Othello, himself, does indicate prejudice. In Titus Andronicus this is even more evident. Shakespeare, it must be remembered, was writing of life as he saw it.

John Bunyan (1628-1688) in, "The Holy War," undoubtedly helped to create greater fear of a black skin. His villain, Diabolus, that is, Satan, is "King of the Blacks, or Negroes" which later are "the lesser devils who make the assault on Mansoul" that is, the soul of Man. (41)

Dryden, English poet and playwright (1631-1700) has Jacintha say to one of her suitors, " 'Tis impossible your love should be so humble as to descend to a mulatto." (42) In R. B. Sheridan's "The Rivals" (1775) Mrs. Malaprop says, " 'Tis safest to begin with a little aversion. I'm sure I hated your poor uncle before marriage as if he were a blackamoor." (43) Both Molineaux and Bill Richmond, American Negro puglists living in London, met color prejudice. A white girl was once insulted because she was in Richmond's company. American color prejudice was at that time taking deeper root among the English, too.

But while some shunned a black skin others thought it attractive. It even told a fascination for some who feared it. Dryden gives an instance of this. When Jacintha told her suitor she was a mulatto he replied that he couldn't help being drawn to her

39. See Sex and Race, Vol. 2, p. 402.
40. Vol. 10, xxxviii. reprint, 1928.
41. p. 5, 1795.
42. Evening Love, Act IV, Sc. 1, 1688.

because "there's something more of sin in thy color than mine."
(43)

Shakespeare has some of his characters express color prejudice which he then attacks. In Love's Labour Lost when the King tells Biron that his sweetheart, Rosaline "is as black as ebony," and that "black is the badge of hell," he replies, "Is ebony like her? O wood divine! . . No fair is fair that is not full so black. . . . And therefore is she born to make black hair." The wordy tilt between the King and Biron ends in favor of a black skin over a white one. The King himself speaks of "the sweet complexion" of the "Ethiopes."

In Troilus and Cressida, Pandarus says of the beautiful Cressida, "I care not an she were a blackamoor." Shakespeare by his frequent mention of a black skin was clearly intrigued by it. Certain writers believe that he had a Negro sweetheart and that he shows clear evidence of it in his Sonnets, especially the 130th, where he speaks of "breasts" that "are dun," (poetic for dark, dusky) and with hair like "black wires" (that is, kinky).

"If snow be white why then her breasts are dun
If hairs be wires, black wires grow on her head
And yet, by heaven, I think my love as rare
As any she belied with false compare."

G. B. Harrison, eminent Shakespearean scholar, thinks that the woman might be "Lucy Negro," and Shakespeare's "black sweetheart." (44)

Then as now there were marriages of Negroes and Englishwomen. T. L. Nicholas write, "In England, Negroes are married

43. The Rivals, Act 1, 2.
44. Shakespeare Under Elizabeth, pp. 64, 310. 1935. There was prejudice, as was said. However L. Winstantley is certainly wrong when she speaks of "The intense moral and physical repugnance that Shakespeare's age felt for Moors", She says, "The Moor was to Shakespeare's England all that the Negro is to southern America." (Othello as The Tragedy of Italy, p. 132. 1924). I think the evidence I have so far given refutes her. Shakespeare speaks well of Negroes several times and so does his contemporary, William Painter, in his "Palace of Pleasure" (Novel 35, p. 697. first pub. 1566). And if they had such repugnance why all those Negroes in the coats-of-arms of the nobility? Why have them as pages and favorites? And in the greatest annual pageant, the Lord Mayor's Show? Nowhere in Britain's literature up to as late as 1919 have I been able to find anything nearly as bad said against Negroes as against the Irish. I gave elsewhere the horrible penalty once inflicted on Englishmen for cohabiting with Irishwomen. The following is a specimen from C. J. Ribton-Turner's History of Vagrants and Vagrancy, (1847)," The Irish are extremely filthy in their habits. The younger Irish women are even more filthy than the men. The younger Irish women appear to be generally prostitutes." He adds, "Similar statements have been repeated without exception at all the workhouses visited." (p. 272. See also IRISH in index). This speaks much better of the Negro vagrants.

to decent seeming white women. One meets them in London escorting fashionably dressed ladies. White women walk the streets with their mulatto children." (45) Professor Silliman of Yale, writing in 1820, tells of mixed marriages and says that on Oxford Street he saw "a well-dressed white girl of ruddy complexion and even handsome, walking arm-in-arm and conversing sociably with a Negro man who was well-dressed as she and so black that his skin had a kind of ebony lustre." (46)

Gustavus Vasa, an African, and great anti-slavery agitator, married "a daughter of Mr. Cullen," a gentleman of Ely (47) William Davidson, son of a white attorney-general of Jamaica and a wealthy Negro woman, who was sent to London to study, had several love affairs and left a white wife and children. (48) Davidson was one of the leaders of the Cato Street conspiracy of 1820, whose aim was to set up a republic in England. There are several others on record.

Most sensational mixed marriage of the early 1800's was that of Lady Jane Ellenborough to Medjuel El Mezrab, a black Arab. Lady Jane was a Digby, one of the bluest of blue-bloods, and a noted beauty with golden hair, creamy rose-petal complexion. George IV called her the most beautiful woman he had ever seen. Three kings were in love with her: Otto and Ludwig of Bavaria and Pedro II of Brazil. She married one of the foremost men of England, Lord Ellenborough, later a viceroy of India. But discontented with him, she took three other husbands, all wealthy and of noble birth but unhappy with them all, she at last found true happiness with El Mezrab. Lady Isobel Burton, her friend said El Mezrab "was darker than an Arab generally is," that the blackness of his skin made her shudder" and that she could not understand how Lady Jane could "contact with that black skin." She admits though that El Mezrab was, except for his color, intelligent and charming. England was shocked at the marriage Lady Jane is the subject of several novels. Balzac, who it seems knew her, has her as the very amorous, Lady Arabelle Dudley in his "Lys Dans La Valee." Her passion, he said, "is quite African." (49)

As regards illicit unions, there is abundant evidence of them. Hogarth, in "Unpleasant Discovery" shows a black woman be-

45. Nicholas, T. L. Forty Years of American Life, p. 339. 1947.
46. Silliman, Vol. 1, p. 272.
47. Gentleman's Maga. Vol. 72, p. 384. 1792.
48. Wilkinson, G. T. Hist. of the Cato Street Conspiracy, 406-13. 1820.
49. O'Donoghue, E. M. Odyssey of a Loving Woman, pp. 189-272. 1936.

ing discovered in the bed of an aristocrat by his friends. (50)
In 1770's, Harriot, a Negro woman from Guinea, was one of the
chief figures in London's gay life. Her master, a Jamaica planter,
finding her intelligent, educated her, made her his mistress and
placed her in charge of his household. A writer of the times said
of her, "Her person was very alluring; she was tall, well-made and
genteel in appearance."

Her master took her to England and installed her as mistress of his mansion there. She ran the house and the servants
and devoted much time to improving her mind. But he died soon
afterwards and with no claim on his property she was penniless.
She ran his affairs "so uprightly that she had no money for
herself."

Having now to find "a new protector" she applied to one
Lovejoy, a procureur for the rich. "She was, "said the same
writer," a perfect phenomenon of her kind. He dispatched immediately a messenger to Lord S. . . ., who instantly quitted
the arms of Miss R. . . . for this black beauty. The novelty so
struck him with her unexpected improved talents that he visited
her several successive evenings and never failed giving her at
least a twenty-pound note.

"She now rolled in money and finding that she had attractions
sufficient to draw the recommendations and applause of so great
a connoisseur in female merit as his Lordship, resolved to vend
her charms as dear as possible; and she found that the caprice
of mankind was so great that novelty could command any price.

"In the course of a few months she could class in the list
of her admirers at least a score of Peers and fifty Commoners
who never presented her with less than soft paper, commonly
called a Banknote."

She grew wealthy, the account continues. She had fine
clothes, plate and furniture. Then she fell in love with an officer
of the King's Guard, and "declined to accept any other admirer."
He, however, fell into bankruptcy and she had to go to Paris to
recuperate her fortunes. Returning to London with a great
quantity of silks and laces "she began to refine our amorous
amusements and regulate them according to the Parisian system." She fitted up a house in elegant style and engaged some
of the most beautiful girls of London and a doctor to examine
them. Only men of the highest rank and wealth were entertained." As for the girls she gave them "such instructions that
enable them to pay their devotions to the Cyprian goddess with
great vigour and purity." She could rouse the most jaded
sex appetites," (51) said this author.

50. Picture reproduced in Sex and Race, vol. 3, p. 97.

The same writer tells of an African Prince who had plenty
of money and was a favorite in a house of Venus near Soho
Square, "Notwithstanding his complexion there was scarce a
'nun' in those seminaries who did not think it an honour to be
distinguished by the Prince De S . . . se." (51a) This person, he
says, was the protege of a duchess and had plenty of money. He
was evidently Soubise. Society ladies were glad to be seen riding
in the parks with him.

A circular of the 1750's advertises a house of colored girls
who perform for customers "the rites of Venus as they are done
in the South Seas." At that time the Caribbean was also called
the South Seas. Mrs. Leigh of Georgia told of the Negro servant
she took to England "and how much the English maidservants
preferred him to a white man" and that "my lady's maid preferred
to marry him." (52) Such preference occurred in high life, too.
Love affairs of mistresses with their Negro butlers and valets were
not uncommon. One lady eloped with the Negro butler of her
husband and took her children with her, declaring "She would
live with no other than the black." (53) The Earl of Craven
caught his Negro servant, with his mistress, Harriette Wilson.
He was reported as saying, "Her dismissal from my cottage was
because I caught her on the knee of my black footman, Mingo,
and I bundled black and white into the coach together to seek
their fortunes." (54) Harriette, most talked-of female writer of
her time, was later mistress of the Duke of Wellington of Water-
loo fame. (Harriette does mention Mingo). (55) Among the lovers of Harriette's sister, Amy, was a banker, who was "almost
a mulatto" with "coarse, black hair." (56)

Dr. Samuel Johnson said that his Negro servant and heir,
Frank Barber, was a great favorite with the women. "Frank," he
said, "has carried the empire of Cupid further than most men."
He had a white wife and children by her. (57)

Mixed marriage were approved in novels. In Anna M.
Mackenzie's "Slavery, or The Times," Adolphus, the African
prince, marries the charming English heiress and it is the girl

51. Nocturnal Revels, or History of King's Place, Vol. 2, pp. 98-105.
1779.
51a. Vol. 1, pp. 210-232.
52. Ten Years on A Georgia Plantation, p. 190. 1883.
53. Ashton, J. Good Old Times, p. 268. 1885.
54. Confessions of Julia Johnstone, p. 28, 1825.
55. Memoirs of Harriette Wilson, Vol. 1, p. 8. 1909.
56. Wilson, Vol. 2, p. 595.
57. Hill, G. B. Johnsonian Miscellany, Vol. 1, 291. 1897.
58. Whitney L. Primitivism and the Idea of Progress, p. 89. 1934.
See also in the same vein E. B. Dykes, "The Negro in England Romantic
Thought."

who is honored by the match. (58) In Miss Edgeworth's Belinda, Juba, the Negro marries the rich farmer's daughter. In "The Peregrinations of Jeremiah Grant, Esq." (whose white grandfather had married a mulatto heiress from Jamaica), Jeremiah is quite a ladies' man. In "Humphrey Clinker" (published 1771) a fashionable English ball is led by a mulatto heiress. (59) In Thackeray's Vanity Fair the enormously rich Rhoda Swartz whose "hair is as curly as Sambo's" and whose color is "mahogany" marries the future Lord Castletoddy. (60) A like marriage did occur in real life about that time. The Scots' Magazine of 1823 reported the marriage of a baronet to a "very dark" West Indian girl with a large dowry. (61) Research would no doubt reveal similar marriages. The mulatto girls were daughters of rich West India planters sent to be educated in England. Their fortunes were a huge attraction.

The cases of mixed marriages and other unions I have so far given in England do not go beyond the middle of the nineteenth century. And they are but a very small portion of those that actually took place from the time of the Romans to then. As I said earlier, men, regardless of color, coming into a foreign environment usually mate with the women there. Now the question is what became of the great number of Negroes brought into England since before the time of Elizabeth. Absorbed into the white population evidently. There is probably only one instance of English Negroes being colonized in Africa that is, in 1787 when 351 were sent to Sierra Leone with their white wives. (62) Therefore, it is clear, that Anglo-Saxon blood is not the hundred per cent pure we have been taught it is. Daniel Defoe called the English race a mongrel one. In naming the many peoples of which it is composed he did not include Negroes but he could well have done so. He did mention, however, a mulatto who was the son of an English gentleman and a black woman. (63)

William D'Arfey mentioned "a grand English family" very rich, whose ancestor, Judge Mountfaucon, of the eighteenth century, was "an indisputable mulatto." (63) The noble Finch family was so dark they were spoken of as "the black, funereal Finches." Lord Finch was so dark that George I described him as a chimneysweep.

59. Sypher W. Guinea's Captive Kings, pp. 88-9. 1942.
60. Chaps. 20 and 21—42, 46, 51.
61. Little K. Negroes in Britain, p. 205. 1948.
62. Falconbridge, A. M. Voyages to Sierra Leone, 1791-2-3, pp. 61-66. Utting, F. A. Sierra Leone. p. 81. 1931.
63. Reproduced in Hope's Everyday Book, Vol. 3 (1st Pt.), p. 626, entitled, "Mixed Breeds, or Education Thrown Away. "1839.
64. Curious Relations, ed, by Wm. Plomer, pp. 82-100. 1946.

From Negro Slave To White English Royalty

1. Abraham Hannibal, "Negro of Peter the Great." 2. Admiral Ivan
Hannibal, his son. 3. Pushkin, great-grandson of Hannibal. 4. Marquess
of Milford Haven, descendant of Pushkin, great-grandson of Queen
Victoria, cousin of George VI and best man at the Wedding of Princess
Elizabeth, heiress to Britain's throne. (See Appendix).

Up to the end of Victoria's reign, there was very little color prejudice in Britain. J. Renner Maxwell wrote, "A resident for more than three years in one of the best colleges in Oxford, I was not subjected once to the slightest ridicule or insult on account of my color or race from anyone of my numerous fellow-students. . . .

"Alaş, in West Africa the Englishman even the educated Englishman degenerates and stoops to practices which he would have depreciated in England." (65)

Mrs. Casely Hayford, wife of the celebrated Gold Coast lawyer, said that she met a similar lack of prejudice in England. Older residents tell me that Negroes found ready employment at all kinds of work then. Such color prejudice as existed in England between say 1900 and 1939 was largely economic. Jobs were scarce and the whites felt that they, not blacks, should have them. In 1950, with a shortage of labor, there was very little prejudice. Labor leaders told me that should there be another shortage, prejudice might return. I saw Negroes working as engineers, electricians, postmen, musicians, clerks, newspaper reporters, cooks, factory workers, not to mention as physicians, dentist, actors, etc.

In England, as on the Continent, interracial love still appeals to many. As Doris Anderson, white wife of the late Garland says, "In England I know the Negro has a very definite social appeal and a very great charm for many white women. In fact this is so much the case that I have often been ashamed of the way white women of all social classes, but notably in the smarter social sets of London, have offered themselves to Negroes whom I know personally." (66)

On my many visits to England between 1925 and 1950 I saw much to confirm this. In 1950 I went almost every night for six weeks to clubs where whites and blacks meet and was more than ever impressed in my belief that there are whites of both sexes who have no color prejudice whatsoever. Some of the fairest women had the dargest men, and with the mixed pair was sometimes a white couple. I met Englishwomen who were very proud of their brown babies.

George Padmore, London correspondent of the Pittsburgh Courier, wrote (Sept. 1, 1945) : of the departure of Negro soldiers from Bristol:

"To hell with the U. S. Army color bars! We want our colored sweethearts!" shouted hundreds of English girls who tried to break into an American Army camp at Bristol when the colored

65. The Negro Question, p. 55. 1892.
66. Nigger Lover, p. 195.

ENGLAND

Upper and lower right: Floyd Henry of the Royal Air Force and his bride. Lower left: "Prince" Monolulu, celebrated racing character.

troops, who recently arrived in this country from Germany, were about to embark for America.

"British police officers had to be called to protect the colored soldiers from being mobbed by the hysterical girls, whose ages ranged between 17 and 24.

"The scene took place early last Sunday morning following the report that the Negroes had been confined to their camp prior to departure for America in order to prevent the Americans from taking farewell of their girl-friends.

"When the news spread throughout Bristol about what was happening, bands of young girls, devoted to their American friends, were seized with anger at the restriction while they watched the Yanks marching to their barracks, singing, "Don't Fence Me In."

"This was too much for the colored men to tolerate, and soon the GI's started breaking down the barbed-wire fences surrounding the barracks and rushed out into the arms of the white girls.

"This former slave-trading port, from which Sir John Hawkins sailed to West Africa in a ship named "Jesus Christ." never witnessed such a public demonstration of romance before. White Southern officers tried to break up the love-makers, but without success, for the English girls beat off the officers as they tried to separate the couples. Kissing and embracing went on for hours until, with a special reinforcement of military police, the couples were separated and the Negroes forced back to their barracks.

"Later in the day the men were removed from the barracks in special Army trucks to the Bristol railroad station, but news of the Negroes whereabouts soon spread around Bristol, and the girls invaded the station. They thronged the roads and pavements approaching the station platforms sobbing for their sweethearts.

"To avoid further incidents, Army authorities ordered the motor trucks to drive into the side entrance of the station, and by the time the girls—assembled in front of the station entrances—realized what was happening and made a rush for the side gates, the Army trucks were safely inside the station gates.

"Once inside the station and surrounded by armed guards. the men behaved quietly, but the girls standing outside pursed their lips at the fence openings for their farewell kisses.

"Not satisfied with this, some fifty girls climbed over the station fence, while others hired taxis and drove through the station gates as though they were legitimate passengers. Once within the station gates, they boarded the trains taking the soldiers away from Bristol, escorting their boy-friends all the way to the embarkation point.

ENGLAND   An Interracial Party in London

"The unfortunate ones left behind when the train steamed out broke into hysterical sobs. British police officers had difficlty in persading the young girls to go home. Most of these girls had been friendly with the colored soldiers for years, before the men were transferred to the European continent. When the men returned to England, the romantic relations were renewed.

"Now the end has come, but many of the girls hope to go to America to rejoin their sweethearts.

"Some of the girls had been waiting outside the assembly barracks in Bristol throughout the night just in order to get a last farewell goodby from their boy-friends who had come thousands of miles to help defend Britain in her darkest historical hour.

"We don't mind getting wet," said one 18-year old girl as she dripped from head to foot in the rain pouring down on the struggling, screaming mob of girls trying to enter the station just before the train pulled out.

The girl added:

"These Southern officers can say what they like, but we girls intend to give our sweeties a good send-off. And what's more, we intend going to America after them.' " (67)

The London Sunday Pictorial said, "The scene was Bristol, most English of all English cities. The time was 2 a.m., yesterday (Aug. 25). The actors were a mob of screaming girls aged between 17 and 25.

"Their hysteria was caused by the news that four companies of American colored soldiers in the city were leaving for home.

"The girls besieged the barracks where the soldiers were and began singing 'Don't Fence Me In.'

67. One soldier wrote similarly, "The girls all over Europe have fallen in love with the black soldier and many of them have cried worse than any American girl ever did when the boys move from a town that they have lived in. I have known the girls to follow them from town to town as far as they could go." (Pittsburgh Courier, July 7, 1945).

Ollie Stewart wrote, "Many European girls who met, danced with and later married Negro soldiers, were never the same afterward. I've known a hundred or more who refused to let any white man touch them after they had once been embraced by color." He tells of an Italian princess who said the thing she remembered best was that of a black man who had taught her how to "cut a rig." (Negro Digest, Sept. 1947).

For similar earlier demonstrations towards black men, dating back to 1889, see Sex and Race, Vol. 1, pp. 206-07. 2nd ed. 1940. For the same in Germany, when the French Negroes were in the first world war, see pp. 180-2. For the same in Denmark, p. 182. Iwan Bloch, noted German sexologist, also mentions this tendancy to flock about Negroes. See sources in Sex and Race, vol. 2, p. 401.

English Beauty of Mixed Parentage. (Ida—, a music student of Miss Ira
Aldridge).

"This was too much for the colored men, who began to break down the barbed wire surrounding their quarters. In a few minutes hundreds of girls and U. S. soldiers were kissing and embracing."

The first world war brought thousands of Negroes to England and the sons of some of these by white women have in turn married white. I have seen a fairly large number of such offspring, which will, in turn, marry white and finally disappear in the white group.

The second world war brought an increase in the number of mulattoes by British and American Negro soldiers. Sylvia McNeil's inquiry gives 549 for the Americans, (68) with all not reported. There is no record of those by British Negroes.

In all the large cities are blacks, mulattoes and quadroons with white wives and sweethearts. In Cardiff is a Negro colony, dating from about 1850, with some 7000 blacks and mulattoes. The mothers were either white, or mulattoes born of white mothers. London had an even larger number of Negroes, some of whom had middle-class wives, and some upper-class sweethearts. Liverpool also had a considerable number of mixed marriages.

Negro physicians, of whom there are a goodly many had white wives, one of them the late Dr. Harold Moody, who was president of the Christian Endeavor Society of the World, and whose son, was the first known visibly colored man to be an officer in the British army. Negroes with Negro wives were very rare, one of the few being J. R. Archer, a photographer, who was elected Mayor of Battersea, one of London's most popular boroughs.

A mixed marriage that caused a colonial storm was that of Seretse Khama, twenty-seven year-old heir apparent to the tribal throne of Khama the Great of Bechuanaland, South Africa, and Ruth Williams, London stenographer.

Marriages of Englishmen and colored women also do take place. I have seen more than a few and have reason to believe that most mulatto girls born in England find white husbands, especially if their parents are well-to-do. Dinah Lee, former stage star, London milliner and owner of a fine mansion in Windsor, has a white husband, and one of her daughters has a white one, too. Robert Moses of Liverpool has eleven children by his mulatto wife. V. P. Bourne-Vanneck, graduate of Cambridge University, and a prominent manufacturer, married Victoria Thomas,

---

68. Illegitimate Children Born in Britain of English Mothers and Coloured Americans. Report of a Survey. 1945.

AFRICANS

Physicians, Lawyers and Other Professions resdent in London.

ENGLAND

Seretse Khama, ruler of Bechuanaland, and his English wife, and daughter, Jacqueline.

Left: Mr. and Mrs. Owen of Windsor. Right: Mr. Owen and daughter. Mrs. Owen is Dinah Lee, former actress, and now a successful London milliner.

Children by White Mothers. All are colored but five.

born in Cardiff of a West African father and an English mother. The couple now live in New York, where they bought a newspaper. Richard Angerolia, a Scot, married Hilda Simms, star of Anna Lucasta.

The present Negro strain in Britain is disappearing into the white one precisely as the past. The descendants of Daniel Taylor, father of Coleridge-Taylor, for instance, are now almost indistinguishable from white. There is no reason to believe that what I, myself, saw in England as regarding racial inter-mixture was essentially different from that in the many centuries preceding.

NOTES ON SAKE DEEN MAHOMED

Erredge, J. A. History of Brighton says, "The personage who acquired the greatest fame for his baths and obtained the highest and most extensive patronage was Sake Deen Mahomed." (pp. 235-82. 1862). See also Gentleman's Magazine, Vol. 189, Jan.-June 1851, p. 444. Melville, Lewis, Brighton, pp. 135-7. 1908. (This has a picture of his establishment). Sala G. A. Life, etc. p. 168. 1876. Sussex Co. Magazine, Vol. 13, pp. 135-7 1939. He married an Irish girl. One of his sons, Frederick, became an eminent physician (Dict. of National Biography, Vol. 12, 777-8. 1921. Brit. Medical Jour., Nov. 29, 1889). Another son, James, who died 1935, was a minister.

Additional Notes On Negroes in England (early 19th cent.) see more illustrations of them by Cruikshank Vol. 1, pp. 4, 13, 26, 53, 55, 80; Vol. 2, pp. 7, 11; Vol. 3, p. 64. 73, 75; Vol. 5, pp. 22, 103, 105, 113. (Illustrations. p. vols. 1820). Scrap-book. Vol. 5, p. 511.

Robert Knox tells how "a fair complexion' "'with Negro features" occasionally crop up in the British face from time to time." Races of Men, p. 112n. 1850.

In March, 1950, Jocelyn Bingham, popular entertainer, known as "Frisco" was named as correspondent in suit brought by Sir Ronald Gunter, who held that his wife had carried on a two-year romance with Frisco in his West End love-nest.

EX - SLAVES: WHITE AND BLACK

HARPER'S WEEKLY.

JANUARY 30, 1864.

Harper's Weekly gives the names of these slaves and says of them:
"EMANCIPATED SLAVES, WHITE AND COLORED. The Children
Are From the Schools Established in New Orleans." (Note the man with
name of master branded on his forehead).

"Emancipated Slaves, White and Colored." Other half of preceding page
from Harper's Weekly.

CHAPTER TEN

NEGRO ANCESTRY IN WHITE AMERICA

"All the great peoples of the world are the result of a mixing of races." Lord Bryce. (1)

It was shown in the foregoing pages that Negroes had been migrating into Europe from the earliest times to the present and being absorbed into the population. This is but a small part of what could be given. Also, in the first and third volumes of Sex and Race much was cited that is not given here.

As regards the whites of the New World it is evident that some were already of Negro-European strain, especially the Spaniards and Portuguese. In Volume Two of Sex and Race considerable evidence was also given of the Negro strain in the American whites as the result of slavery. Evidence given here is additional.

Contact of whites and Negroes in the United States began with the coming of the Spaniards to Florida in 1512. Since these first comers were only men the first mixed-bloods were the offspring of white and Negro men with Indian women. Forty-three years after the first landing, the city of St. Augustine was founded. The Negroes who helped build it lived among the Indians. There is record of a Negro nurse in the hospital there in 1597. (1a)

Spaniards and Negroes continued their exploration, going as far west as Lower California and as far north-west as Kansas. They reached Virginia in 1526 under D'Ayllon but the colony of five hundred broke up when the Indians and Negroes revolted, forcing the Spaniards to return to the south. The Negroes undoubtedly made their homes with the Indians thus it seems safe to say that there was some Negro strain in Virginia before the coming of the English in 1607.

The next to arrive were the French and the English. The latter, mostly men, mated with Indian and Negro women. That is to say, the United States began on mixture of Caucasians, Negroes and Indians. Now four centuries later this still goes on.

About the eighteenth century, the mixture of Caucasian and Indian lessened and that of Caucasian and Negro increased. Especially was this so after the abolition of the slave-trade in 1808. In fact, even before then the marriage of whites and Negroes, which was at first strongly opposed, became legal in some

1. Relation of the Advanced and Backward Races of Mankind, p. 16. 1902.
1a. U. S. Guide: Florida, p. 247. 1930.

191

Southern states, then colonies. Marriage of whites and Negroes were at one time or another legal in such Southern states as Virginia, South Carolina, North Carolina, Alabama, Louisiana, Texas and Florida. In North Carolina mixed couples were taxed and in 1755 they petitioned the legislature for relief. (2) Most of the present opposition to miscegenation arose when the whites were trying to bring Negroes under economic subjection during Reconstruction.

So increasingly white did many of Negro strain become that a great number of them were indistinguishable from Europeans and it was possible to kidnap white children in the North and sell them as Negro slaves in the South, instances of which were given in the second volume of Sex and Race. It was also possible to mistake whites for Negroes, or to "accuse" them of Negro ancestry. Enemies of Thomas Jefferson said he was of Negro ancestry. (2a)

In all the Southern States there was an element of Negro in much of the white population, especially South Carolina and Louisiana. Northerners in the Union Army were often surprised at the great number of fair Negroes, some of them very rich. J. W. DeForest, a Union officer, writing from Louisiana, December 4, 1863, said, "You would be amazed to see the swarming mulattoes and quadroons and octoroons who possess this region and call themselves Americans. Some of the richest planters, men of really great wealth, are of mixed descent . . . These are not the former slaves, observe, but the former masters." (3)

Of other Negroes, he wrote, "When I first saw those hazel or blue eyes, chestnut or flaxen heads and clear complexions, I took it for granted that some of the white children of the village had seized this chance for a gratuitous education. I had met the same persons before in the streets, without suspecting that they were other than pure Anglo-Saxon."

He tells also of white women having children by Negroes and of two having Negro husbands. (3a)

V. Colyer, a Northerner, was also amazed at how indistinguishable from white were many Negroes in North Carolina. He said, "I have had men and women apply for work who were so white that I could not believe they had a particle of Negro blood in their veins except from the broad belief, according to the declaration of St. Paul, 'that God made of one blood all the nations of the earth.' I have spoken elsewhere of the beauty of many of the quadroons who attended my school for the advanced

2. N. Carolina Records, Vol. 5, p. 295. Also Vol. 23, p. 106 (1723).
2a. New ork Sunday News, Sept. 13, 1936, p. 70.
3. A Volunteer's Adventure, p. 157. 1946.
3a. A Union Officer in the Reconstruction, pp. 121, 72, 138. 1946.

scholars. Many of them were as white and as comely as any Italian, Spanish, or Portuguese beauty. So remarkable is the difference in the color of the blacks of the South from those of the North that the conviction is constantly forced upon the mind that slavery, if left to itself but a few generations longer, would have died out of itself from this cause alone." (4)

Ficklen tells, too, of "the rich planters living on the Mississippi, who, in spite of the known fact that they were not entirely white" were regarded as white. In fact there was so much Negro strain in the Southern whites that after the Civil War, the latter thought it best to admit fair Negroes into their cast. Nevins says, "Unquestionably not a few mulattoes of very light complexion decade by decade passed into the category of white folk and there married. Some states, notably Kentucky and Virginia, defined a mulatto as any person who had one-fourth or larger fraction of Negro blood. Georgia's definition was less than one-fourth. In no instance did a state law require that a person having a non-perceptible trace of Negro blood should be deemed a mulatto. More drastic laws would have embarrassed white people with a slight tincture, say one-sixteenth of Negro blood, would have been difficult to enforce. A perfectly legal migration from the Negro to the white race was possible." (5)

Mary White Ovington (white) says in her autobiography, "Southern legislatures were at that time passing laws to make a person with a drop of colored blood a member of the colored race. . . .

"I recall one evening when we examined photographs of families that lived, some in the white, some in the colored world. I had heard of these things but it was a different matter to see pictures of colored persons who had gone white, especially when a brother, still in the colored world, exhibited them." (5a)

ʐ Of the twenty-nine states, which now have laws, against mixed marriages, a few as Virginia, Alabama and Georgia, do not make some provision for those who look white to enter the white caste. In Florida, Indiana, Kentucky, Maryland, Missouri, Mississippi, Nebraska, Nevada, North Carolina, South Carolina, Texas and Utah those with less than an eighth Negro strain may marry white. Oregon fixes it at less than a fourth and Louisiana forbids "any appreciable mixture." (6) As late as 1909, however, marriage of whites and quadroons was legal in Virginia.

4. Services Rendered by the Freed People in the U. S. Army in North Carolina, p. 33. 1864).

5a. Afro-American. Aug. 18, 1951.

6. Murray, Pauli. State Laws on Race and Color. 1950.

As a result of four centuries of miscegenation, Negro ancestry may be seen in many individuals least expected to have it,
even by those with a not too experienced eye. Photographs,
especially candid ones, make this even more apparnt. Some of
these white "Negroes" hold positions in the government, in the
army and the navy and are physicians, scientists, musicians,
novelists, businessmen, motion-picture actors and sporting figure.

Now and then something happens to make the ancestry of
some of them known. I gave instances in the second volume of Sex
and Race. (7) Here are others:

Dr. Albert Johnson of New Hampshire, who with his family
is subject of the book, "Lost Boundaries" and of the movie of
the same title.

Theophilus J. Syphax, prominent Wall Street lawyer and
Yale graduate, who changed his name to T. John McKee and
was known as white for forty years. However in 1948, he acci-
dentally discovered that he was heir to an $800,000 estate left by
his quadroon grandfather, John McKee, Civil War veteran, and
declared his true name and ancestry. He had kept his secret
so well that even his wife did not know it. It made headlines
in the white and the Negro pres. (N. Y. Daily News, March 1,
1948; Baltimore Afro-American, March 13, 1948.)

The New York Daily News (March 8, 1948) had this about
McKee in its Voice of the People, "It is interesting to see in print
the account of T. John McKee, who had always been regarded
as white, and recently declared himself a Negro. But such cases
are far from uncommon, and are well known to Negroes. I myself am a so-called Negro who "passes," as the expression goes.
By "so-called"! I mean that I am 1/8 Negro and 7/8 white. Because I look like an entirely white woman, I for a long time found
it economically and socially advantageous to be completely
"white." The strain of this hypocrisy finally caused me to com-
promise. I now choose to be "white" downtown, where I work,
and "colored" uptown, where I live. It's a comedy life in a way.
But seriously, though, we have the best country in the world today,
and isn't it pretty childish and stupid for some of our citizens to
hold to unreasoning prejudices that, in many cases such as mine,
don't even make sense?"

Lawrence Dennis, Harvard graduate, and a "Who's Who in
America," is another instance of how Negro strain may get lost
in the white. Dennis, who was once an important official in the
State Department, an economist with leading Wall Street banks,
and an author, was, in spite of his ancestry, one of Hitler's leading supporters in the United States. Called "the brains of Ameri-

7. See for instance, p. 376. Also Vol. 3, pp. 22-3, 304.

Mrs. Violetta Adkins of South Charleston, West Virgina, blonde of Negro ancestry. Under state laws which prohibit association of whites and blacks she was arrested when seen with a dark Negro. The police thought she was "white." (Afro-American, Oct. 20, 1951). Lower Lawrence Dennis. (See text)

can fascism," he was received with honor at the Nazi Party Conference in Nuremberg, Germany. In 1944, he was one of the defendants in the seven months' sedition trial in Washington.

C. J. Carlson first called attention to Dennis' Negro strain in 1943 in "Under Cover." (8) In 1947, Leonard Golditch as a result of inquiry in Atlanta, Georgia, Dennis' birthplace, said his parents were of Negro ancestry, that in Washington he was known as colored and lived with colored relatives. He says, "Dennis" neighbors on Vernon Street, Washington, D. C., recall the boy, Lawrence Dennis as being of light complexion and as one of their own, living with his aunt, Cordelia Dennis, whom he called "Mother." (8a)

Another of obviously Negro ancestry who is known as white is Senator Ellender of Louisiana. P. L. Prattis writes, "Ellender is not what you would call white. He is not even on the pink side. He is weathered high brown. Further, his hair is so suspiciously crinkly that Louisiana Negroes who know him are quite in the habit of referring to him jocosely as "Kinky Ellender." But, Prattis adds, Ellender "is one of the most zealous of the devil's advocates for pure white superiority." (Pittsburgh Courier, July 6, 1949).

A remarkable family whose Negro ancestry was known, but not widely, was the Healys of New England, who had an Irish father and a Negro mother from Macon, Georgia. One son James A. Healy (1830-1910) was Catholic Bishop of Maine and New Hampshire: another, Patrick, was president of Georgetown University, Washington, D. C. from 1873-1882; and another, Michael, was captain of the USS Alaska. One sister married a white man.

Thomas F. Meehan, Catholic historian, said in the New York Times, "James A. Healy . . . had a mulatto mother. He was a graduate of Holy Cross College and had a distinguished career as a priest of the diocese of Boston before he was appointed bishop of Portland. His brother, The Rev. Patrick, was a Jesuit, named president of Georgetown University, who during his incumbency modernized most of the buildings of that institution." (9)

The New York Times (Feb. 16, 1922) reported the case of Jose Bornn, native of the Virgin Islands, whose wife, Ingrid, born in Norway, married him in London, England, where he was in the newspaper business. They came to New York, where Bornn became city editor of the New York Tribune and later of the Journal

8. p. 463. 1943. 8a. Reader's Scope, May 1946, pp. 75-8. I have seen Dennis. He looks like a Southern Italian.

9. Our Colored Missions, May 1933, p. 78 and June, p. 93. Gillard, J. T. Colored Catholics in the United States, p. 185. 1941.

Two Noted Catholics of Negro Ancestry (see text).

Rev. Frank White, Unitarian Minister of Norfolk, Virginia and his wife Anne Anderson, social worker of New York. (Afro-American photo).

V. P. Bourne-Vanneck, publisher of the Age, New York and Mrs. Bourne-Vanneck. Both are English-born.

of Commerce. The couple lived happily for fourteen years then once when Bornn was away, his wife went through pictures of his family he had locked away and suspected he was colored himself. She asked for an annulment as a result. They had two daughters.

The Times (May 16, or 17, 1947) also tells how Mrs. Elizabeth Canino, was granted an annulment in Albany, N. Y. when she discovered her husband, Antonio, whom she believed white, was of Negro ancestry.

Most often the Negro ancestry is never discovered even by those who have it. Here is a case which I happen to know quite well. It involves some thirty persons. A light-colored girl born in Jamaica, West Indies, married in New York a white man by whom she had eight children, none of whom, knew their Negro ancestry. Their children in turn, do not know it either. Some hold fairly high positions. One is an army officer.

Another light-colored Jamaican married a white woman in Philadelphia. His children, also believe themselves to be pure white. This man, now dead, had a nephew in Chicago, and wishing to have him visit him sent to him for a photo to judge whether the nephew was white enough in appearance to present to his family. He asked that the photo be sent to General Delivery. It was. But the nephew never saw his uncle. He was too dark.

I have reason to believe that such cases could be multiplied by tens of thousands.

There are, of course, no figures on how many white Americans are of Negro ancestry but there must be millions. The number of Negroes who know at least one of their number who is passing is vast.

The Negro Digest (April 1949) gives an account of the private life of "Four Who Are Passing." One of them, a native of Georgia, came to New York and enjoying the freedom there, made it his home. He is now vice-president of a white insurance company. Ebony in an article entitled "Five Million White Negroes" gives fourteen photos and asks the reader to pick out the Negroes and the whites. It is impossible to distinguish them. (March 1948).

One proof of the number of Negroes who pass into the white group is that very fair Negro women are much more in evidence than very fair Negro males. The latter drift into the white caste while the women remain in the Negro group, where they are much sought after by dark males. In the white group these women would find themselves in competition with white women.

Herbert Asbury (Collier's, Aug. 3, 1946) says that competent authorities think there are from 5,000,000 to 8,000,000 Negroes who live as whites, and that between 15,000 and 30,000 persons classed as Negroes go over to the white side every year, although a few investigators have placed the annual migration as high as 200,000."

These estimates, he adds, are not mere guesswork. They are based on careful studies by experts of census reports, immigration records, vital statistics and the like and show "very conclusively that approximately 20,000 Negroes disappear every year and that their absence from the black population cannot be accounted for otherwise than by passing.

"Two of America's foremost social scientists, Dr. Charles S. Johnson of Fisk University and the late Dr. Edward B. Reuter of the University of Iowa and Fisk University, have made extensive examinations of the census records and other data relating to mulattoes. They found an abnormally low ratio of mulatto men to mulatto women especially in the age groups 15-19 and 20-24. For example, the census of 1910 showed an excess of more than 85,000 mulatto females in the age group 20-44, a ratio of 79.9 males to each 100 females. No such careful studies have been made of later censuses, but most sociologists believe that they will show a corresponding excess of females.

"Since there are no biological or other reasons, both Dr. Johnson and Dr. Reuter have attributed the excess of mulatto females to the fact that large numbers of mulatto men, particularly in the age group 20-44, cross the line, or at least have reported themselves to the census takers as white. Their theory is strengthened by the fact that the low ratio of mulatto men to mulatto women is particularly noticeable in the large cities of the North, where passing is easiest."

Another investigator, he says, after extensive examination of census and other records, concluded that in the two decades from 1890 to 1910, Negroes lost approximately 600,000 persons, an average of about 30,000 a year, and that since there has been scarcely any Negro emigration from the United States he concluded that these 600,000 had gone over to the white side. "In addition to studies of this nature," he says, "there has been a great deal of personal investigation of passing, and several extensive surveys have been made by research projects. The results of these indicate that the estimates made by sociologists and anthropologists are correct."

"Nearly every survey has reported that few Negro families have been found which didn't know of at least one instance of passing. Some families knew of dozens. And contrary to general belief, Negroes who attempt to pass are seldom exposed by other Negroes. When they are, it is usually because of personal enmity that has followed them across the line, or because having turned white, they try to prove their orthodoxy by turning violently anti-Negro. Walter White says he "could name some men in American public life of this type."

Asbury quotes a "very light-skinned man who resembled a South European more than a Negro," who said, "I pass myself. Every day from nine to five I'm a white man. I've got a good job downtown; I do the work well, and I've had two raises. But I'd never have been hired if I had said I had Negro blood. When I applied, I gave my race as white and my nationality as Spanish, and neither statement has ever been questioned. I keep a little room in a white part of town, to bolster my story if necessary, but I seldom go there.

"Nearly every night I come home to Harlem because my folks and all of my friends are colored. I am engaged to a girl who has the same amount of Negro blood that I've got, one eighth. Our children will have no more, but if they tell the truth about their ancestry they'll be classed as Negroes. Maybe after I'm married I'll stay over on the white side, so my kids will have a better chance to get somewhere in the world."

"It is now estimated," says Asbury, "that there are at least between 5,000,000 and 8,000,000 persons in the United States, supposed to be 'white, who actually possess Negro blood. In reality, this is a very conservative estimate. . . .. Hundreds of prominent American men and women who live as whites are actually white Negroes . . ." (10)

Nanette Kutner in "Women Who Pass as White," (Liberty, March 1949), tells of one girl whose "skin is as fair as that of the Hesperus skipper's daughter, her shoulder length hair as straight and golden as Lana Turner's." She attended a white college. Another, she says, is a Phi Beta Kappa, who married a man white as herself and who lives in a white neighborhood.

The Southern Workman has an interesting story of a white Negro girl and her difficulty in getting socially adjusted and how white men took advantage of her whēn her ancestry became known. (11)

Arthur Davis writes, "My friend X is . . . graduate of a colored trade school" and "is now making about $8,000 a year as foreman of a large and nationally known manufacturing plant.

X is not happy, because he doesn't want to be white.

He doesn't want to be white, first of all, because his wife is not light enough to pass.

He therefore lives in a colored neighborhood and spends

10. See also "Who Passes For White." Our World, Apr. 1947.
11. Southern Workman, Vol. 64, p. 368. 1945.

his evenings among his own people—and likes it.

At the same time he has to keep a "downtown" address in case of illness.

He has to be careful when he is downtown with his wife. In stores, on buses, and on the street, he is constantly on the alert for workers and officials from his plant.

It isn't a pleasant way to live, but where can he make $8,000 as a colored man in his particular field?

The best job he would get would be a $2,800-a-year position as teacher in some colored technical high school." (Afro-American) Nov. 10, 1945.

On the other hand are those who wish to be known as Negroes but are taken for whites. These are mostly women married to dark Negroes. I recall how once during a vice drive in Chicago an acquaintance of mine was arrested when with her husband on the belief she was white. She won high damages.

In Cincinnati, Mrs. Francis, blonde, and indistinguishable from white, was arrested when out with her dark husband, because they were taken for a mixed couple. She won a $900 verdict. In court, it developed that her sister, also colored, was married to a white man in Michigan. Mrs. Francis' father was white.

In Chicago, Mrs. Marion Robinson Mallory, former Powers model, blonde, was arrested in Chicago when out with her husband, Edward, by an over-zealous policemen. The couple won a $2,300 verdict. (Amsterdam News, Apr. 24, 1948).

In May 1949, in Indianapolis, the police had orders "to break up white prostitution in colored neighborhoods." Two light-colored women, social workers, taken for white, were among those arrested. With them were two colored men, one a juvenile court judge, and the other a prominent politician. The policemen refused to believe the women, locked them up, but had to apologize in court. (Afro-American, May 21, 1949).

Negro-Indian Ancestry

Considerable Negro strain has entered the white group through the American Indian. The Indian, though less advanced than the Negro, is now considered as of superior ancestry because of his straighter hair. In fact it is even fashionable to boast of Indian ancestry. But up until about the early part of the nineteenth century it was quite otherwise. A common saying then was, "A good Indian is a dead Indian."

But it is quite possible that this Indian ancestry boasted of might have some Negro in it. Negroes and Indians mixed freely from the start in Florida, where they and the whites first met in what is now the United States. H. G. Loskiel, writing in the

1790's said, "The Indians and the Negroes marry without any scruple." (12) G. Catlin, authority on the Indians says they welcomed fugitive slaves. He says, "As they came with a good share of the tricks and arts of civilization they are at once looked upon by the tribe as extraordinary and important personages; and generally marry the daughters of chiefs, thus uniting theirs with the best blood of the nation which produce these remarkably fine and powerful men that I have spoken of above."

"The finest and most powerful men I have ever yet seen have been some of the last mentioned, the Negro and North American Indian mixed of equal blood." Of one Missouri Negro-Indian chief, Pe-toh-pee-kiss (The Eagle's Ribs), he says, "This man is one of the extraordinary man of the Blackfoot tribe . . . His dress is really superb; almost literally covered with scalplocks." There is a portrait of him sketched from life. Of Ta-wah-nah (Mountain of Rocks) Texas Comanche chief, he said, "A perfect personation of Jack Falstaff in size and figure with African face." (13) There are also portraits of him and other Negro Indian chiefs. Negro Indian chiefs have been fairly plentiful especially in Florida. The Wisconsin Indians had considerable Negro strain, and their great chief, Oshkosh, for whom a town was named, was undoubtedly of Negro ancestry. So was his son-in-law, John Baptist DuBe (or DuBay), who was called "a black Ethiopian." (14)

Indians and Negroes have mixed so freely over the centuries that today along the Atlantic Coast and the Southwest, an Indian is more mulatto and Negro than anything else. In certain states, as Virginia, an Indian is only one while on the reservation. Away from it, he is a Negro. The Negro strain in the much-mentioned Indian one of Charles Curtis, vice-president of the United States (1929-33) was apparent.

Negro Origin of the Creoles

The Creoles of New Orleans assert they are of unmixed an-

12. History of the Mission of the United Brethren Among the Indians. p. 58. 1754.

13. North American Indians. Vol. 1, p. 39 ; Vol. 2, p. 75, 250 et seq. See also, Coe, C. H. Red Patriots, p. 250. Also Phylon, 3rd. Quar. 1947. where K. W. Porter gives much detail of Negro-Indian families in Florida.

Relations between Indians and Negroes, Jour .of Negro Hist. Vol. 18, 1933, pp. 283-321. Racial Composition of the Seminole Indians of Florida and Oklahoma, Vol. 19, 1934, pp. 412-430.

Racial Composition of the Seminole Indians. Jour. Negro History, Vol. 19, pp. 412-430. 1934). Negroes in Florida Prior to the Civil War pp. 77-86., p. 339 also.

14. Krug, M .E. DuBay, p. 128. 1946. See also Chap. 35, Sex and Race, vol 2.

NEGRO INDIAN CHIEFS

1. Mickenopah. 2. Pe-to-pee-kiss. 3. Ta-wa-que-na (Sketched from life by Catlin). 4. Osceola (Howard, O. O. Famous Indian Chiefs I've Known).

cestry and object to colored people using the name. But Blumen-
back (1752-1840), Father of modern anthropology, says, "The
word originated with the Ethiopian (Negro) slaves transplanted
in the sixteenth century to the mines in America, who first called
their own children who were born there Criollos and Criollas."
(Anthrop. Treatise, p. 112, 215, 1840). He cites as authority, a
Spanish-American historian of the seventeenth century, Garcilasso de Vega, (Origen de los Incas, p. 255, 1633), first published
in 1609.

There is good reason to believe that this name was passed
on to children borne by black women for white men, also, and
the offspring of these children. Moreau de St. Mery's use of the
word is an instance. St. Mercy was born in Martinique in 1750, and
was one of the leading writers and political figures of his time. In
1793, he visited the United States and wrote his American Journey, in which he said as regards yellow fever, of which Negroes
and those of Negro ancestry are believed to be immune, "It was
said everywhere that I was stricken with it but since I am a
Creole it was highly improper to include me in that number."

This passage has proved a mystery to Kenneth Roberts,
author of "Lydia Bailey" and other novels. In his translation of
"American Journey," he says, "This is confusing. The word
'creole' properly speaking has no connotation of color. It means
a person born in the West Indies of Spanish or French parents,
as distinguished from immigrants direct from France or Spain,
or from Negroes, mulattoes or aboriginals . . . Nowhere is the
indication that Moreau had colored blood. White Creoles were
not supposed to be immune. Why Moreau should imagine he
was immune because he was born in the West Indies is a mystery." (15) In short, it does seem that St. Mery used "creole" in
its right sense, that is, he knew he had a Negro strain. St. Mery
was a relative of Empress Josephine, whose color justified the
belief she was of Negro ancestry.

Since, as was said, "creole" is of Negro origin and since
the first native-born Americans were of Indian, Negro, and Caucasian stock in Florida is it not possible that "creole" still held
its original meaning in that region and that therefore Louisiana
Creoles are originally of this mixed stock?

That a more numerous "racial" group in any given environment usually absorbs the smaller is commonplace fact. The
countries of the New World offer many instances of this. For
instance in the British West Indies, Haiti, and the Dominican
Republic the blacks have been absorbing the whites; in Uruguay
and Argentina, the whites have been absorbing the Indians and

15. p. 236n. 1947.

the Negroes; in the eastern United States, the Negroes are absorbing the Indians; and in the Western States it is the whites who are.

This letter to the open columns of the New York Daily News
might be intended as satire but it is typical of American ancestry:

"What's my nationality, please. My great-great-great-great-
grandfather came over on the Mayflower. He married an Indian;
his son married an African. The son of this child married a German, and their son married a Jew. Their son married a Jap, and the
son of that union married an Italian. Their boy married a Pole
—and so it went. I'm getting married to an Italian in the New
Year. My sweetheart says I am an American, but I would just like
to know for sure, so as to fill out the blanks properly on the
marriage license application. Mixed-Up Jose."

Unless there is a great incoming of Negroes to the United
States, those now there will be absorbed. But whether we have
white absorbing black or black absorbing white we will still have
only humanity for as Emerson said, "If you have man, black or
white is an insignificance. The intellect — that is miraculous!
Who has it has the talisman. His skin and bones though they were
of the color of night are transparent and the everlasting stars
shine through."

Chapter Eleven

SOME RECENT WELL-TO-DO MIXED MARRIAGES MENTIONED IN THE PRESS

Negro Males

Porfiria Rubirosa of the Dominican Republic and Doris Duke, called the world's richest woman. Rubirosa was former husband of Danielle Darrieux, French motion picture actress (N. Y. Daily News, Aug. 31, Sept. 2. Pittsburgh Courier, Sept. 13, 1947).

Frank Marshall Davis, poet and Helen Canfield Peck, artist (Ebony, September 1951).

Fleetwood McCoy, Jr. and Geraldine Martin (Ibid).

William Tibbs of Detroit and Eleanor Sydham Stahl (Ibid).

Allen L. G. Woods, chauffeur, to his wealthy employer, Mrs. Adrian Nicholson. (Courier, June 11, 1949).

Paul Robeson, Jr. and Marilyn Greenberg, July 2, 1949 (White newspapers and Afro-American, July 2, 1949).

William Grant Still, composer conductor, and Verna Arvey, concert pianist, (New York Age, Nov. 5, 1949).

Aubrey Pankey, concert artist, and Katherine Weatherley (Courier, April 28, 1945).

Father Divine (George Baker) and Edna Rose Hitchings (N. Y. Daily News, Aug. 8, 1946 and Negro papers).

George Massengill, auto mechanic, and Clair, formerly of the Women's Army Corps. Their son, Lester, was judged "most perfect" baby in a Detroit contest in which 5,200 babies were entered, most of them white (Afro-American, Dec. 2, 1950).

Billy Daniels, night-club entertainer, and Martha Braun, socialite of Lowell, Mass. (N. Y. Daily News, Dec. 2, 1950. Courier, Jan. 21, Feb. 4, 1950).

Leslie Perry and Ruth Weygand, National Labor Relations Board (Afro-American, Feb. 11, 1950).

Frank Curley Montero, Urban League official, and Ann Mather, of wealthy Boston family, with the approval of their parents. The father of the bride is a Yale graduate, Who's Who. and a member of prominent clubs. The marriage was given extensive publicity in the white press. The story appeared on three pages of the N. Y. Daily News, July 15, 1950.

Ebony Magazine, December 1949, had pictures of mixed couples, among them Richard Wright, author, to Ellen Poplar: Nathaniel O. Calloway, M. D., of Chicago to Doris Howe, nutrition specialist; Max Yergan, Spingarn Medalist to Lena Halpern, M.D. of New York; Robert Angerola of Scotland to Hilda Simms, star of Anna Lucasta. There were also pictures of other mixed couples above-mentioned.

Rev. William Tyree and Rhogene Cobb of Florida. The marriage was approved by the bride's parents (Afro-American, Apr. 9, 1949).

Nat Humphries, 60, sportsman, and Maria Seena, hospital clerk (Amsterdam News, March 3, 1949).

Walter White, NAACP secretary, and Poppy Canner, Magazine editor (Courier Aug. 27, 1949; and white dailies).

Dean Dixon, symphony orchestra conductor, and Vivian Rifkind (Courier, Apr. 28, 1945).

Ebony (Nov. 1950) has pictures of Club Miscegenation of Detroit at one of their outings. There are eighteen pictures of these mixed couples and their children and also of their homes. Some had been married forty years. Detroit also has a Club of Tomorrow and Washington, D. C. a Club International, composed of mixed couples.

White Males

Lennie Hayton, impresario, and Lena Horne, singer-actress (N. Y. Daily News, June 27, 1950. They had been married three years before).

Herman Kobbe, socially prominent New Yorker, and Selma Burke, sculptress (N. Y. Age, Oct. 29, 1949. It was also reported in the N. Y. Times).

John Pratt, socially prominent New Yorker and Katherine Dunham, internationally known dancer (N. Y. Age, Oct. 29, 1949).

Sashu Horowitz, wealthy New Yorker and Gladys Spivey. milliner (N. Y. Age, Oct. 29, 1949).

Rev. Frank White of Virginia, Unitarian, and Anne Anderson of New York (Afro-American, Feb. 2, 1946).

Gustav Woerner, wealthy San Franciscan, and Juanita Smith. The marriage made headlines in the San Francisco Examiner (white) Aug. 10, 1946.

Robert Preiskel, Yale graduate and member of New York business firm, and Barbara Alma Scott (Pittsburgh Courier, Nov. 4, 1950).

James Clark, sea-captain, and Mildred Santiago (Afro-American, Dec. 11, 1948).

Walter Days of Rhode Island and Dorothy August (Afro-American, Aug. 8, 1947).

Marriages In The South That Brought Prison Terms

Ted Sesney, white, Oklahoma farmer, to Josie Douglas. Each was sentenced to a year and ordered to leave the state, when freed (Pittsburgh Courier, Feb. 23, 1946).

Davis Knight, a thirty-two year-old veteran, who had served

in the navy as white was sentenced to five years for marrying a white girl at Ellisville, Mississippi. Research was made into his ancestry and it was discovered that his great-grandmother Rachel, was a slave who had a child by Capt. Newt Knight, white. Knight, who is to all appearances white, claimed that he is part Indian, not Negro.

One witness for the prosecution said that he had seen the great-grandmother as a child and that she had "the characteristics of a colored woman." Those for the defense said she had "straight hair and the appearance of an Indian." (Afro-American, Jan. 1, 1949. Pittsburgh Courier, Feb. 5, 1949).

William Purcell, 35, of Richmond, Virginia, was jailed for marrying Mrs. Ada C. Rhoton, white. Purcell who had registered as white, had the appearance of a dark white person — "a Spaniard." (Baltimore Afro-American, Jan. 15, 1949). Mrs. Rhoton was jailed, too. (Feb. 5, 1949).

Other "Mixed" Marriages

On May 4, 1901, Emma Bethel, 30, of a wealthy Philadelphia family, was married to Howard Lee, a coachman. St. Louis Post-Dispatch, May 4, 1907.

Zachariah Footes of Philadelphia, Married in 1896, they have lived happily. He is an engineer. They have grandchildren (Afro-American, July 7, 1945).

Mrs. Arthur Little of prominent Detroit family sued for divorce on the ground she was colored. (Crisis, Feb. 15, 1915, p. 167).

Acquanetta (Mildred Davenport) of West Virginia, who played top roles in Hollywood, and was known as an Indian, had a son for Luciano Baschuk, millionaire, whom she sued for divorce and a large sum. (Courier, Jan. 21, 1950). A later report said she had married again a white man, Henry Clive, artist.

George White of Valdosta, Georgia, to all appearances white, was arrested with his wife, supposedly white, who claimed she was part Indian, for violation of the state's marriage laws. The wife had complained that their children, also to all appearances white, were barred from white schools on the ground they had "Negro blood." (Afro-American Oct. 29, 1949).

Clark C. Hamilton, a Navy veteran, to all appearances white, and registered as white, was sentenced to three years at Roanoke, Virginia, for marrying Florence Hammond, white (Afro-American, March 12, 1949).

Unmarried Couples

Thomas Johnson, 30, of Goochland, Virginia, was sent to State Industrial Farm for living with Margaret Goosey of England, whom he had met while serving in an army base near her home. She had come to America to marry him but found

that Virginia law prevented her. She was given a six-months'
sentence (Afro-American, Dec. 27, 1947). Horace White, 29, of
Rockingham, North Carolina, was sentenced to life for allegedly
being the father of a child by a white girl.

Dan Cannon, well-known politician, of Louisville, Kentucky,
was sentenced to five years for illicit relations, with Geneva
Davis, white. The girl, who lived in a Negro neighborhood, had
told him she was colored, he said. (News, March 18, 1942).

Harold Webster, wealthy Florida real-estate man, who "passed for white" and married a white woman and had children by
her, shot and killed his mother-in-law when she called him a mulatto and reproached him for his Negro strain. (New York News
March 5, 1927).

Clement Wood, asking for "full social equality for Negroes"
tells of that which already exists through sexual association. He
says, "Erskine Caldwell's Trouble in July" indicates that it is
often the white girl who is the aggressive demander of the Negro
man's attentions. . . . The preference of French, Russian, and
other European women for Negro lovers is also in point.

"Each section of the South has its lore of wealthy white girls
who accepted their colored chauffeurs, or other Negro men as
their lovers — incidents often discreetly shut up by an arranged
marriage of the girl to a complaisant white husband. If the
white girl feels experimental in sex — and increasingly they
appear to — an affaire with a Negro, covered by the group
conspiracy of silence, runs far less risk of detection. White wives
neglected by their husbands or dissatisfied with amatory ama-
teurishness, find a similar outlet the safest. Many of the sexual
vacations of white girls and wives in Bermuda use the Negro
bellhops there as the safest outlet. One does not need to read
Walter Winchell to learn of the pursuit of outstanding Negro
men by even titled English and European women. I once heard
a roomful of white girls and wives in New York declare that each
would rather have an affaire with a leading Negro actor than
with any in the world. Only rarely do such girls publicize the
incident as 'rape'; Bermuda, especially, laughs at this charge:
because it knows. Certain white girls, especially those who have
had Negro lovers, insist that a white girl gains by having her
first experience of this nature. But this forgets that individual
choice ought to rule, in all cases.

"What is the attitude of white men toward all this? The
cloaks of silence about sex makes a definite answer difficult, if not
impossible. One or two facts may aid more than any speculation.
In bordellos exhibiting circuses of the 'House of All Nations' type,
whether in Paris, Cairo, Chicago, New York or elsewhere, the

most popular display is a Negro man enjoying a white girl, preferably a novice. Owners of these illicit erotological laboratories have told me that the girls involved thereafter prefer this experience and that they themselves are much in demand, for a fee, to introduce men to spectators, who desire to employ the men for less public entertainment. The most popular 'stag show' movies have the same theme, fully embroidered; and these circulate on a rental basis in many wealthy or well-to-do homes having private projection facilities. The keen interest displayed in these exhibitions pushes white male opposition to the idea toward the vanishing point." (Atomic Age, March 1946).

A final thought: It has been shown in this book and in Sex And Race that in no matter what age or country white and black meet they have intermixed. We saw them centuries before the Christian era doing so in Egypt, Rome, Greece; we saw them likewise in the Middle Ages in Spain, Italy, France, Britain, and in our own times as far north as Scandinavia.

The two may be pictured as streams which flow one into the other, blending little by little until the color of the smaller yields to that of the larger. In Europe, the white stream was larger: in the West Indies and Brazil, it is the black that was. As in Europe and the United States where the descendants of an unmixed black had become indistinguishable from white in less than a century so the offspring of whites settled in Ethiopia in the seventeenth century became as the result of mating with black women, generation after generation, became indistinguishable from black.

A most evident truth is that color prejudice is not natural to man but is the result of economic and social rivalry, the desire to hold certain groups available for exploitation. It was shown in Chapter Three that while whites in Europe had no prejudice for a black skin they had for women, Jews, Christians and lower-class whites while in Africa the whites centered their prejudice, not on other whites, but on blacks. The blacks, too, had their economic rivalries, not of color, but tribal. Thus color is only a pretext. It is only the outward form on which hate, greed, and jealousy fix themselves for justification. When it's not color, it's religion, nationality, politics, schools of thought, art, music and almost anything on which people can differ. Left to themselves most of the white American colonists would have developed no more color prejudice than they had had for blacks in England, which, as was shown, was almost nil. In fact, in the beginning in America there was much less prejudice for blacks that certain whites as Quakers and the Irish. The slaveholders deliberately built up color prejudice. So well were most whites and blacks getting along together that the master found it necessry to pass laws and exact penalties to promote it. In short color prejudice is a plant that has to be zealously tended to keep it alive, so difficult it is to keep people who have much in common hating one another simply because their color is different.

Bishop Gilbert Haven, white, of the Methodist Episcopal Church, predicted in 1869 that American commonsense would some day reassert itself and that citizens would be judged not by their color but by their worth. As regards so-called intermarriage, he said, "The hour is not far off when the whitehued husband shall boast of the dusky beauty of his wife and the Caucasian wife shall admire the sun-kissed countenance of her husband as deeply and as unconscious of the present ruling abhorrence as is his admiration of her lighter tint . . .

"The Song of Songs will have a more literal fulfilment than it ever confessedly had in America; and the long existing devinely-implanted admiration of Caucasians for black but comely maidens, be the proudly acknowledged and honorably gratified life of Northern and Southern gentlemen."

APPENDIX

Miscellany on Miscegenation

The sexual association of which Clement Wood writes has always existed in the United States. It began with the whites on the slave ships that brought the Negroes across and was continued by the slave masters. Abundant evidence was given in Volume Two of Sex and Race. Here are some other instances:

Johnson Green, Revolutionary War veteran, son of a Negro and a white widow, later hanged for burglary, told in his confession of his intimate affairs with white women, at least four of whom were married (Phylon, 1st Quarter, 1946).

Benjamin Banneker (1732-1806) was the grandson of an Englishwoman, who having purchased a small plantation, bought two Negro slaves, one of whom she married. (Nat'l Cycl. of American Biol. Vol. 5, p. 35, 1907). Banneker, an astronomer, was appointed by Washington to help lay out the city of Washington.

The white daughter of Gen. Robert Howe of Revolutionary War fame had two children by a Negro slave. (Gen. Miranda. Archivo, Vol. 1, pp. 220-1. 1909).

Dehault de la Susse, last Spanish governor of Louisiana, had a quadroon concubine, Hester, to whom he left a fortune. She, in turn, left it to her son by him, who had disappeared years before. He was traced to Baton Rouge, where he passed as white. Rather than admit his Negro ancestry, he refused the legacy. (Pulzsky. White, Red and Black, Vol. 2, p. 83. 1853).

"At one period the marriages between freeborn English women and Negro slaves were so frequent that the Assembly (of Maryland) enacted that the wives of such husbands should be slaves during the lifetime of their husbands." Neill, E. D. Terre Mariae, p. 203. 1867.

Of the 46 original founders of the city of Los Angeles, Sept. 4, 1781, twenty-five were of Negro ancestry. "A strange mixture of Indian and Negro with here and there a trace of Spaniard." says H. H. Bancroft. (History of California, Vol. 1, p. 345; Vol. 2, pp. 230, 248, 293; Vol. 4, p. 755). Pio Pico, last of the Spanish governors of California was undoubtedly of Negro ancestry.

"In the 17th Century in Virginia, Negroes used to import white servants and receive head rights to land. One of them, Richard Johnson, imported two white servants and received 100 acres of land on the Pungoteague River. In 1651, Johnson imported eleven and received 550 acres adjoining his. About 1650 Benjamin Dole imported six and received 300 in Surry County while others did the same." U. S. Guide, Virginia, p. 11. (1940).

"Indeed, for more than twenty years from the time when the Negroes first appear in the courts there was no restriction upon their right to own white indentured servants." (Russell, J. H. The Free Negro in Virginia, p. 91).

E. B. Reuter: "It is, of course, a well-known fact that certain eminent men associated with Negro women and were perhaps the fathers of mulatto children. Washington, Jefferson and Franklin are often mentioned in this connection and Franklin, at least, appears not to have been much concerned to conceal the association." (Race Mixture, p. 46, 1931).

Of the 207 students enrolled at Wilberforce University in 1859 a majority "are the mulatto children of Southern and Southwestern planters. (Jour. of Negro Hist. July 1923, p. 335).

Anthrop. Review, Vol. 2, p. 121. 1864 quotes report from the New Hampshire Patriot of white women going South to teach Negroes and having children by them. There was said to be sixty-four such cases, it says.

E. Dick. The Dixie Frontier, p. 96, 1948 tells of a camp meeting at Sparta, Georgia, where 3000 whites and blacks camped together on the ground at night." Whites and Negroes attended a ball and danced together. "The happiest people in the ballroom were the Negroes. The slaves moved about the room at will." (From Farmer's Gazette, 1807).

General Winfield Scott, hero of the Mexican War, general-in-chief of the United States, and Whig candidate for the Presidency, had a mulatto son. (Crisis Aug. 1916, p. 198).

Zephaniah Kingsley (1765-1843) white, richest man in Florida at that time married Anna Madegigne Jai, a Negro woman of East Africa, daughter of a chief and herself wealthy. Kingsley had large plantations and a fleet of ships engaged in contraband slave-trading. His ships brought thousands of Negroes from Africa, trained them and sold them as high as $1500 each. He had paid $25 for them. Once when a U. S. Coast Guard gunboat captured one of Kingsley's ships with 350 contraband Negroes aboard and the government didn't know what to do with them it turned them over to Kingsley.

James Monroe, President of the United States, appointed him one of the thirteen men to help form the Second Legislative Council of Florida.

Kingsley married his colored sons to white women and his colored daughters to white men. He wrote strongly in favor of intermarriage. He left all his property to his Negro wife. When she died in 1870, she left it to one of her daughters who had married a white man. Whistler's mother, subject of the famous portrait of that name, Kingsley's niece, tried to break his will without success. (Corse, D. Key to the Sea Islands, p. 115, 1931. Florida Hist. Quar. Vol. 23, No. 3, July-April, 1944-5, p. 157. Kingsley Z. Treatise on Slavery, 1829. New York Times, Aug. 6, 1950).

Edwin Belcher, Union officer, who commanded a company of white troops in the Civil War, wrote William Lloyd Garrison, that he was made a captain in 1861. "I was born a slave of my father in South Carolina in 1845." He added, "My complexion precluding a possibility of a discovery" of his Negro ancestry. (Letter, unearthed by WPA project of Boston, Mass.).

Elizabeth Keckley, former slave, who lived in the White House and was the closest friend of Lincoln's wife, and talked often with Lincoln, had a son, who served as white officer in the Union Army. (Keckley, E. Behind the Scenes, p. 105, 1868. Washington, J. E. They Knew Lincoln, p. 208, 1942).

William Wells Brown, says of slaves he saw being taken on a river-boat for sale: "There was, however, one in this gang that attracted the attention of the passengers and the crew. It was a beautiful girl, apparently twenty years of age, perfectly white with straight light hair and blue eyes. But it was not the whiteness of her skin that created such a sensation among those who gazed upon her — it was her unparalleled beauty. She had been on the boat but a short time before attention of all the passengers, including the ladies had been called to her and the common topic of conversation was about the beautiful slave girl . . . the man who claimed this article of human merchandise was a Mr. Walker, well-known slave-trader residing in St. Louis. Her master kept her close to his side." (Narrative, etc. p. 34, 1847).

J. Buel: "Mysteries and miseries of America's Great Cities," says, "Here are Negroes with white women for partners and white men in the arms of oleaginous black wenches all twirling in the lascivious waltz to the music of fiddle and banjo . . . The participants are unconscious of everything save the fun in hand and our weakened stomachs are partly forgotten in the amazement at the loud sounding osculations of a buck Negro practising on a white girl's cheek. When the dance is concluded the enraptured couples march to the bar and sometimes to a strictly retired part of the house." (p. 57, 1883).

Richard K. Fox Gazette, a publication of the 1900's tells of Lizzie Winsweiler, white, who appeared against Samuel Kellum, a Negro, charging him with being the father of her child. Kellums denied the child was his and that its color was due to its mother feeding it black tea instead of milk. The magistrate sent for

APPENDIX

milk. The baby drank it. (Van Every. Sins of New York, p. 155. 1930).

Irene West, vaudeville artist, tells of a rich white girl, who fell in love with a Negro bartender, whom she later had as her chauffeur, and the tragedy that resulted when her family interfered. (Afro-American, Dec. 8, 1945).

George Wolsey in "Call House Madam" tells the adventures of a woman who ran such a house in Los Angeles. She said, "Customers don't know just what it is but they like to be entertained by a black woman. That's telling the truth from the men and the girls. . . . The black girls in my houses were getting the play — and the money . . . I could have made a fortune, though, in black girls alone."

Some actresses, too, preferred Negroes. One, "a great screen bet," liked black prizefighters. "Her passion is to see her white skin against the black skin of a colored lover." This woman picked out the blackest men. (pp. 203, 416, 1942).

The New York Daily News mentioned a de luxe house of prostitution in New York with women inmates in which two Negro men were arrested, one for living on its proceeds, and the other, owner of a Harlem nightclub, for a financial interest in the house. (March 22, 1947).

Charles Montgomery, a mulatto, was named as boss of a Hollywood white slave ring, which had thirty-one houses, of which Ann Forrester, white, was in charge. The inmates of these houses were white. (Daily News, Oct. 2, 1949).

The Mayor's Committee on Human Rights of Milwaukee. names a teen-age club of white girls, the requirements of which was to have sex relations with a Negro or take a beating. (Pittsburgh Courier, Dec. 9, 1950).

AFRICA

Black was the sacred color of the ancient Egyptians (Mythology Of All Races, Vol. 12, pp. 94, 97, 413. It was also that of the Jews. The fire in which Jehovah made himself manifest was black as in the burning bush of Moses. Ginzberg, L. Legends of the Jews, Vol. 2, p. 303, 1925). That of the Greeks and other ancients, too (Higgins G. Anacalypsis, Vol. 1, pp. 286, 332. 1927.

* * *

About 1215 A. D. the king of Nubia, "whose skin was all black," was guest of Emperor Alexius in Greece (Related by Robert of Clari. Conquest of Constantinople, pp. 79-89. Ed. of 1936 (McNeal).

* * *

West Africa in the 18th century had a great number of mulattoes. In Astley's Collection of Voyages one reads, "Of mulattoes born of a white and a black there are great numbers here." (Vol. 3, p. 270. Also Vol. 2. p. 633, 1746). Richard Jobson (Golden Trade, p. 35, 1623) tells of the large number of Portuguese mulattoes in West Africa.

* * *

Prof. Lips says that the white woman was first regarded as a "monster" in Central Africa. The Negroes had so far seen only white men and figred there were no white women. Alexandrine Tinne, first white woman explorer was killed in 1869 by the Taregs, who thought her "an evil spirit." When the white woman did come with the white man, she could do nothing, he says. She had no weapons and nothing to trade; she wore clothing to conceal her person and that she had breasts, hips and the power to bear children did not occur to them." (p. 215)

* * *

White Woman Reared Among Africans Just Like Them

Ruth McBride, ("Keeping House on the Congo," National Geographic Maga., Nov. 1937), tells of African women, each of whom, "would be bent forward, a loaded grass hamper on her back held by native straps, resting upon the forehead and often a pickaninny was strapped to either hip.

"Once in this pitiable file there was a white woman, probably thirty years of age, with fine features and hair coiffed in native style. On her back was a heavy burden. She was clad like the other wives, barefooted, dirty, and wild-looking, and chattered a native dialect."

"We often wondered about her, whence she came, and what could have been her weird history." (White children reared by American Indians were Indian in manner precisely as Indians and Negroes who had group up with whites since babyhood were in white in their ways).

White Man and Negro Woman in Africa

Dr. Fred Puleston (African Drums, p. ix. 1930) says, "the domestic relations of the white man to the black woman have an enormous influence to his comfort and stability while in the Dark Continent." (Chapter: Some Excuse for the Harem).

EUROPE

Ancestry of David Michael Mountbatten, third Marquess of Milford Haven: General Abraham Hannibal's son Joseph, had daughter, Nadejda, who was married to Count Pushkin. Their son, Alexander Pushkin, the poet, had a daughter, Sophie, Countess of Merenberg, who was married to Prince Nicholas of Nassau. A daughter of this couple, Countess Torby, was married to Grand Duke Michael of Russia, brother of the Czar. Their daughter, Nadejda, was married to Prince George Mounbatten, second Marquess of Milford Haven, a grandson of Queen Victoria of England, and father of the present Marquess. One of Prince George's sisters married Czar Nicholas of Russia, thus making a Pushkin descendant a relative by marriage with him.

On Africa and Oriental soldiers in Germany under the Romans (Hertz, F. Race and Civilization, p. 81, 1928).

Moorish heads carved in stone on pillars in the Netherlands (Ray. Jour. Low Countries. From Oxford Dict.)

On Higiemonte, Negro painter (Joachim von Sandraart. Academia Nobilissimae Artis Pictoriae, p. 180, 1683).

White women given over to Negroes to be raped during the French Revolution. (Ryan, M. Prostitution in London, p. 15. 1839).

H. Fleischmann, "Les Demoiselles de Palais Royal," (1911) in a list of prostitutes of Paris of 1790, with their prices, names several Negro women. (p. 110-11).

Alexander Dumas the Elder was rather proud of his Negro ancestry. When his daughter was to marry into an aristocratic family, he invited a large number of the Negroes of Paris. The bridegroom's mother was shocked. To make it still worse, Dumas told her, "They are my relatives who wish to be present." (Gronow, R. H. Recollections and Anecdotes, pp. 119-124. 1863).

Black Sambo (Santa Claus) and the BlackKnight in legend. Holland has a Black Peter that hands out gifts at Christmas (Massey G. A. Book of the Beginnings, Vol. 1, p. 306).

Admiral Sir William Cornwallis, brother of Lord Cornwallis, had a Negro sweetheart, Couba Cornwallis, who probably saved the life of Lord Nelson, England's great naval hero. She was presented to the Duke of Clarence, later King William IV. (Cundall Historic Jamaica, p. 75, 1915).

Froude tells of his seeing a lively little black boy returning from his studies in England and everywhere the white ladies on the ship fondled him as if he were a pet monkey. If, on landing in Jamaica they had done that, both the native whites and mulattoes would have been scandalized, he says.

Some Earlier and Little Known Works on the Negro

William Painter: The King of Maroco in the Palace of Pleasure. Works of. Vol. 3, p. 697, 1813. Reprinted from the edition of 1575. His Novels 7, 14, and 22 also mention Negro subjects.

Alonso de Sandoval, "Naturaleza Policia Sagrada. Sevilla, 1627. This work deals with Negro saints among them Antonio de Cattagirone (1539-1589). Rare. In Biblio. Nationale. Paris.

Dessailly, Abe. Le paradis terrestre at la race negre devant la science. Paris. 1892.

Mailhol, G. Philosophe Negre et les secrets de Grecs. 1755. Count Soden von Sassanfart. Die Negerinnen oder Lilliput. 1788.

A Fair Nymph Scorning a Black Boy Courting Her

◈

Nymph. Stand off and let me take the air
         Why should the smoke pursue the fair?

Boy.   My face is smoke, thence may be guessed
         What flames within have scorched my breast.

Nymph. Thy flaming love I cannot view
         For the dark lantern of thy hue.

Boy.   And yet the lantern keeps love's taper
         Surer than yours that's of white paper
         Whatever midnight can there be
         The moonshine of your face will clear.

Nymph. My moon of an eclipse is 'fraid
         If thou shouldst interpose thy shade

Boy.   Yet one thing, sweetheart, I will ask
         Take me for a new-fashioned mask.

Nymph. Done: but my bargain shall be this
         I'll throw my mask off when we kiss.

Boy.   Our curled embraces shall delight
         To checker limbs with black and white.

Nymph. Thy ink, my paper make guess
         Our nuptial bed will prove a press
         And in our sports, if any come
         They'll read a wanton epigram.

Boy.   Why should my black they love impair
         Let the dark shop commend the ware
         Or if thy love from black forbears
         I'll strive to wash it off with tears.

Nymph   Spare Fruitless tears since thou must needs
         Still wear thy mourning weeds.
         Tears can no more affection win
         Than wash thy Ethiopian skin.

                    John Cleveland, English Poet, 1613-1658

Nazis and the Negro

The Nazis removed St. Maurice, Negro, leading Catholic saint of Germany, from coats-of-arms. Lips, J. E. "The Savage Strikes Back, p. xxv. 1937) says, "A black man's head even in a coat-of-arms, such as that of Coburg, was replaced by the Government with a sword and sickle."

Professor Lips says: "Long before Europe set forth her emissaries in history to discover and capture the colored world, that world had pent the white man in his own land. The age of discovery was, after all, but the bursting of the chain which the coloured world had put around the white." (p. 1).

English and American Color Prejudice at Monte Carlo

Gen. Pierre Polovtsoff, President of the International Sporting Club of France, says, ("Monte Carlo Casino" p. 17), "I am responsible for running the Beach and it occasionally happens that Negroes wish to bathe there. Now in France there is no 'color bar' and if the other bathers were all French not the slightest objection would be made to the presence of Negroes in the swimming-pool. English people, on the other hand, strongly object to mixing with Negroes, and the position therefore becomes extremely awkward. Luckily for me the problem arises only very occasionally but whenever I see a coloured visitor in the streets I always pray that he will not take it into his head to visit the Beach."

"The Insane Man of Ancona"

"The Negro, whom William IV of Prussia, made his adopted son, has just died in an Insane Asylum.

"Berlin, August 25. In an insane asylum at Ancona, Italy, has just died an old Negro, known in German circles as Henri Noel, the insane man of Ancona." The dead man has a strange history. In 1865, the German explorer, Frederick Rohlfs, leaving Tripoli, made an expedition to Lake Chad. On the way, he was called to attend a slave merchant, who was gravely ill. Rohlfs who had served from 1855 to 1860 as a medical major in the Foreign Legion, cured the sick man, who in addition to giving him a large sum of money, made him present of a Negro child of six, son of the native king, Abd el Taradi, who had been made captive and his children sold.

"On his return to Germany in 1867, Dr. Rohlfs presented the young Negro to King William of Prussia, who became emperor of Germany in 1871. William baptised the young Negro and gave him the name of Henri Noel.

"Of course the young Henri Noel received a military education. He was sent to a Prussian Cadet Corps and in 1877, age 18, he served in the Turkish army in war against Russia and was seriously wounded in the head at Plevna.

"Some time after that he met Dr. Rolfs again at Malta . . . Rohlfs realizing that Henri Noel was cerebrally deranged as the result of his wound, wrote the emperor who had his adopted son interned and cared for in the asylum at Ancona, where it was soon seen that he was incurable.

"Henri Noel was completely inoffensive and suffered from delusions of grandeur. Until 1918, the royal court of Prussia through the German ambassador in Italy paid the expenses, Kaiser Wilhelm II, himself being particularly interested. After the first world war, the German government undertook charge of Henri Noel.

"In the pictures of 1867 to 1870 the King of Prussia is seen with a superb young Negro in his suit: it is the poor "fou" of Ancona. (From the Depeche Africaine, Aug. 26, 1931).

African "Prince" with Wine, Women and Song in London

By J. A. ROGERS

One of London's most glittering playboys has just come to grief and it's the talk of the town. I bring him up because he shows how far a black man can go in this that is really a white man's land—because also he makes me think of Negroes, with plenty of money, legitimately earned, in Texas or Oklahoma, who are moldering in jim-crow and who go placidly from birth to death through back doors of whites less well off than themselves.

The playboy in question is "Prince" Olayimiki Fasanya of Nigeria. Thirty years old, he fills the popular conception of the Negro type—coal black, wooly-haired, flat nose, very large mouth. He reached London only five years ago as a deck hand, but in that short time was able to lay his hands on enough money to make him the joy of night club owners, waiters, and lovely blondes. Just how he did it I'll come to in time.

The Prince lived in lordly style. He had a flat in one of the city's most expensive sections and a country home — a Rolls-Royce, two American cars, and a refugee Russian, nobleman as chauffeur at $22 a week, a very good salary here—as well as a valet, butler, housemaids, not to mention three secretaries — all white of course.

His suits, of which there were some forty, were made in Saville-row, high water mark of good tailoring. Though stocky and plump (he's about five nine inches), he looked like a tailor's model — immaculate, impeccable. With nose nearly always in the air, he was most difficult to please. He traveled first-class and was sure to complain to the conductor of the dirt, no matter how "crack" the train. The same when he went on planes to Paris for week-ends. A member of several West End clubs, as well as business clubs, he'd walk up to the bar and order "double Scotch" for everyone present. He had an eye, too, for feminine pulchritude. When he walked into some ultra-fashionable restaurant with a blonde — nearly always a new one — that Hollywood would go ga-ga over, waiters fell over themselves to get him for his lavish tips. The same when he went into some expensive shop, a lovely on his arm, for her to choose whatever her heart desired. At elections, he rode to the polls in his Rolls-Royce, and haughtily cast his vote against the Socialists.

Now how did the "Prince" get all this? He soiled his royal hands, yes, with trade. West Africa is short of all kinds of goods and he decided to supply them. With his staff of secretaries, he sent off thousands of letters promising to supply everything from needles to cement at prices and on credit terms that made merchants and individual buyers sit up. Of course, because of the slowing up of production due the war, the goods would take some time to arrive, but to insure them an advance was necessary, he said.

Money poured in to the tune of 50,000 pounds ($250,000, but worth about $400,000 here in purchase value). Some Africans parted with their life-savings. Others sent ivory, textiles, and native products. Prince Ajanji Lagunja of the Gold Coast sent $960 for cement. Years passed by, however, but no goods came. The "Prince" wouldn't let business interfere with pleasure. Even illiterate folk in the back country began to be disturbed. Finally a Nigerian elephant hunter sent a strange, badly scrawled message to the London police asking for justice against the "Prince."

Scotland Yard sent out a detective, who after following clues for two and a half years was able to get enough evidence pinned together with bamboo clips and signed with thumb prints to convict. The police marched in on the "Prince" in his swell London flat. They found him in pajamas and dressing gown dictating to his secretaries. They found also that his pretentious "National West African Traders Association" of which he was president was only a little empty shop in an obscure neighborhood. His bank account was overdrawn and his only assets were some $900 in a West African bank. English businessmen were victimized too, fooled by the "Prince's" Monte Cristo-like spending.

Scotland Yard, at considerable expense to the government, flew in witnesses, among them Prince Ajanji of the cement order. Now the Gold Coast playboy, after five years of luxury flats, white women, cars, chauffeurs, secretaries and double-Scotch, will spend five years at the prosaic task of making bags for His Majesty's mail. (J. A. Rogers, Pittsburgh Courier, Nov. 18, 1950).

United States

Moreau de St. Mery (Voyage aux Etats-Unis, 1793-78, p. 78, p. 171) tells of a place in New York called "Holy Ground" where prostitutes of all colors were to be seen.

On white sailors and women on slave-ships coming from Africa, Taussig C. W., "Rum, Romance, and Rebellion" (p. 185. 1928) says, "It is not surprising that in the long voyage of the slaves from Africa to America, there should have been intimate relations between white officers and crew and the Negro women. For the most part the crew of the slaves were a lecherous, dissolute lot and on many trips almost the entire passage was devoted to wild orgies."

Negro Pirate with Harem of White and Negro Women

Black Caesar, a Negro ex-slave, and trusted lieutenant of Blackbeard, who died 1718, was a great pirate in his own right. Was known for his cruelty, love of luxury, and ambition had a harem of some hundred women, White, Negro and Indian. His stronghold was an island off the Florida Coast which is still known as "Black Caesar's Rock. (United States: WPA Florida Guide, p. 328. 1939).

White Woman Given Two Years for Teaching Negro Slave to Read the Bible

On July 4, 1847, Martha Christian of Righteous Ridge, Virginia, was indicted by the Grand July for "not having the fear of God upon her eyes but moved by the Devil wickedly, maliciously and feloniously did teach a black woman, named Rebecca, alias Black Beck, to read the Bible to the great displeasure of Almighty God." She was sent to the Richmond Penitentiary for two years. (Jour. of Negro History, Vol. 18, p. 474).

Term "Nigger" Used to Describe White Man Who Favored the Union

From Testimony given in the investigation of two commissioners of police in Baltimore, 1866.
"Tell me what do you mean by word 'kind.' "

"A nigger straight out."

"You mean violent men?"

"Yes, sir. Men who would do anything to accomplish their ends. One was a murderer.

. . . I am a Union man, but no nigger." (Testimony of Charles D. Hiss, justice of the peace. Records of proceedings, pp. 80-81).

In York, S. C., visits were made by the Ku Klux Klan, during the Reconstruction period "to white men living in adultery with Negro women, and to Negroes living in adultery with white women. A former Klansman told of a visit to a house of a white woman, who was found in the company of three Negroes . . . In Union, S. C., a Negro was killed and his step-daughter whipped because the latter had a child for one of its members." (Jour. of Negro Hist. Vol. 12, p. 663).

New Orleans Voodoo Serves For Mating of Whites and Blacks

Whites and Negroes participated in voodoo rites in New Orleans and indulged in sexual orgies together. In a raid on the den of "Doctor" Don Pedro in 1855, the police found a dozen white women, naked except for thin camisoles, and as many Negro men, all "busily amusing themselves" under the direction of Don Pedro. In 1889, in a raid on "Doctor" James Alexander, a tall, slim mulatto from Mississippi, the police found "ten Negro men, half-naked, lying on the floor, while fifteen white women, similarly undressed sat on chairs ranged in a circle about them." Alexander claimed he had been "born with a caul and a gift from God in his hands." His principal confederate in fleecing the gullible and superstitious was Lou Jackson, a white woman, who furnished the women.

These voodoo doctors preyed on superstitious whites, some of whom were rich women. These rites had been brought from Africa and with their ceremonies and incantations had a powerful influence on the minds of the gullible. "Many of the Voodoo queens and doctors acquired fortunes of respectable proportions, for they were consulted not only by practically all the Negroes of New Orleans, but by great numbers of lower-class whites as well. Neurotic and repressed white women were especially easy victims of the Voodoo doctors, particularly of the stalwart mulattoes who prescribed not only charms and powders, but participation in orgiastic rites . . . police raids on the premises of the black sorcerers, over a long period, frequently netted as many whites as blacks."

One "Dr." John, a native African with a tatooed face, made a fortune and had a harem, presided over by a white wife. Most famous of these voodoo doctors was Marie Laveau (1796) who was one of the most important figures in New Orleans, regardless of color. Her tomb is still visited for luck. Her daughter, Marie

NEGROES OF THE PACIFIC

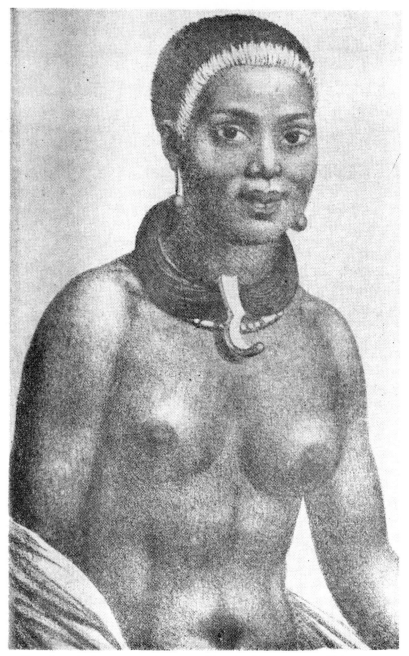

Hawaiian Girl of 1816. Note the Negroid Features and Hair (From Choris ,"Pittoresque Voyage autour du Monde, Pl. VII). See other pictures in Sex and Race, Vol. 3.

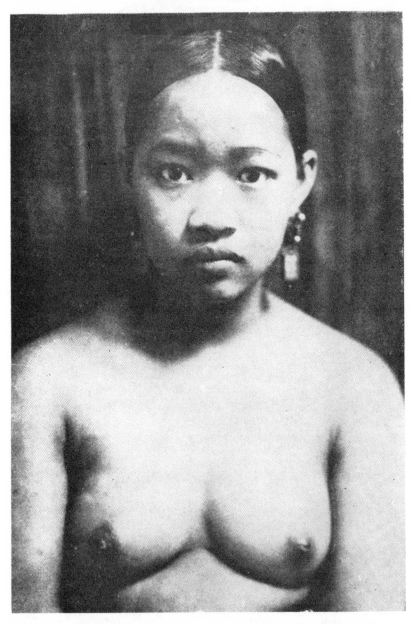

Three parts Malay and One Part Chinese this girl resembles many an American of White and Negro parents (From Hagen's Melanesia).

II, made a fortune, too, principally by catering to whites, telling fortunes and the like. (See chapter IV "VOODOO," Herbert Asbury's "The French Quarter," pp. 225-283. 1938).

For Voodoo and Miscegenation elsewhere in America see, Chapter: Sex and Religion, Sex and Race, Vol. 2.

Says Negro Women not Accepted Socially with White Men

In the fight for white supremacy, the colored woman has been shoved aside by her colored man and his white idol.

A colored man can get woman from any source and she is to be accepted into the best of circles . . . because she is white.

But a white man and a colored woman who would dare become friendly, no matter of what status, are ostracized.

Women of all colored races have suffered and are suffering. Our white sisters are tramping in our faces with the help of our men.

White Man, Colored Woman

Several months ago I was stationed with a WAC unit at a port in the United States. A white clerk in a store treated me awfully nice the couple of times we saw each other.

We saw each other sometimes in the park where we talked. I knew I was falling for him and I wanted to stop seeing him before it got too thick between us.

But I still went back to see him. I wanted to tell him that we couldn't see each other again, when I saw him I was glad to be with him.

One night last month he asked me to marry him and live with him in a town in Pennsylvania. He is waiting for my answer.

I do want to be his wife, but one thing stops me. He is white and I am colored. I want him more than anything in the world, but I am afraid people would talk.

If I marry some other man, I would not be happy because I would be thinking of him always. I wish your readers would help me by giving me advice. — XYZ (Letters to Afro-American Sept. 1, 1945).

Eight Answers to the Question: "Would You Mind Sitting by Negroes in Buses?" From "The South Today."
(Asked of Southern Whites)

1. "No. I prefer to sit by people who don't have colds; that's about all I'd ask of a street car."

2. "I personally don't mind. But you know you can't start that kind of thing down in the South."

3. "If you let a nigger sit where he wants to on street cars and buses, next thing you know he'll be wanting to marry your sister— see?"

4. "It doesn't matter to me the shade of skin. All I hope for is not too much dirt."

5. "Whether I mind or don't seems beside the point. This happens to be a democracy. Anybody has as much right in that street car as I have, if he can pay the fare."

6. "All right, you asked for it, now get it: it's a hell of a question to be asking . . . stirring up trouble between the races like that . . . hurting the war effort."

7. "Anybody can sit on the street car and anywhere else. Listen: I have a boy fighting in the Solomon Islands. There's just one thing on my mind. I want him to come back home when this thing's over, and I want it to hurry and get over.

"If you had real things on your mind like that, you wouldn't be worrying about who sat by you. Things like that just don't matter anymore except to crazy people.

"Didn't priests once spend a lot of time arguing about how many angels could dance on the point of a needle? All right. If you heard a bunch of Church folks arguing about that today, you'd send them to the mental hospital, wouldn't you? This other thing is just as crazy . . . just as crazy, I tell you!"

8. "A nigger sit by me on a street car? Just let one try it!"

Woman Arrested for Being Thought "White"

CHARLESTON, W. Va. — Police Chief Billy W. Mowell of Lester, a suburb near here, is being sued for 5,000 on charges of having arrested and jailed a colored woman he had mistaken for white.

Mrs. Violetta Adkins, complainant, says she was jailed on Sunday, Sept. 2, as a "white woman riding around with a colored man." Mrs. Adkins is colored. Police Chief Mowell's face is red. He denies the charge.

Mrs. Adkins insists that she was placed in jail "without any justification whatsoever."—(Afro-American Sept. 15, 1951).

Gets Two Years on Charge of Having Thoughts About White Girl

YANCEYVILLE, N. C. — Such expressions as "reckless eye-balling" and "mental rape" have long been a part of the Southern Negro's repertoire of grim humor, but the bizarre circumstances upon which a 44-year-old farmer was convicted here recently of attempted assault on a female are inconceivable even to the "unfeeling" of this section.

Mack Ingram, a father of ten children, was arrested here last month and convicted of an attempted assault on 18-year-old Willie Jean Boswell, a white woman who testified that Ingram was never any closer to her than seventy-five feet and that he made no improper advances toward her.

Mr. Ingram told the court that he did not even see the prosecutrix on the day of the alleged crime and was unaware of any trouble until he was arrested, handcuffed, and taken to the Boswell house early the same afternoon.

He was sentenced to two years. (Pittsburgh Courier).

An appeal and retrial resulted in a hung jury in November 1951.

Discharged When Real Ancestry Is Discovered

Mrs. Sarah Grayson, of 2231 Ontario Road, Northwest, Washington, D. C., who operated a Capital Transit Company street car for four months before her employers discovered that she was colored. Mrs. Grayson, without attempting to hide her racial identity, applied for a job and was accepted and trained. Last week she was fired without notice when a neighbor "informed" on her. (Afro-American).

White Adopted Daughter Barred from Inheriting Negro Estate

The claim of an 18-year-old white girl to a share in the estate of Adolphus Humbles, who died in 1926, leaving property estimated to have been worth $150,000, has been denied because she was adopted by a mixed couple, and Virginia laws do not recognize interracial marriage, or the adoption of a white child by a colored person.

The ruling, long pending and believed to be unprecedented in Virginia as well as in the nation, was handed down by Judge S. LuVal Martin in Corporation Court.

Adopted by Daughter

The girl, Miss Doreen L. Armstrong, was adopted by Humbles's daughter, Mrs. Geneva H. Armstrong, whose husband is a white Canadian, Guy R. Armstrong. The couple married in Canada and lived there.

Lawyers for the girl contended that the Armstrong marriage was legal in Canada, as was the adoption of a white child by a colored person, and hence Miss Armstrong was entitled to share in the Humbles estate.

May Appeal Decision

Judge Martin ruled against them and the lawyers indicated that they would appeal.

Basil G. Watkins, attorney for the Humbles estate which opposed the claim, argued that although the adoption was legitimate in Canada, it did not have to be recognized in Virginia, because it is contrary to public policy as expressed in a number of laws.— (Afro-American Feb. 2, 1944).

Experiences of an Indian Thrust into the White Caste

"I am writing to you because I feel that we have something in common in the welfare of the colored race. First to tell you of my personal history: When I was one year old my mother married a colored man, a wonderful man. She died when I was about ten years old. Since then I have been closely associated with the colored people. My rear father, an Indian, died a year after my mother did. My stepfather was really kind to me. He is still living and at my home in Los Angeles. He writes to me constantly, but is seventy years old. He used to train with Jack Blackburn in Los Angeles when that city was in knee pants. His name is Ed Welch. As I grew up, I began to see prejudice creeping up but I still wouldn't leave my adopted people."

"In 1938, I met a colored girl whom I love. After a few objections, I married her in Tia Juana, Mexico, as they refused to marry us in the State of California. The objections were from my relatives on my father's side and my mother-in-law, but she consented. She pointed out to me what I would face, but I was sincere about my intentions so she readily consented. We have three fine children. Two girls and a boy. The oldest is a girl six years old.

"My wife lives at Los Angeles 11, Calif. We had been living happily until I got drafted.

"Here in this white man's army, I am often to myself. It is my first close association with them. After twelve weeks, I can't seem to get along. Everytime I look into their faces I seem to see a meanness and they are mean in their speech and manner. Sometimes they include colored people in their speech and use that word 'nigger.' Some of the officers make a habit of telling jokes about them. Of course, that aggravates my feelings.

"I wish I could get out of the Army or at least serve with the colored troops. What would you suggest, talk it over with the commanding officer about a transfer to the colored troops where I would feel better or just continue on? I have little or no confidence in these officers because of above incidents and other incidents. Texas really presents a problem.

"I attempted to talk with a colored waitress here on the camp, but she told me I wasn't supposed to talk with her. Also 'all Negro establishments are off limits to white personnel,' as one posted bulletin reads. I remember the time I could walk any place on Central Avenue in Los Angeles and enjoy myself. I do not say I am white. I am an Indian. I have six weeks of training left before I go on furlough.

"It's a relief to get off my chest, especially to you, as I feel you would understand. You can make reference to this letter if you so desire, but kindly withhold my name.

"My opinion as to interracial marriage is marry the one you love no matter what color or race and to h—l with what other people think or say. I have been happy taking my family out to parties, picnics and dances."

(From George S. Schuyler's Views and Reviews. Pittsburgh Courier).

Minneapolis once had a Manasseh Society (Negro men, white wives) to which no white man or colored woman was admitted (Pearson's Maga, p. 546, 1910).

Herbert Asbury defines "creole": "The word, Creole, comes from the Spanish and was unknown in Louisiana during the French occupation. Properly, it meant native, so that any native of Louisiana was a Creole. In practice, however, the title was applied only to descendants of the original French and Spanish settlers, and, for convenience, to the native Negroes, live stock, etc. It was used as a noun only in speaking of a white man; otherwise as an adjective as 'Creole Negroes,' 'Creole horses,' 'Creole cattle,' etc. In modern New Orleans, among the whites, it has the same meaning as in earlier times, but among the Negroes octoroons are known as Creoles. ("The French Quarter," 92n. 1938).

The whites, or those presumed to be white, resent, however, the use of Creole by any of Negro ancestry.

* * * *

Another version of maternal impression is this from Gould and Pyle: "A woman had a Negro paramour in America with whom she had sexual intercourse several times, she was put in a convent on the Continent (Europe) where she stayed two years. On leaving the convent she married a white man and nine months after she gave birth to a dark-skinned child. The supposition was that dur-

233

Head of Olmec Deity of about 500 A. D. Reproduced in American Museum of Natural History, New York. Original weights about five tons. See others in Sex and Race, Vols. 2 and 3.

ing her abode in the convent and the nine months subsequently she had the image of her black paramour constantly before her." Anomalies and Curiosities, Vol. 1, p. 85. 1937.

Slavery of Whites in Colonial America

In early colonial days the sale of white slaves was an im-source of revenue. Moreau de St. Mery gives the sum at 1,260,000 English pounds in 1798 which he says leads him to say the progress of America lies not "in the goodness of the soil or the excellence of the laws" but "in the sale of the Europeans who have peopled it." (Voyage aux Etats-Unis, 1793-98, p. 289).

On sale of white children. Mittelberger, G. Journey to Pennsylvania in 1750. "Many parents must sell and trade away their children like so many head of cattle." p. 27, 1898.

Cannibalism Among American Whites

Captain John Smith (1580-1631), founder of Virginia, wrote, "So great was our famine that a savage we slew and buried the poorer sort took him up again and eat him; and so did divers ones another boiled and stewed with herbs. And one amongst the rest did kill his wife, powdered (Salted) her and had eaten part of her," (The General Historie of Virginia. The Fourth Booke p. 294 (1606-1625) ed by J. F. Jameson, 1907.

"One man killed his wife to eat for which he was burned. Many fed on corpsus." (Neill, E. D. Terre Mariae Maryland) p. 30, 1867. From Virginia Assembly).

Daniel Webster's Color

An old acquaintance of Daniel Webster on seeing him after he had become famous. "What, exclaimed the teamster," that little black stable-boy that once brought me the horses?" (Harvey. P. Reminiscences of Daniel Webster," p. 77. 1882).

Note: On page 32, para. 3, line 6 should read: "In the Vulgate, based on the Septuagint, or Greek edition of the Bible . . . " There are many later interpretations of this passage which are different. See Henderson, E. Isaiah, pp. 103-05. 1857. The English Bible (1931) p. 1164, has it, "To a nation, tall and sleek, to a people dreaded near and far ; a nation strong and triumphant." The American Bible has it, "A nation, scattered and peeled . . . a nation meted out and trodden down." p. 58 for 1871 read 871.

THE END

INDEX—AUTHORS

Abd Allah, Ibn, 57
Abdul Baha, 5
Abrantes, Duchess, 66, 123, 149
Acton, R., 163
Aeschines, 48
Aeschylus, 41, 48
Aesclepiades, 34
Alatir, Ibn, 58
Aleman, M., 73
Anderson, D., 177
Anderson, W., 80
Angelo, H., 177
Athair, Ibn, El, 69
Ammianus, 48
Aristotle, 17, 38
Ariz, Pacha, 140
Armandi, D., 44
Arnobius, 49
Arnold, Sir T., 59, 61, 82
Asbury, H., 200, 230, 233
Ashton, J., 174
Astley, T., 218
Atgier, E., 53
Augustine, St., 10, 11, 12
Avezac' D, 72

Babelon, E., 45, 49, 50
Bailey, Nath., 10
Balzac, H., 172
Bancroft, H. H., 214
Barbot, J., 123
Bardsley, C. W., 80
Barry P., 155
Basile, G., 93
Baring-Gould, S., 30
Barrow, R. H., 43
Beardsley, G., 34
Beaumier, A., 58
Beddoe, J., 71
Belcher, E., 216
Bell, R. H., 28
Benedictus, 121
Berejkov, 108
Berkeley-Hill, O., 46, 117
Berry, W., 72, 81, 87
Bertrand, L., 30
Bigelow, J., 130
Binet-Sangle, C., 45
Bloch, A. 41
Bloch, I., 145, 149
Blumenbach, J., 206
Boccalini, T., 110
Boorde, And., 99
Boswell, J., 79

Botsford, J. B., 156
Bourdon, E., 149
Boyce, W. D., 2
Brantome, P., 92, 121, 149
Briffault, R., 155
Brome, R., 40, 74.
Broom, R., 2
Brown, B. C., 157
Browne Sir T., 73
Brown, WM. W., 216
Bryant, J., 31, 53
Bryce, Lord, 191
Byron, Lord. 31, 68
Buel, J., 216
Buffon, G. 5
Bulleid, A., 16
Bulleid & Gray, 71
Bunyan, John, 170
Burckhardt, J., 110, 117, 122
Burke, J. B., 80
Burton, Rich., 117. 140
Busnot, Abbe, 62, 63

Caedmon, 1
Calixte, R., 149
Calixte de Prov., 70
Carcopino, J., 43, 44, 50
Carleton, J. W., 163
Carlson, C. J.,
Carvalho, P. de, 108
Carvajal, M., 30
Catlin, G., 204
Catterall, H., 156
Chambers, Robt., 1, 70
Childe, V., 23
Chapuy, P., 87
Chaucer, G., 99
Chenaye des Bois, 92
Cervantes, M., 66
Cicero, 44, 46, 48
Cinthio, G., 108
Claudian, 52
Cleveland, G., 108
Cleveland, J., 170, 221
Clymer, R. S., 151
Cole, C. H., 204
Cole, C. H., 204
Cole, C. W., 147
Colyer, V., 192
Corse, D., 216
Costello, L. S., 29, 149
Cox, Harold, 14
Crawford, M., 69
Croce, Bene., 74 93,

Cromer, Lord, 7, 36
Cummings, L. V., 34
Cundall, F., 220

Dabney W. P., 31
DaCosta, I., 63
Dan, P., 70
D'Arfey, W., 175
Darwin, Chas., 1, 5
Davis, A., 202
Davis, E. C., 10 8
Decourdemanche, J., 140
DeForest, J. W., 192
Deheque, F. D., 34
Delacroix, J., 149
Dessailly, Abbe, 220.
Deslandres, P., 70
Delisle, F., 15
Desmichels, M.
Dieulafoy, J. P., 41, 123
Dio Cassio, 54
Diodorus, Sicu., 23
Dionysius, 31
Donkine, R., 53
Dozy, F., 59
Dryden, J., 170
Draper, J. W., 61
Driscoll, C. B., 70
Durand-Lefebvre, M., 29
Durant, Will, 58
Duruy, V., 43, 49
Dykes, E. B., 156

Eckhart, J. G., 121
Eden, R., 73, 74
Edmondson, J., 72,
Egan, P., 163, 169
Eisler, R., 40
Ellis, A., 82
Erredge, J. A., 163, 188
Evans, Eir A., 34, 41

Fabre d'Olivet, A., 32, 37
Falconbridge, A. M., 175
Fazil, Bey, 140
Fieffe, E., 145
Finot, J., 1
Fishberg, M., 122, 140
Flaccus, Calp., 51
Flournoy, F. R., 63
Fowler, W. W., 43
Frank, T., 43, 50
Freeman & Simon, 10, 39
Freyre, G., 55, 60, 61
Frichet, H., 41
Frobenius, L., 16
Frost, T., 165

Fulford, R., 163
Fuller, H., 75

Gandia, E., 62, 66
Garcilasso de Vega, 206
Garth, T. R., 1
Georgeakis & Pineau, 74
Gibbon, E., 54
Gilbert, H., 111
Gill, J., 49
Ginzberg, L., 10, 218
Girard, G., 145
Gomez Moreno, D., 57
Goncourt E. & J., 150
Gostling, M., 29
Gottschalk, M., 87
Gould and Pyle, 39, 233
Graindor, P., 41, 54
Grandmaison, C., 77
Gray, H., 16
Gregorovius, F., 69
Gregory, W. K., 1
Griffith, R. H., 56
Gronow, R. H., 220
Gunther, John, 143
Gurowski, A., 41, 130
Gusman, P., 46

Hackwood F. W., 157, 169
Hahn, J. G., 74
Hambly, W., 57
Hamilton, A., 122
Hardy, G., 70
Harrison, G. B., 171
Harrison, Jn., 74
Harper, C. G., 157
Harvey, P., 235
Haven, G., 213
Hawes, S., 170
Hawkins, Sir J., 82
Heliodorus, 39
Helper, H. R., 20
Herbert, Geo., 108
Herodotus, 28, 31, 42
Hertz, F., 18, 40, 99., 122, 219
Herve, G., 16
Higgins, G., 8, 16, 71, 218
Hill, G. B., 174
Hindley, C., 157
Hirschfeld, M., 142
Hitti, P. K., 58
Hogben, L., 61
Homer, 31
Hoorebeke, G., 87
Hopkins, J. T.,
Horace, 48
Huja, Rabbi, 9

Hume, M. A., 161
Hunt, Leigh, 163
Hutchings, W., 80
Hyde, W. W., 50, 71

Inman, T. 2, 40

Jerome, St., 50
Jobson, R., 218
Johnson, Jack, 135
Johnson, Sam'l., 10, 73, 82, 174
Jones, T. W. S., 30
Jonson, Ben, 74, 87
Johnstone, J., 174
Julian, Emperor, 10, 12
Juvenal, 44-46, 50, 144

Khaldun, Ibn, 58
King, C. W., 51
Kingsley, Z., 215
'Knox, Robt., 79, 188
Krug, M. E., 204
Kutner, N., 202

Lamb, C. L., 157
Lane-Poole, S., 61
Larchey, L., 87
Lawrence, T. E., 117
Laubat, Chasse, De, 15
Lavisse, E., 69, 143
Lazarillo de E., 66
Le Cat, C. N., 39
Lindo, E. H., 65
Lips, J. E., 218, 222
Little, K., 175
Liudprand, 111
Livi, R., 117
Lombroso, C., 45
Loskiel, H. G., 203
Lowe, Van R., 16
Lower, M. A., 80
Lea, C. H., 28, 61
Leake, 53
Leakey, L. S., 2
Leared, A., 63
Leeuw H. de, 68
Legrand, E., 74
Leigh, F. B., 174
Lepsius, K., 51
Lespinasse, B., 30
Lucian, 32
Lyons, F. J., 167

Mabbe, J., 75
McBride, R., 218
Mackenzie, A. M., 174
Mackintosh, Mrs., 116

McNeil, S., 183
MacRitchie, D., 69, 70, 72, 77, 79, 87, 99
Madden, R., 114-16, 117
Mailhol, G., 220
Malcolm, J. P., 161
Mangin, Gen., 58
Mandeville, J., 73
Manouvrier, L,. 15
Marcosson, I., 135
Marett, J. R., 15
Marlowe, C., 74-5, 108
Martial, 43, 48, 50, 72, 140
Marx, Karl, 130
Massey, G., 8, 16, 23, 53, 71
Masuccio, T., 75
Mathorez, J., 143, 147
Mayhew, H., 165, 167
Maxwell, J. R., 177
Menander, 28, 34
Mercier, L. S., 149
Michaud ,J., 61
Michel, E., 59
Miles, H. D., 169
Millingen, 114
Miranda, Gen., 214
Mohamet, 34
Montesquieu, C., 20
Moreau, St. M., 206, 236
Murray, P., 193
Moreno-Villa, 65

Nash, Roy, 60
Neill, E. D., 235
Nietzsche, F. W., 5
Nettl, P., 82
Nevins, Allan, 193
Nichols T. L., 171
Nisbet, A., 80-1
Nott & Gliddon, 49
Numantius, 48

Oakesmith, J., 71
O'Donoghue, E. M., 172
Ortiz, F., 55, 65
Ovington, M., 193
Padmore, G., 177
Paine, Thos., 5
Painter, Wm., 73, 171, 220
Paracelsus, P., 20
Park, Mungo, 14
Parkyn, M., 14
Parry, A., 135
Peele, Geo., 74-5 109
Penzer, M., 140
Pepys, Sam'l., 165
Percy, T., 75

Perdrizet, P., 36
Persius, 48
Peyrere, I. de, 21.
Philostrates, 34
Piette, E., 15
Pileur, Le, 28
Pirenne, H., 117
Plutarch, 38
Pliny, 38, 43-4
Polo, Marco, 14
Polovtsoff, P., 222
Pommerol, M. F., 30
Porter, K. W., 204
Porter, Sir J., 114
Poyntz, A., 118
Prattis, P. L., 9, 196
Predergast J. P., 29
Prichard, J. C., 1, 121, 123
Procopius, 55, 72
Puleston, F., 219
Pulzsky, F., 49

Quintilian, 48, 51

Radin, M., 142
Ramanujam, T., 14
Rapoport, S., 10, 51
Rawlinson, G., 32
Raymond, M., 57
Reau, L., 108
Reinaud, J. T., 58, 69
Reinach S., 36
Renesse, T., 87
Reuter, E. B., 215
Ribton-Turner, C. T., 165, 171
Rice, 9
Ricoles, J. B., 147
Rietstap, P. B., 75
Riley, 80
Ripley, Robt., 51
Robert of Clari, 218
Roberts, K., 206
Robertson, W., 66
Rocker, R., 131
Rodocanachi, F., 117
Roland, 56
Ronciere, C., 145, 14 7
Ross, E. A., 29
Rostovtzev, M., 54
Rothery G. C., 34
Russell, J. H., 215
Ryan, M., 219

Saco, J. A., 59, 117
Sackville-West, V., 157
Said of Andalusia, 60
Sala, G. A., 188

Sandoval, A., 66, 220
Sassanfart, S., 220
Sayle, R. T., 161
Schlumberger, 111
Schopenhauer, A., 1
Schuyler, G. S., 140, 233
Schwarzschild, L., 130
Scott, S. P., 59, 61
Scott, Sir W., 59, 61
Shakespeare, Wm., 4, 6, 10, 31,
    36, 51, 73, 75, 99, 108-9, 171
Shaw, Alice, 131
Seneca, 28, 44, 45, 46, 48
Sergi, G., 1
Seth, D., 108
Siebmacher, J., 75, 99
Silliman, B., 157, 172
Simonides, 28
Smeeton, G., 165
Smith, Elliot, 57
Smith, Capt. J., 235
Smith, J. T., 165
Smith, Sir W., 31, 53, 72
Smith, W. G., 132
Snowden, F. M., 31, 44, 52
Snyder, D. J., 109
Socrates, 4
Southey, W., 68
Spearing, H. G., 123
Speke, J. H., 13
Spengler, O., 111
Spratlin, V. E., 66
Springer, B., 131, 150
Stanley, H. M., 4 1
Stephen of Byzantium, 32
Stephens, H. M., 162
Stevenson-Smith, M., 2 5
Stewart, C., 9
Stewart, Ollie, 132, 181
Stoll, E. M., 73, 109
Strabo, 23, 31, 32, 123
Stuart-Glennie J. 41
Suetonius, 51
Sypher, W., 156, 175

Tabourot, J., 82
Tacitus, 48, 71, 123
Tagore, R., 8
Taussig, C. W., 225
Tannenbaum, S. A., 109
Taylor, Griffith, 1
Terence, 4
Thackeray, W. M., 161, 175
Theodectes, 1
Theophrastus, 41
Thorndike, L., 19, 121
Tommaseo, N., 161

Topinard, P., 10, 11
Tores, De, 74
Toynbee, A. J., 18
Turner, J. K., 130
Turton, W. H., 87

Uffenbach, Z., 156
Utting, F. A., 175

Vanini, Luc., 2 0
Vautel, C., 153
Verlinden, O., 59
Verneau, R., 1, 15
Villa Morena, 65
Virenda, V., 31
Virgil, 48, 53
Von Luschan, F., 1
Voltaire, 14, 20

Wade, W. C., 77, 93
Waitz, T., 123
Wanley, N., 155
Washington, J. E., 216
Watson, J. B., 18
Watscn, J. L., 56

Welch, J., 132
Wells, H. G., 1
Welsford, E., 82, 121, 161
Westermann W., 36
Whitelock, B., 121
Whitman, W., 5
Whitney, L., 174
Wilkins, R. N., 48
Wilkinson, G .T., 17 2
Winckler, A., 108
Winstanley, L., 109, 171
Wolsey, G., 217
Wood, Clem, 211
Wood, R. W., 27
Woodson, C. G., 66
Wyndham, H. A., 63

Xenophanes, 31

Yilma, Asfa, 19

Zambaco, D. A., 140
Zimmern, A., 36
Zucrow S., 28

INDEX—SUBJECTS

Arabs on Negro origin, 25

Black Caesar, 225
Black Madonna, 29, 30, 34-5, 40, 50
Blacks admired, 7, 27, 30-3, 39; as favorites, 108, 113, 119, 121, 122, 128, 129, 149, 159, 161, 163, 167, 169, 173, 174, 222-4; shunned, 18, 170; worshipped, 29,59.
Blonds, favored, 6; shunned, 17, 18.
Brunettes, not favored, 6
Buddhas, 8

Cannibalism in Virginia, 235
Christ, his color, 40-1
Cleopatra, 51
Coats-of-arms: Britain, 76, 78, 80-1; Cities, 93, 106, 107; Germany 75, 86, 88, 89, 94, 95, 96, 98, 100, 103-4; Spain, 105; Northern and Central Europe and Portugal, 83, 85, 90, 91-3, 96-7, 101-3.
Creoles, 204, 206, 232.

Egyptians, color of, 41
Ellenborough, Lady, 168, 172

Ethiopians color of 31
Eunuchs, 111, 114, 140

Garibaldi famiy, 122
Goethe, 131
Gordon, John, of Russia, 135

Hair straightening by whites, 130
Ham legend, 13
Hamelin, Fortunee, 150
Harems, 59, 60
Harriot, procuress, 173
Hottentot Venus, 148
Human race, origin of, 4-5

Indian-Negro-White intermixture, 203-05, 232-4.

Jews, Race of, 13, 38-9, 48, 63, 65, 122, 130, 142-3.

Keeckley, Eliz., 216
Kingsley family, 215

Lassalle, Ferdinand, 130
Los Angeles, founding of, 214
Luther, Martin, 131

Mahomed, S. D., 161, 166, 188
Marriage, laws against, 193 ; mixed marriages, England, 172, 174-5, 178, 183, 185-6.
Miscellany, Africa, 218 ; Europe, 218, America (race—mixture) 214-17.
Monnerville, Gast. 152, 155.
Monte Carlo, 223
Moors, their race, 55-7, 72-4, 80-1, 108 ; slave-raids, 69-70 ; in Spain. 55-61, Morris-dance, origin of, 82
Mulattoes in Europe (World Wars,), 131-4, 140, 145-6, 183.

Negro, origin, and use, of word, 59, 73-5 ; beliefs about, 1-4
Negroes, Ancient Britain, 70-3 ; Roman-Britain, 71, 110 ; in British literature, 156 ; in Ancient Europe, 41-2 ; 27-54 ; in Italy, 75, 85, 93 ; prehistoric, 15-16 ; and Spaniards in early Florida, 189 ; in Spain and Portugal, 55-7, 62, Negroes, white wives (USA), 208-09
Negroes, their belief about origin of whites, 13, 15
Norway, Negroes in 137-9
Notitia Dignitatum, 110

Olmec deity, 234
Othello the Moor, 108-110, 122.

Popes, their severity against race prejudice, 20, 21
Prejudice, color: its real origin, 17-18.
Prejudice color: in Ancient India, 7-9 ; Egypt, 8-9 ; Europe, 20-1 ; Rome, 45-6, 52 ; in Jewish legends, 9-10 mulattoes for blacks, 13, 25-6
Prejudice, white men against white women, 28 ; for other whites, 27-9

Pass for, or thought, white, 194-5, 196-7, 202-03, 231
Queens and their Negro lovers, 74-75

Race unity among early Christians, 10
Race, as viewed by Greeks, Romans Jews, 10
Race mixture among early Christians, 52-3 ; ancient Egypt, 23 ; resulting from wars, 37-8.
Racial origin from names, 52-3
Randolph, P. B., 151
Rape (by thought), 231
Red hair, thought evil, 18
Roman wives and Negroes, 50-52
Royalty ,Negro "blood' 'in, 66, 87, 94, 122, 131, 143, 147, 149, 150-1, 176.

Schweninger, Dr. E., 131
Slaves, white and black: in France, 143 ; in Rome, 43-4 ; in Eastern and Southern Europe, 111-12, 121 ; among Moors, 59.
Slaves and servants in England, 156-8, 160-1, 165.
Slaves, white and colored (USA) 188-9, 235

Turks and NeNgroes, 111

Voodoo and race mixture, 226
Vulgate, 32, 235.

Webster, Daniel, color of, 235.
White men, Negro wives (USA), 198-9, 209
White servants (USA) imported by Negroes, 214
White Skin, beliefs about its origin, 1-3, 13-15

FOR MORE SUBJECT MATTER ON RACE MIXTURE SEE: INDEX, "SEX AND RACE" VOLUME THREE.

A BLACKAMOOR MAID WOOING A FAIR BOY

Stay lovely boy, why fliest thou me
That languish in these flames for thee?
I'm black, 'tis true, why so is night
And love doth in dark shades delight
The whole world do but close thine eye
Will seem to thee as black as I
Or open it and see what a black shade
Is by thine own fair body made
That follows thee where ere thou go
(Oh, who allowed would not do so?)
Let me forever dwell so nigh
And thou shalt need no other shade than I.

Translation of the Latin poem "Aethiopissa ambit cestum Diversi Coloris Virum" of the English poet, George Herbert, (1593-1633) by Henry Rainolds, his contemporary.

Henry King, Bishop of Chichester (1592-1699) replied:

BOY'S ANSWER TO THE BLACKAMOOR

Black Maid, complain not that I fly
When fate commands antipathy
Prodigious might that union prove
Where night and day together move
And the conjection of our lips
Not kisses make but an eclipse
In which the mixed black and white
Portends more terror than delight
Yet if my shadow then will be
Enjoy thy dearest wish: But see
Thou take my shadow's property
That hastes away when I come nigh
Else stay till death hath blinded me
And then I will bequeath myself to thee.

During the French Revolution L. Mole wrote a play, "Zamore and Mirza" which was a strong plea for justice to Negroes. Since the principal characters were Negroes and these were apparently no Negroes competent to play the roles, it would be necessary to blacken whites. A tempestuous actress, Marie le Gouge, was chosen to play the lead but the theatre at which is was to be played resolutely opposed any blacking up. Marie fought furiously and eventually won her way, "In what way," she demanded. "do whites differ from Negroes" except in the matter of color (Fleischmann H. Les Femmes et La Terreur, p. 259-60. 1910).

242

J. A. Rogers

J. A. Rogers has engaged continuously in research on the Negro since 1915. Published himself his first book, "From Superman to Man," in 1917, after it was refused by the publishers.

Wrote and published his second book, "As Nature Leads," in 1919.

Began writing for the Negro press in 1920 and has been doing so since.

In 1924, '25, and '26, toured the North and South, lecturing and selling "From Superman to Man" (4th edition).

In 1925 went to Europe for research in the libraries and museums there.

In 1927 returned for research lasting three years. Went to North Africa.

In 1930 went on his own initiative to the coronation of Haile Selassie, who presented him with the Coronation Medal. The same year published his "World's Greatest Men of African Descent."

From 1930 to 1933 continued his researches in Europe.

In 1934 published his "100 Amazing Facts About the Negro" which went into 19 editions.

In 1930, 1935 and '36 continued his researches in Egypt and the Sudan.

In 1935 published his "Real Facts About Ethiopia" and went the same year as war correspondent to Ethiopia for the Pittsburgh-Courier.

In 1940 began publication of his "Sex and Race" in three volumes.

In 1947 published his "World's Great Men of Color, 3000 B. C. to 1946 A. D." in two volumes.

In 1950 returned to Europe for further research on "Nature Knows No Color-Line."

In 1930, he was elected to membership in the Paris Society of Anthropology and is now a member of the American Geographical Society, the Academy of Political Science and the American Assn. for the Advancement of Science. Listed in Who's Who in the East, Who's Who in New York, etc.

His knowledge of Negro history represents but a small part of his general information on world history.

ALSO BY J. A. ROGERS

Africa's Gift to America
ISBN 978-0-8195-7516-6

The Five Negro Presidents
ISBN 978-0-9602294-8-2

100 Amazing Facts about the Negro
ISBN 978-0-9602294-7-5

Sex and Race, Volume 1
ISBN 978-0-8195-7507-4

Sex and Race, Volume 2
ISBN 978-0-8195-7508-1

Sex and Race, Volume 3
ISBN 978-0-8195-7509-8

From Superman to Man
ISBN 978-0-9602294-4-4

Books available from University Press of New England,
One Court Street, Suite 250, Lebanon, NH 03766
phone: 1-800-421-1561; or visit www.upne.com